THE KINGFISHER
SOCCER
ENCYCLOPEDIA

Brazil and England contest their 2002 World Cup quarterfinal in Japan's Shizuoka Stadium Ecopa. The 50,600-capacity arena hosts the bigger games of two Japanese J-League teams, Jubilo Iwata and Shimizu S-Pulse.

THE KINGFISHER
SOCCER
ENCYCLOPEDIA

CLIVE GIFFORD

KINGFISHER
NEW YORK

Copyright © 2006 by Kingfisher Publications Plc
KINGFISHER
Published in the United States by Kingfisher, an imprint of
Henry Holt and Company LLC, 175 Fifth Avenue, New York,
New York 10010. First published in Great Britain by
Kingfisher Publications plc, an imprint of Macmillan
Children's Books, London.

Distributed in Canada by H. B. Fenn and Company Ltd.

Library of Congress Cataloging-in-Publication Data
Gifford, Clive.
  The Kingfisher soccer encyclopedia / Clive Gifford.—1st ed.
    p. cm.
  Includes index.
  1. Soccer—Encyclopedias. I. Title.
  GV942.2.G54 2006
  796.33403—dc22

                              2005023899

ISBN: 978-0-7534-5928-7

Kingfisher books are available for special promotions and
premiums. For details contact: Director of Special Markets,
Holtzbrinck Publishers.

Printed in China
10 9 8 7 6 5 4 3
3TR/0708/WKT/MA(MA)/C

Note to readers: The website addresses listed in this
book are correct at the time of publishing. However,
due to the ever-changing nature of the Internet, website
addresses and content can change. websites can contain
links that are unsuitable for children. The publisher cannot
be held responsible for changes in website addresses or
content or for information obtained through third-party
websites. We strongly advise that Internet searches
should be supervised by an adult.

CONTENTS

THE BEAUTIFUL GAME

Pelé described soccer as the "beautiful game," and the emotion and loyalty that soccer inspires in its fans means that this simple sport has a lot to live up to. But soccer delivers it all—cramming dynamic action, breathtaking skills, and heart-stopping tension into 90 minutes of play. It is dramatic, making heroes and villains out of its players, coaches, and referees. From its recognized beginnings in the 1800s to its global dominance today, soccer has provided great moments of excitement, celebration, and despair; no other game has the same power to unite and divide.

RAPID GROWTH

In a little more than 100 years soccer has boomed from a casual game played by a small group of amateur gentlemen to a highly sophisticated, money-focused sport that is played and watched by millions of people. As soccer has grown, dozens of changes have occurred. Some have involved the rules of the game—from the two-handed throw-in, introduced in 1883, to the back-pass rule for goalkeepers that was adopted 99 years later. Other changes—such as the arrival of promotion and relegation up and down a league—have shaped the competitions of which games are a part.

Soccer's adaptability has been one of its strengths. Another big part of its appeal is that people of all ages and skill levels can play the game. At its most basic, soccer is a simple sport that can be enjoyed without expensive equipment and played almost anywhere—from a sandy beach to an office or hallway with a crumpled ball of paper.

The simplicity of soccer is a big selling point with new fans. The finer details of rules and tactics may not be understood at first, but the basics of the game and the skills of star players—their speed, ball control, passing, shooting, and tackling—can be admired by almost anyone.

▲ Soccer is a sport that generates very strong bonds between supporters and their teams. This fan, whose face is painted in the national colors of Portugal, awaits the semifinal of the 2004 European Championships between the Netherlands and Portugal.

▲ Soccer arouses the emotions of players, as well as fans. Here, Bayern Munich's Carsten Jancker (left) and Thomas Helmer are inconsolable after their team was beaten by Manchester United in the last minute of the 1999 Champions League final.

▼ *Barcelona's Ronaldinho (right) is one of the most famous soccer players on the planet. Here, he holds off Michel Salgado of Real Madrid during a derby game between Spain's two biggest teams in November 2004.*

THE NUMBERS GAME

In its full version soccer is a game in which two teams of 11 people each play two halves of 45 minutes. Today more than 50 million soccer players around the world play in official competitions. Many millions more play the game on a regular basis—a survey by world soccer's governing association, the *Fédération Internationale de Football Association* (FIFA), estimates that figure to be more than 240 million.

Top leagues, such as Serie A in Italy, the German Bundesliga, and Spain's La Liga, attract millions of viewers globally. In 2003 games or highlights of the English Premier League were broadcast to more than 140 countries, attracting a television audience of 550 million. The final of the 2006 World Cup, between Italy and France, was watched by more than 600 million television viewers, while the overall tournament had a cumulative audience of more than five billion.

▲ *Soccer can be played practically anywhere, in almost any conditions. These South African schoolchildren are enjoying a casual but competitive game only days before their country won the right to host the 2010 World Cup.*

▲ *A mural of Brazil's Ronaldo brightens the wall of a building in Paris, France. Soccer's top players are global superstars at the center of mini industries. Money is generated away from the players' work on the field, through personal appearances, endorsements, advertisements, and merchandise.*

THEN AND NOW

Going back in time 140 years, a modern soccer fan would be surprised to find no referees, corners, or field markings at a game. Players wore coats and even top hats; they handled the ball in the air and wrestled with each other on the ground. Over time soccer has evolved into the game that we know today.

▶ *The referee's whistle was first blown at a soccer game in 1878. British company Acme Whistles has sold an astonishing 160 million Acme Thunderer whistles, which have been heard at World Cups and in top leagues around the globe.*

THE FIELD

Unlike most sports, the field in soccer can vary in size. Most are around 328 ft. (100m) long and 213–230 ft. (65–70m) wide. Back in the 1860s, a field could be as long as 590 ft. (180m). The first markings arrived in 1891, including a center circle and a line running the width of the field, 36 ft. (10.98m) in front of the goal line. A penalty could be taken from any point along that line. It was another 11 years before the field markings that we know today were introduced. Since then only two additions have been made—the penalty arc at the front of the penalty area (in 1937) and the corner quadrants (in 1938).

▶ *Referee Ken Aston came up with the idea of red and yellow cards after a stormy World Cup game in 1966. Here, he sends off Italy's Georgio Ferrini in 1962.*

▲ *At the 2002 World Cup, held in Japan and South Korea, the grass at the Sapporo Dome was grown away from the stadium and then was moved as an entire field into the arena on a "cushion" of air.*

GOALS

To score a goal, a team has to propel the entire ball over the goal line, between two posts that are set 24 ft. (7.32m) apart. On many occasions controversy has occurred over whether the ball crossed the line— from the 1966 World Cup final between England and West Germany to the

THE MEN (AND WOMEN) IN BLACK

Referees did not feature in early games of soccer because the sport's founders believed that gentlemen would never intentionally foul or cheat. Instead each team had an umpire to whom they could appeal. By 1891, games were controlled by a referee in order to cut down on controversial decisions and long interruptions for debates, and the two umpires became linesmen. (Since 1996 linesmen have been known as assistants.) Despite often being described as the "men in black," referees have played in all types of colors. Early referees tried to keep up with play while dressed in the popular fashions of the time—pants, a blazer, and even a bow tie.

Champions League semifinal in May 2005 between Chelsea and Liverpool.

Early goals consisted of only two posts. Following arguments over the height of a shot, a white tape was attached to the posts, 8 ft. (2.44m) above the ground. Wooden crossbars began to replace tape in the 1870s. Goal nets came later, invented by an engineer from Liverpool, England, John Alexander Brodie. They were first given a trial in January 1891, when Everton's Fred Geary became the first player to put the ball in the back of the net. Incidentally, that game was refereed by Sam Widdowson, who had invented shin pads 17 years earlier.

FACT FILE The Belgian referee at the 1930 World Cup final, Jean Langenus, wore a suit jacket, golfing plus fours, and a red striped tie.

CLEATS AND BALLS

No game is complete without the soccer ball, 40 million of which are sold every year. It is the referee's job to inspect the game ball and spare balls for size (26.5–27 in./68–70cm), weight (14–16 oz./410–450g), and correct air pressure. Modern balls are made from leather or synthetic materials, with a waterproof outer coating. Brazilian team Santos pioneered the use of a white ball (instead of the traditional brown leather ball) for better visibility during evening games. Early soccer balls were made from the inflated bladder of a pig or sheep, covered in a leather shell that was secured with a set of laces. Contrary to popular myths, soccer balls of the past were not heavier than today's, at least when they were dry. Without a waterproof covering, however, early balls soaked up moisture and gained weight.

Soccer cleats were certainly heavier in the past. Originally, players used their heavy work boots, tying them up over the ankles. The boots often had reinforced toe caps, and players sometimes nailed metal or leather studs into the soles. Modern cleats are lightweight and flexible, allowing a player to "feel" the ball on his or her foot. Their soles come in a range of stud, dimple, and blade patterns. Each design gives the right level of grip for a particular field condition.

> **FACT FILE**
> India withdrew from the 1950 World Cup when FIFA refused to allow their players to be barefoot.

▲ Some modern cleats have molded dimples for playing on hard or artificial fields; others have screw-in studs to increase the grip on wet or soft fields.

▲ Alex James, a star for Arsenal in the 1930s, tries out a muscle-enhancing machine. Today's players undergo carefully planned exercise routines and eat a diet that is scientifically monitored by their teams.

ALL DRESSED UP

Today's lightweight soccer uniforms are the result of years of research and development. During the first-ever international game, in 1872, the Scotland and England teams wore knickerbockers (long shorts), long shirts, and "bobble" hats or caps. Gradually, soccer uniforms developed to give players more freedom of movement, although shorts remained almost knee length until the 1960s. Numbers appeared on shirts regularly for the first time in the 1930s, but player names did not arrive until the late 1980s. In 1924 the English Football Association (FA) began to insist that teams have a second shirt (known as an away shirt) that could be worn in the event of a color clash. Today uniform manufacturing is a highly profitable business. Teams often have two or even three away shirts; they update their uniform design every season and sell many thousands of replica shirts to supporters.

▼ Samuel Eto'o wears Cameroon's radical all-in-one uniform at the 2004 African Nations Cup. The figure-hugging design gave opponents little material to tug or pull but broke FIFA's rule that shirts and shorts have to be separate. An earlier Cameroon uniform with sleeveless shirts—worn for the 2002 World Cup qualifying games—was also declared illegal.

SOCCER'S ORIGINS

A tavern in Victorian England seems to be an unlikely place to launch a sport that would become the world's biggest and most popular. Yet that is exactly what occurred in 1863 at the Freemason's Tavern in London, England. There, representatives of 12 clubs met to form the Football Association (FA) and drew up a single set of rules for the game.

HISTORY MYSTERY

No one knows where the first forerunner of soccer was played. The ancient Greeks took part in a team ball game known as *episkyros* or *pheninda*, while the Romans played *harpastum*. Paintings dating back more than 2,000 years show men and women enjoying the ancient Chinese game of *tsu chu*, in which players tried to propel a ball made of stuffed animal skin through bamboo goalposts up to 33 ft. (10m) tall. During the Ch'in dynasty (255–206 B.C.) a form of *tsu chu* was used to help train soldiers.

In medieval Europe games of mob soccer were so unruly and violent that the leaders of several countries, including Charles V in France and Oliver Cromwell in England, attempted to ban the sport. In contrast to mob soccer, the Italian game of *calcio* was first played in the 1500s by aristocrats and religious leaders, including three popes. Each team was made up of 27 players, and goals were scored by kicking or throwing the ball over a certain spot on the edge of the field.

GETTING ORGANIZED

By the late 1700s and early 1800s, a kicking-and-rushing ball game was played in schools and universities across Great Britain, but rules varied from place to place. In 1848 players at Cambridge University drew up soccer's first set of rules. This attempt to bring order into the game only had limited success, and so in 1863 representatives of 12 teams (including the Crusaders, No Names of Kilburn, and Crystal Palace) met in London. They formed the FA, developed the laws of the game, and, eight years later, set up the world's oldest surviving cup competition, the FA Cup. The first-ever international game, between England and Scotland, was played in 1872, and in 1888 the first soccer league was founded in England.

▼ *This illustration shows a friendly international game between England and Scotland in 1878. Between 1873 and 1888, Scotland lost only one out of 31 international games.*

▼ *The Japanese game of kemari is at least 1,500 years old. Players had to stop the ball from touching the ground by juggling and passing it with their feet. This reenactment was held to celebrate Japan's cohosting of the 2002 World Cup.*

HIT THE NET

www.11v11.co.uk
The Web site of the Association of Football Statisticians has historic photos and features on soccer's early history.

www.womensoccer.com
An online magazine with news and features on international women's soccer.

www.innotts.co.uk/soccer/hist1.htm
Featuring articles on the history of the game, plus a time line of soccer milestones.

▼ Malin Mostroem, the captain of Sweden, turns past Nigeria's Effioanwan Ekpo at the 2003 Women's World Cup, held in the U.S.

WHAT'S IN A NAME?

Around the world many teams have taken their names from European teams. Here are just a few:

ARSENAL LESOTHO
Lesotho Cup winners 1989, 1991

LIVERPOOL
Namibia, league champions 2002

BARCELONA
Ecuador, league champions 1995, 1997

EVERTON
Chile, league champions 1950, 1952, 1976

JUVENTUS
Belize, league champions 1999

MANCHESTER UNITED FC
Gibraltar, league champions 1999

AJAX CAPE TOWN
South Africa

QPR FC
Grenada, league champions 2002

THE WOMEN'S GAME

Women's soccer struggled from the beginning against male prejudice that it was "unladylike" for females to play the game. Interest in women's soccer reached its first peak after World War I thanks to the exploits of the Dick, Kerr Ladies team (see page 81). The women's game was then stifled for almost 50 years following the introduction of a ban on women playing at the grounds of FA member teams. Between 1969 and 1972, bans were lifted in a number of countries, and women's soccer slowly began to expand. The first European Championships for women were held in 1984, while an Olympic competition was launched in 1996. More than 60 nations entered the qualifying competition for the first Women's World Cup in 1991.

SOCCER EXPORTS

Soccer spread rapidly around the globe in the late 1800s. The game was exported first by British players and then by players from other European nations, especially to their colonies. Soccer was introduced to Russia in 1887 by two English mill owners, the Charnock brothers, while resident Englishmen founded Italy's oldest league club, Genoa, six years later.

In 1885 Canada defeated the U.S. 1-0 in the first international game to be played in the Americas. In Argentina, British and Italian residents encouraged the formation of South America's first team, Buenos Aires, in 1865. The first league in South America was set up 28 years later.

In 1904 FIFA was founded in Paris, France, with seven members: Belgium, Denmark, France, the Netherlands, Spain (represented by Madrid FC), Sweden, and Switzerland. Over time FIFA became the dominant organization in world soccer. In 1930 it had 45 member nations; in 1960 that figure stood at 95. In May 2004 FIFA welcomed the Pacific island nation of New Caledonia as its 205th member.

▶ W. R. Moon of the Corinthians, an amateur English team, poses for a photograph in his uniform. The Corinthians helped spread soccer's popularity by touring the world. Their 1910 trip to South America inspired the formation of the famous Brazilian team Corinthians Paulista.

THE GLOBAL GAME

FIFA is in control of world soccer. At continental or regional levels, the game is organized by six confederations. The traditional powerhouses of international soccer have been Europe and South America, home to the world's richest teams and the winners of every World Cup. But as other regions begin to exert more influence, the global game is changing.

▲ Steve Mokone was the first black South African to play professionally in Europe. From the 1950s, he played for England's Coventry City, Dutch team Heracles, Spain's Valencia, Marseille in France, and Italy's Torino. Mokone later played in Australia and Canada.

BALANCE OF POWER

Huge advances have been made by the federations and national teams of regions outside of Europe and South America. More and more national soccer teams have become truly competitive on the world stage, thanks to the emergence of dozens of high-quality players, primarily in Africa, but also in Asia. Australia, for example, performed well at the 2006 World Cup (its first since 1974), narrowly losing to the eventual winners, Italy, in the second round. African teams have won two out of the last three Olympic Games, and at the end of 2006 the continent had three teams— Nigeria, Cameroon, and the Ivory Coast— ranked in FIFA's top 20. There have also been strong showings by Japan, South Korea, and the United States at recent international tournaments. Today, FIFA is working hard to promote the game outside of its traditional strongholds. African and Asian nations have been chosen to host many tournaments, including the World Cups of 2002 (South Korea and Japan), 2010 (South Africa), and the Women's World Cup of 2007 (China). Additionally, Africa and Asia now enjoy more automatic places at the World Cup than ever before.

FACT FILE A European team has reached the final of all but two World Cups (1930 and 1950).

◄ Argentina line up to play Germany in the 2006 World Cup. At the time, only goalie Roberto Abbondanzieri played club soccer in Argentina. After the tournament, he signed with Spanish club Getafe.

CONCACAF
Confederation of North, Central American, and Caribbean Association Football
www.concacaf.com
Founded: 1961
Members: 40

Mexico and the U.S.—traditionally the strongest CONCACAF nations—have hosted three World Cups, while smaller nations, such as Costa Rica, have reached the tournament. CONCACAF teams have often been invited to play in South America's Copa America competition, and the federation actually includes two South American nations, Guyana and Suriname.

UEFA
Union of European Football Associations
www.uefa.com
Founded: 1954
Members: 52

As the most powerful confederation, UEFA was awarded 14 of the 32 places at the 2006 World Cup. It runs the two largest competitions after the World Cup—the European Championships and the Champions League. Thousands of foreign players work in Europe, but UEFA clubs may soon be forced to include a minimum number of homegrown players on their teams.

CONMEBOL
Confederación Sudamericana de Fútbol
www.conmebol.com
Founded: 1916
Members: 10

CONMEBOL teams have won nine of the 18 World Cup finals. Brazil and Argentina are rarely out of the top five in FIFA's rankings, while Uruguay, Chile, Colombia, and Paraguay frequently field strong teams. Domestic leagues are suffering, with clubs in debt and top players heading to Europe. Despite a disappointing World Cup in 2006, Brazil was still ranked as FIFA's number-one team at the end of that year.

CAF
Confédération Africaine de Football
www.cafonline.com
Founded: 1957
Members: 54

Africa was not awarded an automatic World Cup place until 1970, but the rise of soccer in this continent meant that the CAF sent five teams to the 2006 tournament. While national teams continue to improve, the domestic game struggles because of a lack of money and the movement of its best players out of Africa. In 2001, for example, 979 African players were playing in Europe and 102 in Asia.

AFC
Asian Football Confederation
www.the-afc.com/english/intro.asp
Founded: 1954
Members: 46

Asian soccer is booming. The highly successful Asian Champions League was set up in 2002, and national leagues are increasingly well supported. Many foreign players play in Asia—more than 30 Brazilians are based in Japan, for example. Australia joined the AFC in 2006, but all eyes are now turning on China, which has the world's largest pool of potential players and supporters.

OFC
Oceania Football Confederation
www.oceaniafootball.com
Founded: 1966
Members: 11

Soccer has struggled for support in Oceania. In the larger countries it has to compete with more popular sports, while smaller nations suffer from a lack of money, facilities, and players. Australia, the OFC's biggest and most successful nation, became frustrated by the lack of an automatic World Cup place for the confederation. In January 2006 it left the OFC to join the Asian Football Confederation.

> **FACT FILE** New Zealand was the last OFC team to reach a World Cup, back in 1982.

HAVE CLEATS, WILL TRAVEL

Soccer is flourishing all over the world, but Europe remains the most attractive destination for the world's top players. The globe's 20 richest teams are all European, and this situation is unlikely to change for some time as a result of the huge amounts of money that teams receive from television rights, advertising, and qualifying for the Champions League. This revenue enables European teams to hire the best players from around the globe. Out of more than 700 players at the 2006 World Cup, 102 played club soccer in England, 74 in Germany, 60 in Italy, and 58 in France. Not one member of the Ivory Coast team played club soccer at home, and only one played in Africa.

In the past South American soccer teams held onto many of its stars. Every member of Brazil's 1970 World-Cup-winning team played for a team in his home country. This has changed, with hundreds of players moving to Europe in search of higher salaries and the chance to play in the most prestigious competitions, from Serie A and La Liga to the Champions League.

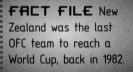

◄ *Emmanuel Olisadebe was born in Nigeria, plays soccer in Greece, and represented Poland at the 2002 World Cup. Many other African-born players now play for a European country, including Djibril Cissé of France, Norway's John Carew, and Belgium's Mbo Mpenza.*

HIT THE NET

www.worldsoccer.com
World Soccer magazine's Web site focuses on global soccer and its best players, teams, and competitions.

www.afcchampionsleague.com/en/news
The official Web site of the Asian Champions League, with the latest news, results, standings, plus team profiles.

www.soccerstats.com
Get the latest soccer news and competition standings from around the world.

Alfredo di Stefano (in white) kicks Real Madrid's second goal past Eintracht Frankfurt goalie Egon Loy. Despite making a number of fantastic saves, Loy conceded seven goals.

MADRID'S MAGNIFICENT SEVEN

Soccer's capacity to surprise, excite, and, above all, entertain has rarely been better showcased than in the final of the fifth European Cup in 1960. Real Madrid, the winner of the first four competitions, played Eintracht Frankfurt in front of a record crowd of more than 130,000 at Scotland's Hampden Park. Eintracht took an early lead. Was Real's reign as the unrivaled master of Europe about to end? The answer was an emphatic "no." Led by Hungarian genius Ferenc Puskas and Argentinian virtuoso Alfredo di Stefano, the Spanish team put on a dazzling display of attacking soccer. In an electrifying 45 minutes Real went from 1-0 down to 6-1 ahead, courtesy of goals by both Puskas and Di Stefano. But the enterprising German team was just as committed to attacking. They fought back, scoring two goals and hitting the woodwork twice, while Real countered with its seventh and Di Stefano's third goal to eventually triumph 7-3. No one who witnessed the game would ever forget the spectacle of Europe's best team playing at the peak of its skills.

BASIC SKILLS

In the words of former Liverpool coach Bill Shankly, "Soccer is a simple game based on the giving and taking of passes, on controlling the ball, and on making yourself available to receive a pass." Shankly's words highlight the most important skills in soccer.

BALL CONTROL

The world's top players, such as Zinedine Zidane and Ronaldinho, appear to control the ball effortlessly. Their easy command and movement of the ball hides thousands of hours of practice and training, often from a very early age. As children, many great players spent long hours playing games with a tennis ball, a crumpled ball of paper, or a battered piece of fruit.

Players can control the ball with any part of their bodies except for their hands and arms. Cushioning is a technique in which a player uses a part of the body to slow down a moving ball and then bring it under control with his or her feet. High balls can be cushioned using the chest, thigh, or a gentle header to kill the ball's speed and bring it down. For a low, incoming ball, the foot is preferred—either the inside of the shoe or its instep (where the laces are). A ball that is rolling across the field can be stopped with the sole of the foot— a technique known as trapping.

▲ French female players practice their close control skills by keeping the ball up using their heads and feet. Good ball control only comes after hundreds of hours of practice.

► David Beckham leans back to perform a chest cushion during a Real Madrid training session. A good chest cushion sees the ball drop at the feet of the player, who can then pass, run, or shoot.

▲ Real Madrid's Zinedine Zidane brings the ball down during a Champions League game against Italian team Roma. He uses a side-foot cushion to leave the ball at his feet.

◄ An instep cushion is used to control a ball that is arriving from the front. Here, the player meets the ball with his shoelaces and instantly pulls back his foot, stopping the speed of the ball.

SHIELDING AND OBSTRUCTION

When players have the ball at their feet, they are said to be in possession and have a number of options. These include: running with the ball; dribbling with the ball close to the feet; passing; shooting; and shielding the ball. Shielding or screening involves a player putting his or her body between the ball and an opponent in order to prevent the other player from gaining possession. This gives the shielding player crucial time to decide on the next move, which may be a pass backward to a teammate or a sharp turn and an attempt to play the ball around the opponent. Shielding players have to be careful not to hold, push, or back into the other player. They must also keep the ball close by and under control, or otherwise the referee may award an indirect free kick for obstruction (in which a player unfairly blocks an opponent's path to the ball). An obstruction usually occurs when a player steps into the path of an opponent when the ball is several feet away.

◀ Sergiy Nazarenko of Ukrainian team Dnipro Dnipropetrovsk shields the ball from FC Utrecht's Etienne Shew-Atjon during a 2004–2005 UEFA Cup game.

▶ Pavel Nedved of Juventus hits a long instep drive pass during a Serie A game against Messina in 2004.

PASS MASTERS

Passes can be made with a thrust of the chest or with a carefully directed header. Usually, however, they are made with one of three parts of the shoe—the outside, the instep, or the inside. The inside or side-foot pass is the most common and accurate pass, allowing players to pass the ball with a high level of precision. Some players attempt as many as 60 or 70 passes in one game, most of which are side-foot passes. At Euro 2004 Denmark's Thomas Gravesen averaged 81 attempted passes per game.

For longer passes, players tend to use the instep. This allows them to propel the ball with force. The instep can also be used for lofted drives that send the ball into the air as a cross or a clearance, as well as to stab down on the back of the ball. This makes the ball rise up at a steep angle, known as a chip. A pass' weight—the strength with which it is hit—is as important as accuracy in order for the pass to be successfully completed. At Euro 2004 strong passers such as France's Claude Makalele, Stilian Petrov of Bulgaria, and Germany's Dietmar Hamann all completed 88 percent or more of their passes.

◀ Wigan's Jason Roberts (left) and QPR's Danny Shittu compete shoulder to shoulder for the ball.

▲ Arsenal striker Thierry Henry hits a perfect side-foot pass, keeping his eye on the ball and letting his kicking leg follow through and point toward the target.

MOVEMENT AND SPACE

Soccer is a dynamic, fast-moving sport. Throughout a game pockets of space open and close all over the field. A player who has an awareness of where space exists or where it will shortly open up is a great asset to a team. Just as valuable is the ability to move into that space to receive a pass. The more space a player has, the more time he or she usually has to receive the ball, control it, and attack with it.

SPOTTING AND CREATING SPACE

The ball can zip around a field much more quickly than even the quickest player. Good players make the ball do the work, moving it around with quick, accurate passes. Vision is the priceless ability to spot a pass, space, or goal-scoring opportunity that other players do not see–or before they see it. Players with good vision try to move into a space, timing their run to give a teammate who has the ball a chance of making a pass that cannot be intercepted by an opponent. Once the ball has left the passer's control, he or she often moves into a position to receive a return pass. All players, not just midfielders and attackers, must be capable of passing well and moving into space in order to receive passes in return.

Players can create space for themselves or for teammates through quick, agile movements and the use of feints or dummies, with which

► Germany's Michael Ballack advances upfield against Iceland in 2003. Keeping the ball under close control, he holds up his head in order to assess the options for a pass or run.

they attempt to fool a nearby opponent into thinking that they are moving one way, before sprinting off in another direction. World-class players like Zinedine Zidane, Michael Ballack, Pavel Nedved, and Arjen Robben are especially skilled at outwitting an opponent in this way in order to find space.

◄ A wall pass (also known as a one-two pass) is a classic way to cut out an opposition player. It involves two passes that must be hit quickly and accurately, with the first passer running to collect the return ball.

FACT FILE
At Euro 2004 Portugal completed more passes than any other team—2,504 in only six games.

▲ Making space can be crucial to winning the ball at a throw-in. Here, one player makes a decoy run toward the thrower, dragging a defender with him and creating space in which a teammate can collect the ball.

▲ Dutch winger Arjen Robben (right) attempts to move around the outside of Portugal's Miguel in the semifinal of Euro 2004.

OFFSIDE

Teams have to stay aware of Law 11, the offside law, throughout a game. In 1847, under the rules of Eton College in England, being offside was known as "sneaking." A player was caught sneaking when there were three or fewer opposition players between him and the goal at the moment a teammate passed the ball forward. The rule has been altered over the years. The most notable change came in 1925, when the number of players between the attacker and the goal was reduced from three to two. The result was a goal avalanche, as defenses struggled to cope with the rule change and attackers took advantage. In the English leagues, for example, 1,673 more goals were scored in the 1925–1926 season than under the old law in the previous year.

Today a player is offside if, at the moment the ball is played, he or she is in the opposition half and is closer to the opponent's goal line than both the ball and the second-from-last opponent. That opponent can be an outfield player or the goalkeeper. Players cannot be offside in their own half or if they receive the ball directly from a goal kick, throw-in, or corner.

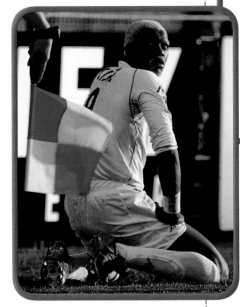

▲ Auxerre's Djibril Cissé (now at Liverpool) looks ruefully at the referee's assistant after being signaled offside in a 2004 French league game against Toulouse.

Being in an offside position is not an offense in itself. Referees must judge whether the player in an offside position is involved in active play at the moment that the ball is struck. This controversial aspect of the law tests an official's judgment to the limit. Is a player who is offside but a long way from play, for example, involved or not? What if he or she is drawing defenders out as markers? If a referee does stop the game, an indirect free kick is awarded to the opposing team at the place where the player was judged offside.

▲ Here, the player at the top left of the picture is in an offside position when the ball is struck. The referee decides that he is not interfering with play, however, and awards the goal.

▲ You cannot be offside if you are behind the ball when it is played. This scorer receives the ball from a teammate who is ahead of him, so he is onside, and the goal is given.

HIT THE NET

www.dynamic-thought.com/OffsideClicketteLo.html
A site featuring diagrams and animations that explain the key points of the offside rule.

www.fifa.com/en/regulations/regulation/0,1584,3,00.html
View the latest laws of the game as approved by FIFA or download them in PDF format.

www.asktheref.com
A site for budding referees—learn more about the laws of the game and the jobs of soccer officials.

www.futsalplanet.com
A Web site dedicated to futsal, with tournament news and results, as well as links to the laws of the game.

SMALL-SIDED GAMES

In many countries children under the age of 11 play games that feature six, seven, or eight players per team. These small-sided games give young players an invaluable chance to see more of the ball and improve their control, passing, and movement skills. Around the world small-sided games are played by children, teenagers, and adults of all skill levels on indoor or outdoor fields at schools and parks. Futsal is FIFA's official five-on-five game. A game lasts for 40 minutes (two halves of 20 minutes) and is played on a field the size of a basketball court, without surrounding boards or walls. Futsal was devised by a Uruguayan, Juan Carlos Ceriani, in 1930. The game flourished and developed throughout South America, with the first international competition—the South American Cup—taking place in 1965. The first futsal World Championship was held in 1989.

▲ Spain and Brazil battle it out in the final of the 2004 futsal World Championship, held in Taipei, Taiwan. Spain won the 40-game tournament, beating the Brazilians 5-4 in a penalty shoot-out after a 2-2 tie.

OFFICIALS

Frequently abused by players, coaches, and fans, referees are soccer's guardians and the enforcers of its laws. Their job is to impose order throughout a game and to prevent intimidation, injury, and cheating.

THE REFEREE'S ROLE

Referees perform a surprisingly large number of tasks before and after a game. These include checking the goals, nets, and balls and deciding whether the field and weather conditions are suitable for the game to go ahead. Afterward they write a report containing details of disciplinary actions and other important incidents. On the field, the referee runs the game. His or her duties range from adding on time because of injuries, other stoppages, and time wasting to deciding whether the ball is in or out of play or has crossed the goal line. If a player commits a foul or breaks a law, referees must stop play and order a restart such as a drop ball or a free kick. They can caution players and team officials and even abandon a game if weather, crowd trouble, or another factor makes the game unplayable. Referees have to follow the laws of the game, but they have a certain amount of freedom to interpret aspects of the rules as they wish. For example, if a player is fouled when his or her team is in a promising position, a referee may let the game continue, playing the advantage rule to keep it flowing.

ASSISTANTS AND THE FOURTH OFFICIAL

A referee relies on his or her assistants as extra pairs of eyes. Referee's assistants indicate when the ball goes out of play and whether a goal kick, corner, or throw-in should be awarded. They also use flag signals to point out that a substitution has been requested, a player is offside, or whether an offense has taken place out of the view of the referee. A referee can consult with an assistant if he or she was closer to the action, but it is up to the referee to make the final decision. In some competitions a fourth official carries out duties before and after a game and also performs touchline tasks. These include helping with substitutions and displaying the amount of time added on at the end of a game for stoppages.

▲ The fourth official checks the shoe studs of Paraguayan substitute Nelson Vera in a World Youth Championship game against Uruguay.

> **FACT FILE** In 1998 English referee Martin Sylvester sent himself off after punching a player during a game in the Andover and District Sunday League.

▲ Referee Dermot Gallagher shows attention to detail by asking Manchester United's Cristiano Ronaldo to remove his jewelry before continuing play in a 2004 Premiership game against Everton.

▼ Coaches and team officials can be cautioned or sent off if they use abusive language or do not behave responsibly. Here, Celtic coach Martin O'Neill is sent off during a 2002 UEFA Cup game against Celta Vigo.

◄ Early in a game a good referee talks to players to calm them down or issues verbal warnings rather than yellow and red cards. Here, Nicole Petignat tries to soothe AIK Solna's Krister Nordin in the first UEFA Cup game to be refereed by a woman, in 2003.

HEAVY PRESSURES

Thousands of amateur referees give up their weekends and evenings for free, purely to give something back to the game they adore. In contrast, officials in charge of major championship games are minor celebrities who are paid significant amounts of money. This is a reflection of the importance of their job. Top referees have their performances assessed, attend training seminars, undergo regular medical checkups, and are tested for fitness. A referee may run between 5.6–7 mi. (9.5–11.5km) during a game (even farther if extra time occurs) and often has to sprint to keep up with play. Referees work in a harsh, unforgiving environment in which footage from multiple cameras and slow-motion television replays are broadcast over and over again, highlighting every poor decision. At the 2006 World Cup, for example, British referee Graham Poll mistakenly issued three yellow cards to Croatia's Josip Simunic, before finally sending him off.

▲ Referee Horacio Elizondo shows the red card to France's Zinedine Zidane during the 2006 World Cup final. The midfielder was sent off for headbutting Italian defender Marco Materazzi in the chest during extra time.

CAUTION

A player is shown a yellow card if he or she:

• is guilty of unsporting behaviour such as simulation;
• shows dissent by word or action;
• persistently breaks the rules, by making repeated foul tackles for example;
• delays the restart of play;
• fails to stand at the required distance at a corner kick or free kick;
• enters or leaves the field of play without the referee's permission.

A player is sent off if he or she receives two yellow cards or one red card. Red-card offenses include a very dangerous tackle, spitting, and stopping a goal with a deliberate handball.

SIMULATION

Watching for contact in the penalty area during a fast-moving attack is especially difficult for an official. In the modern game attackers appear to fall to the ground under the slightest pressure from an opponent. Referees have to judge if a foul was committed or whether the attacker was guilty of "simulation." Many people think that simulation is only about diving without contact in order to win a free kick or a penalty. It is actually defined as pretending to be fouled in any way in order to gain an advantage. In a game at the 2002 World Cup, Hakan Unsal of Turkey kicked the ball at Brazil's Rivaldo, hitting his leg. Unsal was penalized for foul play, but Rivaldo fell to the ground, pretending that he had been hit in the face. Unsal was sent off, but video replays clearly showed Rivaldo's simulation. The Brazilian received a FIFA fine of $8,000 and widespread condemnation.

▲ Deportivo La Coruña's Juan Carlos Valeron goes flying after a lunging tackle by Gianluca Zambrotta of Juventus. The referee has to decide in a split second if a foul was committed and, if so, whether it is serious enough to book or send off a player.

RED-CARD RECORDS

FASTEST IN A TOP LEAGUE
Ten seconds—Giuseppe Lorenzo, Bologna v. Parma, 1990

FASTEST IN THE WORLD CUP
55 seconds—José Batista, Uruguay v. Scotland, 1986

MOST IN ONE GAME
20—Sportivo Ameliano v. General Caballero (Paraguay), 1993

DEFENDING

Compared to strikers or creative midfielders, defenders are rarely praised as game winners. Yet the foundation of every successful team is a composed, secure defense. Defending consists of a range of individual skills allied to good teamwork and an understanding between players so that they defend as a unit. Defenders require strength and excellent heading and tackling skills, along with intense concentration, quick reactions, and bravery. But, in truth, all players must defend if their team is to remain competitive during a game.

▲ *Portugal's Nuno Gomes (left) and Russia's Alexei Bugaev challenge for the ball. Forceful tackles that target the ball, not the player, are a key part of defending.*

▼ *With Joseph Yobo (right) in support as defensive cover, Nigeria's Nwankwo Kanu challenges Freddie Ljungberg of Sweden for the ball during a game at the 2002 World Cup.*

TRACKING AND TACKLING

The two keys to defending well are denying the opposition the chance to score and winning back the ball. As soon as an opponent gets the ball, defenders try to get between the ball and their goal and eliminate space. Defenders spend most of a game tracking opponents as they make runs and closing in on the player with the ball in order to delay his or her progress. This is called jockeying. The aim is to slow down an attack until the defending team is in a stronger position. The defender tries to guide the attacker into a weaker position such as near the sideline where there is little support. When a defender has cover from nearby teammates, he or she may make a tackle. The defender should stay on his or her feet in order to gain possession.

▶ *This attacker has spotted a weak pass by an opponent and reacts quickly to make an interception. Sometimes attackers drop back to help their team defend.*

FALLING FOUL OF THE LAW

Many of soccer's laws, such as obstruction (see page 17), apply to defenders. A defender who is jockeying must be careful not to commit a foul such as pushing, holding, or shirt pulling. A poorly timed tackle may result in a foul being awarded for kicking or tripping. Tackles from behind are especially risky, often leading to a yellow or red card if the defender makes contact with the attacker. A professional foul is a deliberate foul made to deny an attacking team a clear goal-scoring chance. Two of the most common types are using the hands or arms to stop a goal-bound ball and bringing down an attacker with the ball when he or she has a clear path to goal. Both should result in a sending off.

DEFENSIVE FORTRESS

During periods of open play defending teams "mark" opponents man to man or with a zonal system (see page 62). At corners and free kicks from a wide position they tend to mark man to man. A team may also try to catch attackers by playing an offside trap (see page 62). Communication between defenders is crucial in order to prevent attackers from getting free and into space to score. Certain teams that are equipped with highly skilled defenders who work well together have been able to squeeze the life out of opposition attacks. The AC Milan team of 1992–1993, for example, scored 26 goals and conceded only two during its entire nine-game Champions League campaign. In England, Chelsea holds the record for conceding the fewest goals in a season (2004–2005)—only 15 goals in 38 games.

▲ Central defender John Terry shouts to Frank Lampard as Chelsea defend an attack by Portsmouth. With Petr Cech in goal and world-class defenders such as Ricardo Carvalho, Chelsea won the 2005 and 2006 Premier League titles.

SHUTOUTS

Goalkeepers and defenders are especially proud of a shutout— a game in which their team does not concede a goal. Shutouts are usually credited to goalkeepers, but, in truth, they depend on a solid defense as well as midfielders and strikers who are willing to chase, track, and tackle. Italy has a reputation for producing some of the world's best defenders. Between 1972 and the 1974 World Cup, the Italian defense helped goalie Dino Zoff play 1,142 minutes—more than 12 games— without conceding a goal. The run was finally ended by Haiti. Another Italian goalie, Walter Zenga, holds the record for shutouts in the World Cup. He did not let in a goal for 517 minutes (almost six games) in 1990. The world record in professional soccer is held by Brazil's Geraldo Pereira de Matos Filho, better known as Mazaropi. Playing for Vasco da Gama in 1977–1978, he did not concede a goal for more than 20 games—a total of 1,816 minutes.

FACT FILE In 1968 Peñarol of Uruguay went unbeaten through the league season. The team conceded only five goals in 18 games.

▲ Real Madrid's Ivan Helguera and David Beckham hurl themselves bravely into the path of the ball to block a fierce shot from Asier del Horno of Athletic Bilbao.

LONGEST UNBEATEN LEAGUE RUNS (IN GAMES)

108	ASEC Abidjan (Ivory Coast), 1989-1994
104	Steaua Bucharest (Romania), 1986-1989
85	Esperance (Tunisia), 1997-2001
62	Celtic (Scotland), 1915-1917
60	Union Saint-Gilloise (Belgium), 1933-1935
59	Boca Juniors (Argentina), 1924-1927
	Pyunik Yerevan (Armenia), 2002-2004
58	AC Milan (Italy), 1991-1993
	Olympiakos (Greece), 1972-1974
	Skonto Riga (Latvia), 1993-1996
56	Benfica (Portugal), 1976-1978
	Peñarol (Uruguay), 1966-1969
55	Dalian Wanda (China), 1995-1997
	Empire (Antigua), 1997-2000
	Shakhtar Donetsk (Ukraine), 2000-2002

▶ Italian defender Paolo Maldini makes a defensive header above Sweden's Hakan Mild, clearing the ball high into the air and safely away from his penalty area.

GOALKEEPING

Goalkeepers are a breed apart. They have a different role from their teammates and even look a little different since they must wear a shirt that distinguishes them from other players and officials. The crucial last line of defense, goalies can be forgotten when things are going well but are singled out for abuse when they make a mistake that leads to a goal. Goalkeepers can also be game winners thanks to their saves and decisions and their agility and bravery.

▲ *Irish goalie Shay Given stretches to make a diving save during a Premier League game between Newcastle United and Manchester United.*

KEEPING CONTROL

Goalkeepers are allowed to control the ball with their hands and arms, but otherwise they must obey most of the same rules as outfield players. Until 1912, goalies could handle the ball anywhere in their own half, but now handling is restricted to their penalty area, with several key exceptions. Goalkeepers cannot handle the ball:

• after releasing it and without it touching another player;
• after receiving it directly from a throw-in;
• if it has been deliberately kicked to them by a teammate.

If a goalkeeper handles the ball in any of these situations or if the referee judges that the keeper is wasting time with the ball in hand (known as the six-second rule), an indirect free kick is awarded. This can be dangerously close to the goal. In the 1990s a law was passed to reduce time wasting and speed up play. It banned goalies from controlling a ball from a throw-in or a back pass with their arms or hands.

▲ *The Czech Republic's Petr Cech gathers the ball cleanly at the feet of Andy van der Meyde of the Netherlands.*

In the past goalkeepers could be tackled, but today they are well protected by referees. Even so, they have to be brave to dive at an opponent's feet, risking injury. If goalies foul or bring down an attacker, they may give away a penalty and even be sent off if the referee decides that a professional foul has been committed.

◀ *At the 2003 Women's World Cup Norway's Bente Nordby clears a dangerous ball by punching it firmly away from the goal.*

A GOALIE'S SKILLS

To achieve a shutout, goalkeepers need more than supreme agility and the ability to make diving saves. Top goalies train hard to improve their handling skills, learning to take the ball at different heights and from different angles. They must be able to stay alert for the entire game. Many minutes can go by before, suddenly, they are called into action. Goalies need good decision-making skills, too, since a cross or shot may call for them to choose whether to try to hold the ball in a save, punch it away, or tip it over the bar or around a post. Goalkeepers are in a unique position to see opposition attacks developing, and they must communicate instructions to their teammates. They line up walls at free kicks and command their goal area, urging defenders to pick up unmarked opponents. A defense and goalie that communicate well can be a formidable unit.

▶ *Italian goalkeeper Gianluigi Buffon instructs his defenders during the 2006 World Cup. Clear, decisive communication between a goalkeeper and his or her outfield teammates can stop many opposition attacks.*

DEFENSE INTO ATTACK

With the ball in hand, goalies have several ways in which they can move the ball to a teammate or upfield (known as distribution). They can roll it out on the ground, looking for options to kick the ball; they can kick it straight from their hand; or they can throw the ball. Goalies launch the ball from their hand into the opposition half by using their shoe instep to strike it on the volley or half volley. Sometimes goalies aim their kick for a tall winger or wide midfielder who is close to the sideline. This move is often rehearsed on the practice field. Goalies can bowl the ball out underarm, usually to a nearby teammate, or they can use a more powerful sidearm or overarm motion for maximum distance. A third option, the javelin throw, is often the quickest way to get the ball moving. Fast, accurate distribution from the goalie can be vital in turning defense into a rapid breakaway attack.

HIT THE NET

www.goalkeepersaredifferent.com
A fantastic Web site that is dedicated solely to goalies and is packed full of quirky facts.

http://finesoccer.com/keepers.htm
This newsletter contains advice, drills, and tips from the world of goalkeeping.

www.jbgoalkeeping.com
An impressive coaching Web site, with short online videos, covering all aspects of the goalkeeper's game.

▲ Germany's Oliver Kahn rolls the ball out underarm. In 2002 Kahn was FIFA's Goalkeeper of the World Cup. During the following league season with Bayern Munich, he set a Bundesliga record of 737 minutes without conceding a goal.

▶ Spain's Iker Casillas practices handling the ball while on the ground. Goalies work hard in training to improve their handling, flexibility, and reactions.

FACT FILE
The world's first black professional soccer player was a goalkeeper. Born in the Gold Coast (now Ghana), Arthur Wharton played in 1889 for Rotherham United in the English league.

▶ In a one-on-one situation many goalies come off their line to narrow the angle—reducing how much of the goal that the attacker can see. They stay upright for as long as possible to increase the chance of the shot striking them.

GOAL-SCORING KEEPERS

In 1882 goalkeeper James McAulay was pressed into service as a center-forward and scored in Scotland's 5-0 defeat of Wales. Since then many goalies have scored goals for their team or country. Some goals have been scored from long goal kicks that have surprised a defense or by goalkeepers running into the opposition's penalty area in the dying seconds of a game. Others have come from spot kicks in a penalty shoot-out (see page 31). A well-taken penalty by Portuguese goalie Ricardo knocked England out of Euro 2004, for example. A few goalies, mostly in South America, have become legends for their goal-scoring feats from regular penalties and free kicks. The German Jan-Jorg Butt scored 28 goals, while Paraguay's José Luis Chilavert struck 62 times. This staggering tally was passed in August 2006 by Brazilian goalkeeper Rogério Ceni, playing for São Paulo. Ceni has hit 65 goals, including 42 free kicks, and his team has never lost a game in which he has scored.

ATTACKING

As soon as a team gains possession of the ball, with time and in space, its players' thoughts turn to attacking. There are many ways in which a team can launch an attack, from a fast drive into space by a player who is sprinting forward and pushing the ball ahead to a slow, probing attack in which many players keep the ball securely in possession and look for an opening.

TEAM ATTACKS

Many attacks rely on two or more teammates working together to create a promising position. The wall pass (see page 18), for example, is a good way of propelling the ball past a defender with two quick movements. Attacking players also make decoy runs that pull defenders in one direction, creating space for another attacker to run into. Using the full width of the field can be vital to the success of an attack. Fullbacks, wingbacks, or wingers who are in space near the sideline may join an attack and make an overlapping run down the line. Receiving the ball, they may be able to head farther forward to put in a cross or cut infield and move toward the goal. An overload is a situation in which the attacking team has more players in the attacking one third of the field than the defending team. Classic ways of creating an overload are through a counterattack—in which one team's attack breaks down, and the opposition launches a rapid, direct attack—and an accurate long pass that is received by an attacker who is supported by teammates, with only an isolated defender to beat.

▲ Atlético Madrid's Hugo Leal tries to weave past a trio of Espanyol defenders during the final of Spain's Copa del Rey in 2000.

BEATING OFFSIDE TRAPS

Some teams play an offside trap (see page 62), in which defenders move up in a straight line to catch opponents offside. Beating an offside trap takes cunning, skill, and awareness. A perfectly weighted through pass can unlock the trap if the ball is collected by a player who stays onside until the moment the ball moves ahead of him or her. A long diagonal pass that switches play forward and across the field may also work. The receiver makes a run from a deep position, staying onside until the ball moves ahead, and then collects the ball behind the defense. Individual brilliance—such as dribbling or playing a short "push and go" pass—can also beat some offside traps.

▲ Ludovic Giuly of Barcelona threads an accurate through pass between Shakhtar Donetsk defenders Anatoliy Tymoshchuk and Mariusz Lewandowski in a 2004 Champions League game.

▲ A "push and go" pass can beat a lone defender or an offside trap. The attacker pushes the ball past the defender and then sprints to collect it.

SET PIECES

Set pieces are often planned in training. They are attacking moves made from a restart such as a free kick, corner, or throw-in. If a team has a player who can throw the ball a long way, it may treat a throw-in that is level with the penalty area as if it was a corner. Often a target player who is just inside the penalty area will attempt to flick the throw into the goal area. Mostly, set pieces are planned from corners and attacking free kicks (see page 30). At a corner a team's tallest players or its best headers of the ball move up, usually from defense, to join strikers and attacking midfielders in the penalty area. Corners are sometimes played short in order to catch the defending team off guard, but usually they are whipped into the goal area. The attacking team looks for a header, shot on goal, or a flick on to a teammate.

Schollen

Ibrahimovic 4

Mendes
da Silva 2

Ibrahimovic 2

Mendes
da Silva 3

Zonneveld

Stam

Ibrahimovic 3

Mendes
da Silva 1

Ibrahimovic 1

GAME ACTION

Swedish international Zlatan Ibrahimovic moved from Ajax to Juventus for around $19 million in late August 2004, but one week earlier he had given the Ajax fans a solo goal to savor. In a Dutch league game against NAC Breda, Ibrahimovic received a pass with his back to the goal, defender David Mendes da Silva on his back, and another Breda player, Mike Zonneveld, close by. Winning a tackle with Zonneveld, Ibrahimovic twisted past Da Silva and headed toward the goal. Weaving his way to the edge of the penalty area, Ibrahimovic's options looked limited, with four defenders around him. Yet with supreme balance and a series of feints and turns, he avoided the lunging tackle of Ronnie Stam. At the very last moment, when a shot with his right foot looked likely, Ibrahimovic switched the ball to his left foot in order to slide a shot past goalkeeper Davy Schollen. Ajax won the game 6–2.

▼ *Ghana's captain, Stephen Appiah, attempts to twist and turn sharply past Zimbabwean defender Cephas Chimedza in the African Nations Cup. Fake-out movements, step overs, and sharp turns are all ways of disrupting a defender.*

GAME MAGICIANS

Some attacks are inspired by a piece of individual skill, trickery, and brilliance. A player may be able to break free from a defense with a sudden change of speed and direction or a trick move such as the Cruyff turn or a drag back. Some players can simply outrun a defense, bursting through to score. Dribbling—kicking and moving with the ball under close control in order to beat defenders—is one of the most exciting sights on a soccer field. Stanley Matthews, Maradona, and Garrincha were all electrifying dribblers, while today's dribbling superstars include Ronaldinho, Cristiano Ronaldo, Ryan Giggs, and Arjen Robben. Weaving, high-speed dribblers can sometimes open up a game by themselves. They strike fear into defenders who know that one false move or a poorly timed challenge will allow the dribbler to go past or perhaps give away a free kick or penalty.

▲ *An unexpected piece of brilliance can open up a defense or result in a goal. Here, Edmilson launches a spectacular overhead kick to score Brazil's third goal against Costa Rica in the 2002 World Cup. In a game full of attacking soccer by both teams, Brazil finished as the 5–2 winner.*

GOAL SCORING

Players who score goals regularly are the most valuable of all. But scoring is not just reserved for the strikers. A successful team needs its midfielders to contribute a number of goals each season, while tall defenders who are experts at heading often score five or six goals per year from set pieces. For true strikers, goals are what they play for and are judged on. As Argentinian striker Gabriel Batistuta once said, "Goals are like bread. I need them to live."

THE GOAL SCORER'S ART

Speed, power, accuracy, confidence, and a deadly eye for a chance are just some of the qualities required to be a top goal scorer. Some skills can be honed in training—close ball control or swerving a shot, for example. Other qualities, such as confidence and vision, are harder to master. Soccer has gotten quicker at the highest level, and most strikers need a lot of speed in order to break past increasingly mobile defenders or into space to receive the ball before anyone else. Strength to hold off a challenge can be an asset too. Some strikers, however, rely more on their intuition, fast reactions, and ball skills to dribble through a crowded penalty area. Others are taller, stronger players who can score with towering headers or blasted shots. Most crucially of all, strikers have to be able to spot a chance for a goal and go for it. They need to react instinctively, using their vision to time runs into a scoring position. Once on the ball, they rarely have long to shoot. In an instant, strikers have to weigh their options, know where the goal, defenders, and goalie are, and hit a shot with enough speed, bend, or accuracy to beat the goalkeeper.

FACT FILE In 1998 Atlético Mineiro's Edmilson Ferreira celebrated a goal by eating a carrot in front of the fans of rival Brazilian team America MG. His actions caused crowd trouble and incensed America's players, one of whom was later sent off for a foul on Edmilson.

OWN GOALS

An own goal is technically any goal in which the last person to touch the ball before it crossed the line was a player on the defending team. In practice, however, an own goal is awarded not only when the ball has been deflected but also when a defending player has made a genuine error or caused a major change in the course of the ball. The history of professional soccer is littered with outrageous own goals. Among the most common are goalkeeping errors, skewed defensive clearances that are sliced into the net, and misdirected headers. Spare a thought for goalkeepers Gary Sprake of Leeds United (in 1967) and Barte Flem of Norwegian team Tromso (in 1988). Both went to throw the ball out, failed to release it, and ended up hurling it into their own goal.

◄ Manchester United's Wayne Rooney hits a volley to score against Liverpool in a 2005 Premiership game. His thunderous shot is ideal for striking at the goal from outside the penalty area.

FACT FILE
The world record for own goals in one game is a staggering 149! In the last game of the 2002 Madagascan league season, against champions AS Adema, Stade Olympique L'Emryne repeatedly scored own goals from the kickoff in protest at a refereeing decision in their previous game.

► Germany's Miroslav Klose bears down on the goal during a semifinal of the 2006 World Cup against Italy. Klose's five goals made him the top scorer of the tournament and helped take Germany to third place.

▲ When a scoring chance arrives, strikers need deadly accuracy and an ice-cold temperament. Here, Ruud van Nistelrooy calmly kicks the ball into the net despite the dive of Czech Republic goalkeeper Petr Cech.

▶ Goal-scoring midfielders are highly prized. French legend Michel Platini (far left) regularly found the back of the net. Here, at the 1984 European Championships, he scores one of three goals in a 5-0 thrashing of Belgium.

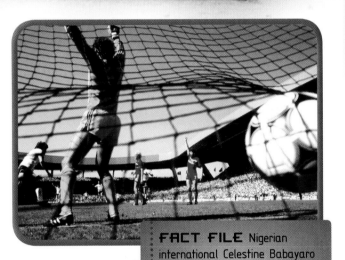

FACT FILE Nigerian international Celestine Babayaro scored on his debut for Chelsea in a 1997 preseason game against Stevenage Borough. By celebrating with a somersault, however, Babayaro broke his leg.

GOAL-SCORING RECORDS

ALL-TIME LEADING GOAL SCORERS
Artur Friedenreich (Brazil)
1,329 goals (1909–1939)

Pelé (Brazil)
1,281 goals (1956–1977)

Franz Binder (Germany)
1,006 goals (1930–1950)

MOST INTERNATIONAL GOALS
109—Ali Daei (Iran), 1993–January 2007

MOST GOALS IN ONE INTERNATIONAL GAME
13—Archie Thompson (Australia), 2001

FASTEST INTERNATIONAL GOAL
8 seconds—Davide Gualtieri (San Marino) against England, 1993

FASTEST INTERNATIONAL HAT TRICK
Inside 3.5 minutes—Willie Hall (England), 1938

MOST HAT TRICKS IN CONSECUTIVE GAMES
4—Masahi Nakayama (Japan) for Jubilo Iwata, 1998

FASTEST GOAL
2.8 seconds—Ricardo Olivera (Argentina) for Rio Negro, 1998

FASTEST OWN GOAL
8 seconds—Pat Kruse (England), playing for Torquay United, 1977

GOAL CELEBRATIONS

As fans celebrate a goal, so do players. For many years celebrations were no more flamboyant than a simple punch in the air and a hug from a nearby teammate. That all changed in the 1980s and 1990s, partly thanks to the acrobatic backflips and handsprings of Mexican striker Hugo Sanchez. Since then players have rocked imaginary babies, danced the conga, and pulled off spectacular gymnastic moves. Nigerian international Julius Aghahowa, for example, is famous for performing six or seven backflips in a row. Referees can penalize teams for time wasting owing to overlong celebrations, and the authorities often take action against players who stir up opposition fans with rude or provocative gestures.

▲ Brazil's Mauro Silva (left), Leonardo (center), and Bebeto pretend to rock babies at the 1994 World Cup. The celebration—during a 3-0 victory against Cameroon—was in honor of striker Bebeto's newborn son.

FREE KICKS AND PENALTIES

Referees award a free kick when a player breaks one of the laws of the game. Common free-kick offenses are mistimed tackles, shirt pulling, obstruction, and offside. There are two types of free kicks—indirect, which cannot be scored from without a second player touching the ball, and direct, which can be scored from directly and is awarded for more serious fouls. If a direct free-kick offense is committed by the defending team inside its penalty area, the referee may award a penalty.

FREE KICKS

Both types of free kicks are taken from where the foul or offense was committed, although a recent rule change means that in some competitions the referee can move a kick around 30 ft. (9m) closer to the goal if the other team wastes time or shows dissent. Opposition players must move around 30 ft. (9m) away from the ball, giving the team that is taking the kick valuable possession in space and with time. Some free kicks are taken quickly to get the ball moving in the middle of the field. Wide free kicks are often crossed with speed toward the goal.

Attacking free kicks engage the two teams in a battle of wits. Players on the defending team mark attackers in the penalty area and usually form a defensive wall to block a direct shot. The free-kick taker may pass to a teammate in space or try to hit a cross or shot past the wall. Some great free-kick takers, such as Brazil's Roberto Carlos, rely on awesome power to blast the ball; others, including David Beckham, are famous for the bend that they put on the strike.

THE KICK OF DEATH

Originally nicknamed the "kick of death," the penalty kick was introduced in 1891. It has created more drama and controversy than any other aspect of the game. The reason is simple. A penalty is an excellent opportunity to score since the taker is one-on-one with the goalkeeper and all the other players are outside the penalty area. In certain situations the referee can order the kick to be retaken— if the taker misses but a defender entered the area before the kick, for example. Penalty takers must hit the ball forward and cannot make contact with the ball again until it has touched another player. Some penalty takers favor accuracy over power, aiming the ball low into the corner of the goal; others blast the ball. For the goalie, trying to figure out where the ball will go is a guessing game.

◄ The Czech Republic's Marek Heinz curls a free kick into the penalty area, aiming for the head of a teammate.

▲ Juventus goalie Gianluigi Buffon shows excellent reactions to save a penalty from AC Milan's Christian Brocchi during the Italian Super Cup in 2003.

▼ *Monaco's defensive wall jumps in an attempt to block a free kick from Rivaldo (playing for Greek team Olympiakos). A wall reduces the options for a free-kick taker, but highly skilled players can bend the ball around or up and over it.*

PENALTY SHOOT-OUTS

Tense and nail-biting, a penalty shoot-out is guaranteed to bring fans to the edge of their seats. Professional soccer's first shoot-out took place in England in 1970. In the semifinal of the Watney Mann Invitational Cup, lowly Hull City held a full-strength Manchester United team to a 1-1 tie. In the shoot-out that followed, Manchester United's Denis Law became the first player to miss a shoot-out spot kick, but his team ended up as the 4-3 winner. The first shoot-out in a major tournament was in the 1972 Asian Nations Cup, when South Korea beat Thailand in the semifinal. Germany lost the first European Championships shoot-out to Czechoslovakia in 1976 but defeated France in the first World Cup shoot-out six years later.

▲ *Portuguese goalie Ricardo (left) looks nervous before his shoot-out penalty against England's David James. Ricardo's effort proved to be the winning spot kick, taking Portugal into the semifinal of Euro 2004.*

In a shoot-out five players per team are chosen to take one penalty each, all at one end of the field. A shoot-out is not considered to be part of the actual game, meaning that a goal is not added to a player's season or career tally. Neither penalty takers nor their teammates are allowed to score from a rebound–each player has only one shot at glory. The goalie knows this and often does his or her best to intimidate a penalty taker. If the scores are tied after each team has taken five penalties, the competition goes into "sudden death." Teams take one penalty each until one team misses and the other scores. On the rare occasion that all of the players on the field, including the goalkeeper, have taken a penalty and the scores are tied, the cycle begins again in the same order. Does this ever happen? Occasionally and spectacularly. In 2005, in the Namibian Cup, 48 penalties were needed to separate KK Palace from Civics (see box below), with several players taking three penalties each.

FACT FILE Tied games at the knockout stage of a competition used to be settled by tossing a coin or drawing straws. In 1954 Spain and Turkey tied 2-2 in a play-off to decide who would qualify for the World Cup. A blindfolded Italian boy, Luigi Franco Gemma, drew straws to decide the winner. Spain was knocked out.

MOST PENALTIES IN A SHOOT-OUT

PENS.	SHOOT-OUT SCORE	COMPETITION
48	KK Palace 17 Civics 16	Namibian Cup, 2005
44	Argentinos Juniors 20 Racing Club 19	Argentinian league, 1988
40	Obernai 15 ASCA Wittelsheim 15	French Cup, 1996
34	Gençlerbirligi SK 17 Galatasaray 16	Turkish Cup, 1996

▲ *Oliver Neuville of Germany keeps his nerve to place a penalty past Argentina's Leonardo Franco. Germany won the shootout 4–2 to book a place in the last four of the 2006 World Cup.*

SNAPSHOT
BAGGIO'S PENALTY MISS

"The difference between heaven and hell is one minute," said Spanish international Josep Guardiola after an epic 4-3 win over Yugoslavia at Euro 2000. For Italy's Roberto Baggio, six years earlier, it took mere seconds. In the final of the 1994 World Cup Italy and Brazil were locked in a 0-0 stalemate. Extra time ended, and a nerve-shredding penalty shoot-out began. With Italy 3-2 down, Baggio stepped up to take his team's pressure-filled fifth penalty. He decided to drive the ball down the middle, as he knew that Taffarel, the Brazilian goalie, tended to dive to one side.

Taffarel did dive, but Baggio sent the ball sailing high over the bar, handing the World Cup to Brazil. Baggio later wrote, "It was the worst moment of my career. I still dream about it. If I could erase a moment from my career, it would be that one." What is often forgotten is that two Italians before Baggio, Daniele Massaro and the highly experienced Franco Baresi, missed their penalties. Even if Baggio had scored, Brazil would have had the chance to win with its fifth spot kick. That said, the photograph of a crushed Baggio remains the iconic image of the 1994 World Cup.

Roberto Baggio hangs his head in disbelief as the Brazilian players celebrate victory in the final of the 1994 World Cup.

SOCCER LEGENDS

From France's Alain Giresse to Brazil's Zico, the game of soccer has been lit up by the talents of thousands of highly committed and skillful players, all of whom have enthralled spectators and inspired their teams to great achievements. Packed into this section are profiles of more than 75 of the finest players to have graced the game.

KEY
Country = international team
Caps = international games
Goals = international goals
(to January 2007)

GOALKEEPERS

PETER SCHMEICHEL
Denmark, born 1963
Caps: 129   Goals: 1

After playing for Hvidøvre and then Brøndby, Schmeichel became one of the best keepers of the 1990s after Alex Ferguson took him to Manchester United in 1991 for the modest fee of $1.1 million. The high point of his international career came with winning the 1992 European Championships, while the wins poured in at the team level. The hugely committed Dane redefined one-on-one goalkeeping, standing menacingly tall or bravely sprawling at an attacker's feet. After winning a triple (English Premiership, FA Cup, and Champions League) with Manchester United in 1999, he moved to Sporting Lisbon and helped the Portuguese team win its first league title in 17 years. He made a surprise return to the English Premiership in 2001, with Aston Villa and then Manchester City, before injury forced him to retire.

▶ Andoni Zubizarreta was Spain's first-choice international keeper for more than 10 years.

ANDONI ZUBIZARRETA
Spain, born 1961
Caps: 126   Goals: 0

While notching up a record 126 games for his country, Zubizarreta played hundreds more games for four Spanish clubs: Alaves, Athletic Bilbao, Barcelona, and Valencia. He won two league titles with Athletic Bilbao, as well as a European Cup, a Cup Winners' Cup, and a league title with Barcelona. He retired from international soccer in 1998, after captaining Spain in his fourth World Cup.

GAO HONG
China, born 1967
Caps: more than 100   Goals: 0

An instinctive shot stopper, Gao Hong (see page 74) began playing soccer for her factory team before moving to the Guangdong team in southeast China. She became a member of the Chinese national team in 1989 and played in both the 1995 and 1999 World Cups. Gao was in goal for China's two Asian Games successes in 1994 and 1998, and she also won a silver medal at the 1996 Olympics. At the end of her international career she appeared in the WUSA league for the New York Power.

◀ Peter Schmeichel makes a typically brave save for Manchester City in 2002.

FACT FILE As an amateur, Peter Schmeichel played as a striker. He showed those skills in the 1995–1996 UEFA Cup, when he came up for an attack and scored with a header against Russian team Rotor Volgograd.

BEST GOALKEEPER AT THE WORLD CUP

Since the 1994 World Cup, FIFA has given the Lev Yashin Award to the best goalkeeper of the tournament.

YEAR	WINNER
1994	Michel Preud'homme (Belgium)
1998	Fabien Barthez (France)
2002	Oliver Kahn (Germany)
2006	Gianluigi Buffon (Italy)

LEV YASHIN
Soviet Union, 1929–1990
Caps: 75   Goals: 0

In South America, Yashin was called the "Black Spider." In Europe he was the "Black Panther"; but everywhere he was regarded as the finest goalkeeper of his era and, possibly, of all time. Blessed with extraordinary anticipation and agility, Yashin made countless, seemingly impossible saves and stopped as many as 150 penalties during his career, which was spent completely at Moscow Dynamo. In 1954 he made his debut for the national team. Yashin's bravery, vision, and shot-stopping skills helped the Soviets win an Olympic title in 1956, the European Championships crown in 1960, and a semifinal place at the 1966 World Cup. With Moscow Dynamo, Yashin won six league titles and two Soviet Cups. In 1963 he became the first—and still the only— goalkeeper to win the coveted European Player of the Year award.

▲ Lev Yashin makes a great save at the 1966 World Cup.

GORDON BANKS
England, born 1937
Caps: 73   Goals: 0

"Banks of England" was as reliable a goalie as any nation could call upon in the 1960s. During his ten-year international career he played 35 shutouts and was on the losing team only nine times. His professional career began at Chesterfield before a $20,000 move took him to Leicester City. In 1962 Banks made his debut for England, with whom he won the 1966 World Cup. The following year he moved to Stoke City, but a car accident in 1972 caused Banks to lose sight in his right eye. The accident ended his career in Great Britain, although he did play in the U.S. for the Fort Lauderdale Strikers in 1977–1978.

FACT FILE Gordon Banks won FIFA's Goalkeeper of the Year award a record six times.

▲ Gordon Banks in action for Stoke City in 1972. Throughout his career Banks trained tirelessly on angles and repeat drills in order to improve his strength and agility.

GAME ACTION

Brazil and England played a tense yet thrilling game in the group stages of the 1970 World Cup, with Brazil winning 1-0. In the tenth minute Jairzinho slipped a high cross into the English penalty area. Rising high, Pelé headed the ball down fiercely toward the far post, with Gordon Banks seemingly stranded. The ball bounced just short of the line, and a goal seemed certain. Yet Banks showed electrifying reaction time, scrambling across his line and clawing the ball almost vertically upward and over the crossbar. Pelé was stunned and later called it "the greatest save I ever saw." Few who witnessed it would disagree.

Tommy Wright

Pelé

Alan Mullery

Banks 2

Banks 1

Tostao

PAT JENNINGS
Northern Ireland, born 1945
Caps: 119 Goals: 0

Calm, gentle, and seemingly unflappable, Northern Ireland's Pat Jennings famously received no formal coaching before joining his local team, Newry Town. A short stint with Watford followed before he moved to Tottenham Hotspur in 1964. There he won the FA Cup, two League Cups, and the UEFA Cup. In the 1967 Charity Shield game against Manchester United a kick from Jennings sailed over the head of the opposing goalie, Alex Stepney, recording a memorable goal. Jennings was sold to Tottenham's north London rivals, Arsenal, in 1977, where he played for eight seasons. He came out of retirement to play his 119th game for his country at the 1986 World Cup.

▲ Pat Jennings tips the ball over the bar during a World Cup qualifying game against England in 1985.

> **FACT FILE** Between 1966 and 1977, Sepp Maier played an astonishing 422 consecutive games for Bayern Munich.

▶ Dino Zoff organizes Italy's defense during the 1982 World Cup. Voted the Italian goalkeeper of the century, Zoff once remained unbeaten in the goal for Juventus for ten games.

▲ Sepp Maier won four league titles, three European Cups, and a Cup Winners' Cup with Bayern Munich.

SEPP MAIER
West Germany, born 1944
Caps: 95 Goals: 0

Josef-Dieter "Sepp" Maier played for local team TSV Haar before becoming an almost ever-present member of the dominant Bayern Munich team of the late 1960s and 1970s. At his acrobatic best in the 1974 World Cup (which West Germany won) and in the 1975 and 1976 European Cup finals, Maier seemed impossible to beat. He was named the German Player of the Year three times, a rare achievement for a goalkeeper. The 1978 World Cup was his last— a car accident forced him to retire one year later. Since then he has coached goalkeepers, including Germany's Oliver Kahn.

DINO ZOFF
Italy, born 1942
Caps: 112 Goals: 0

A true goalkeeping legend, Dino Zoff was rejected as a 14 year old by both Juventus and Internazionale for being too small. He finally signed to Udinese—where he let in five goals on his debut—before moving to Mantova and then Napoli. In 1972 Zoff was bought by Juventus, where he won six Italian league titles, two Italian Cups, and a UEFA Cup. Only one club title, the European Cup, eluded him—although he did win runners-up medals in 1973 and 1983. Zoff's first international call came during the 1968 European Championships. He debuted in the quarterfinals and was part of the team that won the final. A model athlete with intense concentration, Zoff broke many goalkeeping records (see page 23), and in 1982, at the age of 40, he captained Italy to its first World Cup success in the modern era. The oldest player to win a World Cup, Zoff retired shortly afterward and went on to coach Italy's Olympic team, Juventus, and Lazio. He coached Italy to the final of Euro 2000, where they lost narrowly to France.

MOHAMMED AL DEAYEA
Saudi Arabia, born 1972
Caps: 181 Goals: 0

Mohammed al Deayea can lay claim to being the finest goalkeeper that the Middle East has produced. An agile shot stopper, he was part of the Saudi team that won the 1989 World Under-16 Youth Cup—an impressive feat for a country that had no national team until 1976. Al Deayea lived up to his early promise, starring for his country at three World Cups (1994–2002). He performed heroically in a penalty shoot-out to win the 1996 Asian Cup and has won the Gulf Cup twice. At club level, he has spent most of his career at Saudi Arabia's dominant Al-Hilal team.

DEFENDERS

MARCEL DESAILLY
France, born 1968
Caps: 116 Goals: 3

Marcel Desailly is world-famous as one of the French players who won the World Cup and European Championship crowns in 1998 and 2000. He was born in the African nation of Ghana and came to France as a young child. A skillful and commanding central defender, Desailly began his career with FC Nantes and then Olympique Marseille. In 1993 he won the Champions League with Marseille before moving to AC Milan and winning the Champions League again the following year. After a series of outstanding performances at the 1998 World Cup, Desailly moved to Chelsea, where he proved to be a popular leader. In 2004 Desailly retired from international soccer and left Chelsea to join Qatar's Al-Ittihad club.

▲ *Marcel Desailly hits a long pass during France's 1998 World Cup game against Denmark.*

FACT FILE World Cup winner Marcel Desailly became the third player to be sent off in a World Cup final when he was dismissed against Brazil in 1998 after receiving two yellow cards.

▲ *In 1978 Daniel Passarella captained Argentina to the World Cup trophy on home soil.*

DANIEL PASSARELLA
Argentina, born 1953
Caps: 70 Goals: 22

Passarella was a gifted central defender who made surging runs into midfield to build attacks. He was exceptionally good in the air despite being of average height and struck devastating free kicks. In 298 Argentinian league games he scored an astonishing 99 goals. Passarella had success with River Plate before a move to Europe in 1982, first to Fiorentina and then to Internazionale. In 1985–1986 he scored 11 goals for Fiorentina, a record for a defender that lasted for 15 years. He won the 1978 World Cup, played in the 1982 tournament, and was chosen to play in 1986 but was sidelined because of an injury. After retiring, Passarella became a coach, managing Argentina at the 1998 World Cup.

ELIAS FIGUEROA
Chile, born 1946
Caps: 47 Goals: 2

This elegant and skilled defender played almost all of his soccer in the left-back position. Figueroa appeared in three World Cups—1966, 1974, and 1982—and in 1974 he was voted the best defender of the tournament. He won the South American Footballer of the Year award an unprecedented three times in a row (1974–1976). At club level, Figueroa won league titles in three different countries—the Chilean league with Colo Colo twice, the Brazilian league with Internacional on three occasions, and the Uruguayan league with Peñarol five times. He ended his career in the U.S. playing for the Fort Lauderdale Strikers alongside Gerd Müller and Teofilio Cubillas, the great Peruvian striker.

RUNE BRATSETH
Norway, born 1961
Caps: 60 Goals: 4

Rune Bratseth began his soccer career with Rosenborg Trondheim but did not go professional until the age of 23. In 1986 he moved to Germany's Werder Bremen for only $117,000. Bremen had bought a bargain, as Bratseth became their defensive linchpin, using his great speed and skills to operate as a center-back or a sweeper. Bratseth won two Bundesliga titles and a European Cup Winners' Cup with Bremen and was twice voted Germany's best foreign import. One of his proudest moments came in 1994, when he captained Norway to their first World Cup finals since 1938. After the tournament, he retired and went on to became the director of coaching at Rosenborg.

◀ *Rune Bratseth powers away from the Republic of Ireland's John Aldridge at the 1994 World Cup.*

◄ Bobby Moore, England's captain, celebrates with the 1966 World Cup.

BOBBY MOORE
England, 1941-1993
Caps: 108 Goals: 2

England's best-ever defender, Moore appeared to lack the speed and the commanding physique to be a great central defender. However, he was blessed with a wonderful eye for the game and always appeared to be one step ahead of opposition attackers. His tackling was clean and precise, and he was rarely cautioned. One of soccer's truly outstanding captains, Moore led England in 90 games—a record shared with Billy Wright—including the 1966 World Cup triumph. He spent most of his career at West Ham, only joining Fulham (alongside George Best) at the age of 32, before finally moving to the U.S. to play for the Seattle Sounders and San Antonio Thunder. His close friendship with Pelé was cemented in 1970 when the two men played out an epic struggle for supremacy in England's World Cup game against Brazil. Pelé called Moore the greatest defender he had ever played against.

▲ Matthias Sammer (left) was the first defender to win the European Player of the Year award since Franz Beckenbauer in 1976.

MATTHIAS SAMMER
East Germany/Germany,
born 1967 Caps: 74 Goals: 14

Matthias Sammer followed in the footsteps of his father, who played in midfield for East Germany and Dresden. As a midfielder, Sammer led East Germany to victory at the 1986 European Youth Championships. After Germany reunified in 1990, he moved into defense and was a commanding sweeper in the 1994 World Cup and two European Championships. A move to the Italian club Internazionale was short-lived, and he returned to Germany to join Borussia Dortmund, with whom he won two Bundesliga titles and the 1997 Champions League. In 1996 he became the first player from the former East Germany to win the European Footballer of the Year award.

PAOLO MALDINI
Italy, born 1968
Caps: 125 Goals: 7

One of the best defenders in world soccer, Paolo Maldini is, unusually, a one-club player. He made his first-team debut for AC Milan in 1985 and has played more than 600 games for the Italian club, mostly at left-back, although he can also play as a central defender or as a sweeper. Maldini is able to read the game extremely well, tackle cleanly, and move the ball forward accurately. He debuted for Italy in 1988 and soon became a regular on the national team. He played in four World Cups and four European Championships, eventually retiring from international soccer after the 2002 World Cup. In 2003 Maldini lifted the Champions League trophy for AC Milan, and one year later he won his seventh Serie A league title.

◄ Paolo Maldini, Italy's longest-serving defender, clears the ball out of his penalty area during the 1994 World Cup final against Brazil.

MASAMI IHARA
Japan, born 1967
Caps: 123 Goals: 5

Ihara was one of the most recognizable stars of the Japanese league before his retirement in 2002 after 297 J-League games. A strong, skilled defender, excellent in the air and on the ground, Ihara played in central defense or as a sweeper. He began playing for the Yokohama Marinos before the J-League was formed (in 1992) and enjoyed eight seasons with the club before joining Jubilo Iwata for one season and finishing his career with two years at Urawa Reds. By that time, Ihara had already become the first Japanese player to reach 100 caps, and he was a proud member of Japan's 1998 World Cup team, the first Japanese team to play in the World Cup finals.

▲ *The Netherlands' Ruud Krol at the 1980 European Championships, which were held in Italy.*

FACT FILE
Ruud Krol held the record as the most-capped Dutch player for 21 years. His total was finally overtaken in 2000.

▲ *Franz Beckenbauer at the 1974 World Cup. Sixteen years later he became the second man—after Brazil's Mario Zagalo—to win the World Cup as both a player and a coach.*

RUUD KROL
Netherlands, born 1949
Caps: 83 Goals: 4

Krol was a vital part of the great Ajax and Netherlands "total soccer" teams of the late 1960s and 1970s, comfortable playing in almost any defensive position. With Ajax, he won six league titles and two European Cups (1972 and 1973). Krol was the last of the Ajax greats to move away when, in 1980, he played for the Vancouver Whitecaps in Canada. He returned to Europe the following year to play for Napoli and later for Cannes in the French second division, where an injury forced him to retire in 1987. He has since coached teams in a variety of countries, including Switzerland, Egypt, and Belgium.

FRANZ BECKENBAUER
West Germany, born 1945
Caps: 103 Goals: 14

Der Kaiser ("The King") made his debut for Bayern Munich in 1964 as an attacking inside-left. Only 27 games later, he was on the national team. At the 1966 World Cup, Beckenbauer played in midfield and scored four goals on the way to the final. By the 1970 tournament, he had moved into defense, where he revolutionized the ultradefensive role of the sweeper with his astonishing vision and smooth on-ball skills. Time and time again he would turn defense into an attack, striding up the field to release teammates or to take a chance himself. With his stylish attacking play, it is sometimes forgotten that he was a masterful defender, always cool under pressure. In 1972 Beckenbauer won the European Championships with West Germany and was the European Footballer of the Year. Two years later he won the first of three consecutive European Cups with Bayern Munich and also captained his country to World Cup glory. In 1977 he made a surprise move to the U.S., playing in a star-studded New York Cosmos team before returning to Germany in 1980 with Hamburg. He became West Germany's coach in 1984, leading the team to two World Cup finals and winning one.

HIT THE NET

www.planetworldcup.com/LEGENDS/wcstars.html
A selection of profiles of many great soccer players, including Austria's Hans Krankl, Belgium's Jan Ceulemans, and West Germany's Karl-Heinz Rummenigge.

www.rsssf.com/miscellaneous/century.html
A regularly updated list of players with 100 or more international caps. Clicking on a player's name reveals a list of all of their international games.

www.ifhof.com/hof/halloffame.asp
The Web site of the International Football Hall of Fame, with detailed biographies of 25 of the world's soccer legends.

▲ *Franco Baresi won three European Cups with AC Milan, including this triumph in 1989.*

FRANCO BARESI
Italy, born 1960
Caps: 81 Goals: 1

A tough, intelligent defender, Baresi made his first-team debut for AC Milan in 1978. He played 716 games for the club, winning six Serie A titles. But Baresi had to wait until 1990 to completely break onto the Italian national team. Although part of the 1982 World Cup team, he was not chosen to play and refused to appear for Italy while Enzo Bearzot remained the coach. He played in both the 1990 and 1994 World Cups and superbly wiped out the threat of Brazil's Romario and Bebeto in the 1994 final, which Italy lost only on penalties. Milan paid him the ultimate tribute on his retirement in 1997, dropping the number six shirt from its lineup.

HONG MYUNG-BO
South Korea, born 1969
Caps: 135 Goals: 9

An excellent passer of the ball, Hong played for the Pohang Steelers in South Korea and for Bellmare Hiratsuke (now Shonan Bellmare) and Kashiwa Reysol in Japan. He is South Korea's most capped player and is a veteran of four World Cups. At the 2002 tournament, where South Korea reached the semifinals on home soil, Hong was voted the third-best player of the World Cup behind Oliver Kahn and Ronaldo. In November 2002 he became the first Korean to play in the American MLS when he signed for the Los Angeles Galaxy.

LINDA MEDALEN
Norway, born 1965
Caps: 152 Goals: 64

Medalen started her career as a striker, making her debut for Norway in 1987 and going on to win the 1988 unofficial Women's World Cup and the 1993 European Championships. At the 1991 World Cup she was her team's top scorer, with six goals, with Norway finishing as runner-up. As Medalen's career progressed, she moved into defense, where her skill in the air and strong tackling helped Norway win the 1995 World Cup, conceding only one goal in six games. Medalen played in the 1999 tournament, but a knee injury kept her out of the 2000 Olympics, which Norway won. At club level, she won five league championships and three cup competitions for the Norwegian team Asker SKK.

◄ *Linda Medalen holds off China's Ying Liu in the 1999 World Cup semifinal. The Norwegian retired one year later.*

JOHN CHARLES
Wales, 1931-2004
Caps: 38 Goals: 21

The amazingly talented Charles was equally skilled as a bustling, powerful center-forward or as a hugely commanding central defender. In both positions he was world-class. Appearing in attack for Leeds United, he scored a record 42 goals in one season, while playing internationally as a central defender. On the Welsh team Charles was joined by his brother, Mel, and teammates Ivor and Len Allchurch—the first time that any national team had included two pairs of brothers. In 1957 the British transfer record was smashed as he moved to Juventus for $188,000. Charles became a genuine legend in Italy for his towering perrformances, kind behavior toward fans, and his sportsmanship. In a highly defense-focused league he scored an astonishing 93 goals in 155 games, helping Juve win three Serie A titles and two Italian Cups. He later moved back to Leeds and then on to Parma, Cardiff City, and Hereford United before retiring.

◄ *John Charles (right) battles for the ball at the 1958 World Cup. Charles' name is still revered by Juventus fans, who nicknamed him Il Buon Gigante— the Gentle Giant.*

MIDFIELDERS AND WINGERS

JAY JAY OKOCHA
Nigeria, born 1973
Caps: 70 Goals: 13

Okocha was playing in Nigeria for the Enugu Rangers when he visited a soccer-player friend in Neunkirchen, Germany, and was asked to stay and play for the team. From Neunkirchen he moved first to Saarbrücken and then, in 1991, to Bundesliga team Eintracht Frankfurt. He was not yet 18. Okocha shone as an attacking midfielder for the German team before transferring to Fenerbahçe, where he scored 30 goals in two seasons and won the Turkish league. Internationally, Okocha was part of the emerging Nigerian team that won the African Nations Cup in 1994 and the Olympic title two years later. In 1998 he became the most expensive Nigerian player when he moved to Paris Saint Germain for around $28 million. He played in the Premier League for Bolton Wanderers from 2002, before joining Qatar SC in 2006. In the same year, he played his final game for Nigeria.

◀ *Jay Jay Okocha stretches for the ball in Nigeria's 2004 African Nations Cup semifinal against Tunisia.*

STANLEY MATTHEWS
England, 1915–2000
Caps: 54 Goals: 11

The "Wizard of the Dribble" made his first-team debut for Stoke City in 1932 and went on to amaze crowds with his sensational wing play, supreme ball control, and ability to dribble through a defense at will. Matthews' dedication to physical fitness, years ahead of his time, ensured that his career was one of the longest in British soccer. He joined Blackpool in 1947 and inspired them to an incredible FA Cup triumph in 1953, in what is remembered as the "Matthews final." His England career ran from 1937 to 1954, although he only played in 54 of the 119 internationals that the team strived to win, to the outrage of his many fans. He became the first winner of the European Footballer of the Year award in 1956, and in 1961 he returned to Stoke, for whom he played his last game in 1965, at the age of 50 years and five days. In the same year he became the first-ever serving player to be knighted.

▲ *Stanley Matthews (left) exhibits supreme poise, balance, and skill on the ball as he takes on Scotland's George Young in 1948.*

FACT FILE Stanley Matthews was praised as one of the most modest and fair players to ever grace the game. In his 33-year-long career he never received a booking.

CARLOS VALDERRAMA
Colombia, born 1961
Caps: 110 Goals: 10

Famous for his flamboyant style of play and hairstyle, Carlos Valderrama was an exquisite passer of the ball in midfield, who would often link with the attack for a devastating effect. He played for three Colombian teams—Union Magdalena, Millionarios, and Deportiva Cali—before moving to France in 1988, where he won the league title with Montpellier. In 1996 he moved to the U.S. to play for the Tampa Bay Mutiny and then Miami Fusion. Valderrama captained Colombia to three World Cup tournaments in a row (1990–1998) and retired from international soccer after the 1998 tournament. Yet, even past his 40th birthday, Valderrama was still one of the biggest stars in the MLS.

▶ *Carlos Valderrama on the ball during Colombia's 1998 World Cup game against England.*

ALAIN GIRESSE
France, born 1952
Caps: 47 Goals: 6

At 5 ft. 3 in. (1.63m) tall and weighing around 130 lbs. (60kg), Giresse was small for competitive soccer, but his tireless work in midfield caught the eye both at club level, for Bordeaux and Olympique Marseille, and with the French national team. Giresse appeared at two World Cups (1982 and 1986) and also won the 1984 European Championships. He played more than 500 games for Bordeaux and scored the winning goal in the 1986 French Cup final against Marseille, whom he joined a few weeks later. Giresse went on to manage Paris Saint Germain and Toulouse, where his son Thibault Giresse now plays. In 2004 he was appointed the head coach of the Georgian national team.

HRISTO STOICHKOV
Bulgaria, born 1966
Caps: 83 Goals: 37

As an attacking midfielder or a striker, the strong, stocky Stoichkov was surprisingly quick over a short distance and possessed unstoppable power, especially in his left foot. He emerged as a skilled young player at CSKA Sofia before moving to Barcelona. Unpredictable and with a fiery temper, Stoichkov became dissastisfied with Barcelona coach Johan Cruyff when he was asked to play out wide. He later moved to Italy's Parma, Japanese team Kashiwa Reysol, and the Chicago Fire in the MLS. He arrived at the 1994 World Cup as the star player on an underrated Bulgarian team that sensationally knocked out Germany before losing the semifinal to Italy. Stoichkov finished the tournament as the joint top scorer.

FACT FILE Stoichkov was banned for the 1985-1986 season for his part in a riot involving players and fans at the 1985 Bulgarian Cup final.

▲ *Stoichkov during the Euro '96 game against Romania. The midfielder's goal won the game.*

DAVID BECKHAM
England, born 1975
Caps: 94 Goals: 17

David Beckham is one of the most recognizable soccer players on the planet. He began his career as a youth-team player at Manchester United and then had a short loan stint with Preston North End before announcing his arrival in English soccer with a Premiership goal from inside his own half against Wimbledon. At the 1998 World Cup he was heavily criticized for kicking out at Argentina's Diego Simeone and then receiving a red card. But Beckham's excellence for team and country, especially his trademark swerving free kicks, won back public support—notably when he ensured England's qualification for the 2002 World Cup by scoring with a last-gasp free kick against Greece. Having won a Champions League, FA Cup, and Premiership triple with Manchester United in 1999, Beckham joined Real Madrid in 2003 for a fee of $50 million. He failed to win a trophy in Spain, and in January 2007 he announced a move to Los Angeles Galaxy. The deal is expected to earn him more than $260 million over five years.

▶ *In 2006 David Beckham became the first English player to score in three World Cups. He resigned as captain right after the tournamet.*

WOLFGANG OVERATH
West Germany, born 1943
Caps: 81 Goals: 17

A midfield dynamo, good at defensive duties and strong in attack, Overath started with SV Siegburg as a junior before moving to Cologne at the age of 20. In his first season he won the Bundesliga and received his first call to the national team. Overath played in three World Cups and shares with Franz Beckenbauer the record of being the only player to finish first, second, and third in the tournament. He retired from international soccer after West Germany's triumph in 1974 but continued to play for Cologne until 1977, making more than 750 appearances.

▲ *Nakata shields the ball during a Serie A game.*

HIDETOSHI NAKATA
Japan, born 1977
Caps: 77 Goals: 11

Nakata began his career playing for Japan's Bellmare Hiratsuke in 1995. He became the most outstanding player in the J-League and was voted the 1998 Asian Footballer of the Year. The same year Nakata moved to Perugia, Italy, as the first Japanese player to play in Serie A. He was transferred to Roma in 2000, with whom he won the Serie A title, before making a series of moves within the Italian league. Nakata starred in Japan's World Cup campaigns of 1998 and 2002 and is a superstar in his home country. He retired from soccer at the age of 29 in July 2006.

MICHEL PLATINI
France, born 1955
Caps: 72 Goals: 41

A truly great attacking midfielder, Platini was the glittering jewel in a French team that suffered semifinal heartbreak at the 1982 World Cup. Two years later he was the top scorer at the European Championships, with nine goals, as France won the title. Forming a magnificent partnership with Alan Giresse and Jean Tigana, Platini exhibited immense skill and vision. At club level, Platini played for AS Joeuf, Nancy, and Saint Etienne before turning down a transfer to Arsenal in favor of a move to Italian giant Juventus in 1982. He was Serie A's leading marksman three times and was crowned the European Footballer of the Year three times in a row (1983–1985)—a unique feat. Retiring in 1987, he went on to coach France and then led his country's bid to host the 1998 World Cup.

▲ *Dragan Dzajic (left) and Willie Morgan wave to the crowd after Yugoslavia's 1-1 tie with Scotland at the 1974 World Cup.*

GARRINCHA
Brazil,
1933-1983
Caps: 50
Goals: 12

Manuel Francisco dos Santos was nicknamed "Garrincha"—meaning "little bird"—at a young age. A small player at only 5 ft. 6 in. (1.69m) tall, a childhood illness had left his legs distorted, with one bent inward and the other 12 in. (6cm) shorter. Yet those who saw Garrincha play remember him as the greatest dribbler in the history of soccer. He also perfected the bending banana kick, which he used to great effect for his club team, Botafogo, scoring 232 goals in 581 games. He also played in Colombia, Italy, and in France for Red Star Paris, but it was on the international stage that Garrincha became famous. He starred in the 1958

DRAGAN DZAJIC
Yugoslavia, born 1946
Caps: 85 Goals: 23

A left-winger for his entire career, Dragan Dzajic boasted lightning-fast acceleration and an eye for a delicate pass. He made more than 580 appearances for Red Star Belgrade, scoring 287 goals, winning five Yugoslav league titles and four Yugoslav Cups. Dzalic also spent two seasons in France, where he scored 31 goals for Bastia. He was part of the Yugoslav team that entered the 1964 Olympics and reached the final of the 1968 European Championships, knocking out World Cup holders England along the way. Dzajic finished the tournament as the top scorer. After retiring from soccer in 1979, he went on to become the sports director of Red Star.

▼ *England defender Ray Wilson fails to stop the mesmerizing Garrincha as he surges down the wing in the 1962 World Cup quarterfinal. Brazil won 3-1.*

World Cup, which Brazil won, but went on to top those performances at the 1962 competition. Voted the player of the tournament, he was the joint leading scorer as he struck two goals to knock out England in the quarterfinal and then two more goals to beat Chile in the semifinal. Sadly, his life away from soccer was troubled, and he died of alcohol poisoning at the age of 49.

▲ *Platini skips a challenge during France's 4-1 win over Northern Ireland at the 1982 World Cup.*

LUIS FIGO
Portugal, born 1972
Caps: 127 Goals: 32

Luis Figo's glittering career started on a high—he was part of Portugal's "golden generation" that won the European Under-16 Championship in 1989 and the World Youth Cup in 1991. A darting wide midfielder, with exceptional dribbling and passing skills, Figo has twice been at the center of transfer controversy. The first time was in 1995, when both Parma and Juventus claimed that he had signed contracts with them to leave his first club, Sporting Lisbon. In the end, Figo moved to Barcelona, with whom he won the European Cup Winners' Cup in 1997 and consecutive Spanish league titles in 1998 and 1999. He then moved for a world-record fee to Barcelona's fiercest rivals, Real Madrid, winning two league titles and the Champions League in 2002. Figo played in three European Championships, reaching the semifinals in 2000 and the final four years later. In 2005 he came out of international retirement to help Portugal qualify for the 2006 World Cup, where they reached the semifinal.

> **FACT FILE** Luis Figo has played 14 games in the European Championships, a record he shares with Zinedine Zidane, Lilian Thuram, and Karel Poborsky.

▲ *Portugal's Luis Figo lines up a cross during the third-place playoff game against Germany at the 2006 World Cup. Germany won 3–1.*

ZINEDINE ZIDANE
France, born 1972
Caps: 108 Goals: 31

The son of Algerian immigrants, Zidane grew up in Marseille, France, with posters of his idol, Uruguayan striker Enzo Francescoli, on his wall. His first club was Cannes, followed by Bordeaux, where he won France's Young Player of the Year award in 1992. His international debut in 1994 was sensational—he scored both of France's goals in a 2–2 tie with the Czech Republic. In the 1995–1996 season Zidane played 57 games—more than any other French player—and he appeared jaded as he underperformed at Euro '96. But a move to Juventus in the same year saw him regain his best form as he helped the Serie A giants win two league titles. Zidane was a key part of the world-beating French team that captured a double World Cup (1998) and European Championships (2000). As the best midfielder in the world, he won World Player of the Year titles in 1998, 2000, and 2003. Zidane's last tournament, the 2006 World Cup, was memorable in many ways. He led France to the final, scoring three goals on the way and being voted FIFA's player of the tournament. He was sent off in the final, however, for a headbutt to the chest of Italy's Marco Materazzi.

ENZO SCIFO
Belgium, born 1966
Caps: 84 Goals: 18

One of only a handful of players to have taken part in four World Cups, Vicenzo "Enzo" Scifo (see page 87) was born to Italian parents and became a Belgian citizen at the age of 18. He was a teenage soccer prodigy, scoring a staggering 432 goals in only four seasons as a junior. After joining Anderlecht in 1980, his smooth midfield skills helped the club win three Belgian league titles in a row (1985–1987), while with the national team he reached the semifinals of the 1986 World Cup. Scifo's moves to Internazionale and then Bordeaux were both failures, but his career was reignited at Auxerre. He went on to enjoy stints at Torino, in Italy, and Monaco before rejoining Anderlecht toward the end of his career.

WORLD-RECORD TRANSFERS

PLAYER	FROM	TO	FEE	YEAR
Zinedine Zidane (France)	Juventus	Real Madrid	$68.43m	2001
Andriy Shevchenko	AC Milan	Chelsea	c. $60m	2006
Luis Figo (Portugal)	Barcelona	Real Madrid	$59.2m	2000
Hernan Crespo (Argentina)	Parma	Lazio	$56.8m	2000
Christian Vieri (Italy)	Lazio	Internazionale	$51.2m	1999
Gianluigi Buffon (Italy)	Parma	Juventus	$48.9m	2001
Rio Ferdinand (England)	Leeds United	Manchester United	$43.65m	2002
Gaizka Mendieta (Spain)	Valencia	Lazio	$43.5m	2001
Ronaldo (Brazil)	Internazionale	Real Madrid	$42.74m	2002
Juan Veron (Argentina)	Lazio	Manchester United	$42.15m	2001
Rui Costa (Portugal)	Fiorentina	AC Milan	$42m	2001

JOHAN NEESKENS
Netherlands, born 1951
Caps: 49   Goals: 17

After making his debut for the Netherlands in 1970, the exceptionally talented Neeskens played international soccer for a decade. He starred in two World Cup campaigns, which both led to heartbreaking defeats in the finals. In 1974 Neeskens scored a beautiful chip against Brazil and converted the first penalty to be awarded in a World Cup final, against West Germany. Neeskens won three Dutch league titles and three European Cups with Ajax, the European Cup Winners' Cup with Barcelona, and spent six seasons in the U.S. before retiring in 1986.

▲ *Hagi pushes forward at the 1994 World Cup.*

GHEORGHE HAGI
Romania, born 1965
Caps: 125   Goals: 34

Moody, unpredictable, and extremely skillful, Hagi played for Steaua Bucharest from 1987, either in midfield or in a free role in attack. His superb ball skills and vision helped his club win three league titles in a row, as well as the 1989 European Cup final. Hagi then played for Real Madrid, Brescia, Barcelona, and Galatasaray, with whom he won the 2000 UEFA Cup. A linchpin of the Romanian team, Hagi scored an amazing goal from 115 ft. (35m) out against Colombia at the 1994 World Cup, but he was sent off in his final international game, at Euro 2000.

▲ *Boniek scored all three goals in this 3-0 victory for Poland over Belgium at the 1982 World Cup.*

ZBIGNIEW BONIEK
Poland, born 1956
Caps: 80   Goals: 24

A hardworking attacking midfielder, Boniek won two league titles with Widzew Lodz and starred when the Polish team knocked Juventus out of the 1980 UEFA Cup. He joined the Italian club two years later and formed a deadly midfield partnership with Michel Platini. At Juventus, he won Italian league and cup titles, the European Cup Winners' Cup, and the 1985 European Cup (scoring the two winning goals). A member of three World Cup teams, Boniek scored four goals in 1982, with Poland finishing third. After joining Roma in 1985, he operated deeper and deeper in midfield, and he played as a sweeper in the 1986 World Cup.

FACT FILE Michael Laudrup is the only player to have appeared for Real Madrid in a 5-0 win over Barcelona and also for Barcelona when they beat Real 5-0.

▶ *Michael Laudrup challenges for the ball during Denmark's Euro '96 game with Portugal.*

SOCRATES
Brazil, born 1954
Caps: 60   Goals: 22

Named after the ancient Greek scholar, Brazil's Socrates played as an amateur for Botafogo while studying to become a doctor. He turned professional with the Corinthians in 1977. The tall, elegant midfielder became a firm favorite with the fans, scoring spectacular goals and threading superb passes around the field. He captained two hugely talented Brazilian World Cup teams in 1982 and 1986, but neither team did its talent justice.

FACT FILE
In November 2004, at the age of 50, Socrates played for English nonleague team Garforth Town in the Northern Counties League.

MICHAEL LAUDRUP
Denmark, born 1964
Caps: 104   Goals: 37

The peak of Michael Laudrup's international career came in the quarterfinals of the 1998 World Cup, where Denmark lost narrowly to Brazil 3-2—despite his younger brother, Brian, scoring a goal. Laudrup was much in demand as an attacking midfielder, playing for Lazio and Juventus in Italy and winning five league titles in Spain with Barcelona and Real Madrid. Sadly, he missed out on Denmark's finest hour— its Euro '92 championship triumph, when he argued about tactics with the coach and was dropped from the team.

▲ *Lothar Matthäus, Europe's most capped player.*

LOTHAR MATTHÄUS
West Germany/Germany, born 1961 Caps: 150 Goals: 23

Matthäus began his career at Borussia Mönchengladbach before moving to Bayern Munich in 1984. A powerful midfielder with great stamina, Matthäus could play as a midfield anchor or be more creative, using his passing and vision to bring others into the game. He won six Bundesliga titles at Bayern Munich, plus the Serie A with Internazionale. A veteran of five World Cups, Matthäus played in a record 25 tournament games. He led West Germany to World Cup glory in 1990, and in the same year he was voted the World Footballer of the Year. He retired from international soccer after Euro 2000.

MARIO COLUNA
Portugal, born 1935 Caps: 57 Goals: 8

Like Eusebio, Mario Coluna was born in Mozambique and played for Portugal. Coluna was often overshadowed by the great striker, but he was a superb player in his own right. His 17-year-career with Benfica began in 1954. He captained the team in the early 1960s and appeared in five European Cup finals (1961–1963, 1965, and 1968). He also led Portugal to third place in the 1966 World Cup. Coluna moved to Olympique Lyonnais toward the end of his career and later became Mozambique's minister of sports.

SUN WEN
China, born 1973 Caps: 152 Goals: 106

A legend in women's soccer, Sun Wen won seven regional championships with Chinese team Shanghai TV before moving to the U.S. in 2000 to play for the Atlanta Beat. Playing in midfield or attack, she has become one of the world's leading international goal scorers thanks to her strong shooting, vision, and eye for a goal. Sun Wen won both the Golden Boot (top scorer) and the Golden Ball (top player) awards at the 1999 Women's World Cup, where China was narrowly beaten on penalties in the final by the U.S. In 2000 she was named FIFA World Player of the Century alongside the U.S.'s Michelle Akers. After China's surprise World Cup exit at the hands of Canada in 2003, she retired.

▲ *Sun Wen goes past Ghana's Mavis Danso at the 2003 World Cup. China won the game 1-0, courtesy of a goal from Sun.*

JAIRZINHO
Brazil, born 1944 Caps: 82 Goals: 34

Jair Ventura Filho, better known as "Jairzinho," was an electrifying right-winger in a similar mold to his childhood hero, Garrincha. First capped for Brazil in 1964, he was moved to the left wing to accommodate Garrincha in the 1966 World Cup. At the 1970 tournament Jairzinho was moved back to his favored right side, where he shone, scoring in each of the six stages of the competition— a record until this day. At club level, Jairzinho spent most of his career at Brazil's Botafogo, also having short stints with Marseille in France, Portuguesa in Venezuela, and the Brazilian team Cruzeiro, with whom he won the Copa America in 1976.

◄ *Jairzinho surges forward during the third-place play-off at the 1974 World Cup. Brazil was defeated 1-0 by Poland.*

STRIKERS

JOHAN CRUYFF
Netherlands, born 1947
Caps: 48   Goals: 33

Cruyff was one of the game's best-ever players and a pivotal part of the Dutch "total soccer" revolution. Blessed with great vision and remarkable ball skills, he is the only player to have a move named after him—the Cruyff turn. He won three European Cups in a row at Ajax before following his ex-boss, Rinus Michels, to Barcelona in 1973 and helping them win Spanish league and cup titles. Cruyff played as a center-forward but would drift around the field, creating confusion among defenders. His total of 33 goals for the Netherlands would have been higher were it not for his refusal to play in the 1978 World Cup (see page 112). Cruyff later coached both Ajax and Barcelona to success in Europe.

▶ *Johan Cruyff was the European Footballer of the Year three times.*

PAOLO ROSSI
Italy, born 1956
Caps: 48   Goals: 20

As a teenager, Paolo Rossi was released by Juventus owing to a knee injury, but he went on to star for Italy at the 1978 World Cup. Juve tried to buy him back from Vicenza but was outbid by Perugia, who paid a world-record fee of $7 million. A two-year ban for alleged game fixing ended just before the 1982 World Cup, by which time Rossi was back at Juventus. After failing to score in the first four games of the tournament, the pressure was mounting. He responded with a fine hat trick against Brazil, followed by two goals in the semifinal and one in the final to emerge as a World Cup winner and the tournament's leading scorer. Sadly, he was overcome by injuries, and he retired in 1987, aged 30.

▼ *Puskas (left) fires in a shot in the 1954 World Cup final against West Germany. His goal-scoring ratio at international level—almost one goal per game—was extraordinary.*

FERENC PUSKAS
Hungary, 1927-2006
Caps: 84 (4 for Spain)
Goals: 83

A star for his club, Kispest (which became Honved), and his country, Puskas was short, stocky, and an average header of the ball. But his sublime skills, vision, and thunderbolt of a left-foot shot made him a devastating striker. After the Hungarian revolution in 1956, Puskas searched for a club in western Europe for more than one year. In his 30s and overweight, he was eventually signed by Real Madrid in 1958. He repaid Real's faith in him by leading the Spanish goal-scoring table four times, netting four goals in the 1960 European Cup final and a hat trick in the 1962 final. In 1966 he began a coaching career, which saw him take Greek team Panathinaikos to the 1971 European Cup final. In 1993 an emotional Puskas was welcomed home to act as the caretaker coach of the national team.

GEORGE BEST
Northern Ireland, 1946-2005
Caps: 37   Goals: 9

Best was only 17 when he made his first-team debut for Manchester United. He was the most gifted player to emerge from the British Isles—and its first superstar. A free spirit both on and off the field, Best's goal-scoring exploits and his eye for outrageous passes or moves quickly made him a legend. He was also a fearless tackler and great dribbler and was Manchester United's leading scorer five seasons in a row. Sadly, he was denied the biggest stage of all since Northern Ireland failed to qualify for the World Cup during his playing career. In 1974 Best sensationally retired from the game. He made a series of comebacks in England, the U.S., and, finally, Australia, where he played for the Brisbane Lions in 1983.

◀ *George Best was first capped for his country, Northern Ireland, at the tender age of 17.*

ROBERTO BAGGIO
Italy, born 1967
Caps: 57 Goals: 27

Blessed with great skill and vision, Roberto Baggio made his professional debut with Vicenza, in the Italian third division, at only 15 years of age. He broke into Serie A with Fiorentina in 1985, but when Baggio was transferred to Juventus in 1990, Fiorentina fans rioted for three days. The fee of $15.5 million made him the world's most expensive player at the time. Crowned World Footballer of the Year in 1993, Baggio scored spectacular goals for his country and the Italian clubs AC Milan, Bologna, and Internazionale. In 2004, while playing for Brescia, he scored his 200th Serie A goal. He appeared in three World Cups and scored five of Italy's eight goals in the 1994 competition. However, Baggio will always be remembered for his costly penalty miss in the final of that tournament (see pages 32–33). The striker was given an emotional international send-off in 2004, when he played for Italy for the first time in five years in a friendly against Spain.

▶ Baggio chases the ball in his final game for Italy.

DENNIS BERGKAMP
Netherlands, born 1969
Caps: 79 Goals: 37

Named after the Scottish striker Denis Law, Bergkamp was a product of the famous Ajax youth academy. He played in the Dutch league for the first time in 1986. The most technically gifted Dutch player since Johan Cruyff, Bergkamp often played in the space between midfield and attack, where he used his eye for an unexpected pass, plus a world-class technique, to create as many goals as he scored. After an unsuccessful time at Internazionale, Bergkamp moved to Arsenal for $15 million in 1995. In 11 years at the club, he won three Premier League titles and scored or set up more than 280 goals. He retired in May 2006 after the final of the Champions League against Barcelona.

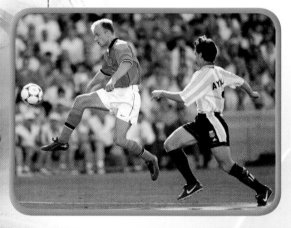

▲ Dennis Bergkamp brings the ball down moments before his sublime goal against Argentina at the 1998 World Cup.

FACT FILE Dennis Bergkamp's fear of flying has caused the striker to miss many international and European games for Arsenal.

GAME ACTION

Dennis Bergkamp broke the deadlock in a tense 1998 World Cup quarterfinal against Argentina with a sensational goal. On the stroke of 90 minutes, Frank de Boer hit a 164.-ft. (50-m) pass into the penalty area. Controlling the ball with one delicate touch of his right foot, Bergkamp took a second touch to turn Argentinian defender Roberto Ayala, before shooting powerfully past goalie Carlos Roa. The goal saw Bergkamp become the Netherlands' leading international scorer.

Roa

Ayala 2

Bergkamp 1

Bergkamp 2

Ayala 1

▲ *Fontaine is chaired off the field after scoring four goals in France's 6-3 defeat of West Germany in the third-place play-off at the 1958 World Cup.*

JUST FONTAINE
France, born 1933
Caps: 21   Goals: 30

Fontaine was born and brought up in Morocco before coming to France in 1953 to play for Nice. A relatively slight center-forward with a real eye for the goal, he scored 45 times in three seasons at Nice before moving to Stade de Reims, where he achieved 116 goals in only four years. Yet, going into the 1958 World Cup finals, Fontaine was the third-choice striker behind Raymond Kopa and René Bliard. An injury to Bliard allowed Fontaine to start the first game against Paraguay, in which he scored a hat trick. He followed this with a further ten goals in five games. His record of 13 goals at a single World Cup is unlikely to be beaten. In 1962 Fontaine retired after suffering a second double fracture to his right leg. The following year he became the first president of the French soccer players' union.

RAÚL
Spain, born 1977
Caps: 102   Goals: 44

Raúl González Blanco made his debut for the Real Madrid first team at 17—their youngest-ever player—and went on to score six times in his first 11 games. In the years that followed Raúl became the biggest star in Spanish soccer and the country's all-time leading goal scorer. At club level, he has won two Spanish league championships and three Champions League titles with Real Madrid. Twice the top scorer in the Spanish league, Raúl's goals in the 2003–2004 Champions League campaign saw him become the first player to score more than 40 times in the competition.

GERD MÜLLER
West Germany, born 1945
Caps: 62   Goals: 68

"The Bomber," as Gerd Müller was nicknamed, holds a series of goal-scoring records. From 1963, he scored a club record 365 goals in 427 league games for Bayern Munich. During 16 years with Bayern, he won four Bundesliga titles, four German Cups, and three European Cups. For his country, Müller held one of the greatest international striking records, scoring more than one goal every game. His two strikes against the Soviet Union helped West Germany win the 1972 European Championships. Müller's tally of 14 goals remained a record until 2006, while his final international goal won West Germany the 1974 World Cup on home soil.

▼ *Gerd Müller shoots during West Germany's win over Morocco in the 1970 World Cup.*

▲ *Spain's Raúl was the top scorer during the qualifying rounds for Euro 2000, with ten goals from eight games. Here, he chases down the ball during Euro 2004.*

ZICO
Brazil, born 1953
Caps: 72   Goals: 52

The youngest and smallest of three soccer-crazy brothers, Artur Antunes Coimbra (known as Zico) was given a special diet and training program to build him up when he first arrived at the Brazilian club Flamengo. Sharp, quick-witted, and with the ability to hit an explosive shot or take a deadly, curling free kick, Zico won four Brazilian league titles with Flamengo, as well as the Copa Libertadores and the World Club Cup (both in 1981). He scored a staggering 591 goals in his first 11 seasons with Flamengo and returned to the club in 1985 after a stint at the Italian Serie A team Udinese. Zico retired from international soccer after the 1986 World Cup final but went on to play in Japan for the Kashima Antlers. In 2002 he became the coach of the Japanese national team.

BOBBY CHARLTON
England, born 1937
Caps: 106 Goals: 49

Except for a final season with Preston North End, Charlton was a one-team player with Manchester United, for whom he made his debut in 1956. Known around the globe for his trophy-winning exploits at both the World Cup and the European Cup, Charlton was one of the few survivors of the devastating Munich, Germany, airplane crash, which claimed the lives of many of his Manchester United teammates. As a player, he showed great sportsmanship and dedication—in training he even wore a slipper on his right foot to encourage him to pass and shoot with his weaker left foot. Playing as a deep-lying center-forward with a phenomenal shot from either foot, Charlton remains the record goal scorer for both England and Manchester United, scoring 245 times and making 751 appearances in total for the club. He was knighted in 1994.

▼ Bobby Charlton's 1970 World Cup campaign was his fourth in a row as part of the England team.

◄ Roger Milla challenges for the ball during Cameroon's second-round victory over Colombia at the 1990 World Cup.

FACT FILE In 1990 Andriy Shevchenko played for the Kiev under-14 team in a youth tournament in Wales. Welsh striker Ian Rush was so impressed that he gave the young Ukrainian his soccer cleats.

ROGER MILLA
Cameroon, born c. 1952
Caps: 81 Goals: 42

Roger Milla's celebratory corner-flag dance remains the most memorable image of the 1990 World Cup, as his four goals helped Cameroon become the first African team to reach the quarterfinals. In the same year the veteran striker was voted the African Footballer of the Year. He had won the award before, in 1976, the year that he moved from Cameroon's Tonnerre Yaoundé to play for Valenciennes in France. Milla went on to play for Monaco, Bastia, and Saint Etienne and won the African Nations Cup twice with Cameroon (1984 and 1988). At the age of 42, he came out of retirement for the 1994 World Cup to become the oldest-ever player and scorer in the competition.

ANDRIY SHEVCHENKO
Ukraine, born 1976
Caps: 71 Goals: 33

Shevchenko scored only one goal in 16 games in his first season on the Dynamo Kiev first team. He later made amends with a series of goal-scoring feats to propel Kiev to five Ukrainian league titles and strong showings in the Champions League. A multimillion dollar transfer to AC Milan followed in 1999 for the striker who has a perfect blend of pace and power. On three occasions Shevchenko scored 24 goals per season in what is regarded as an ultratough league for strikers. In 2004, Shevchenko was voted European Footballer of the Year. Two years later, he moved to Premier League champions, Chelsea, for just over $60 million.

▲ Andriy Shevchenko shoots for Ukraine against England during a friendly international in 2000.

CAROLINA MORACE
Italy, born 1964
Caps: 153 Goals: 105

Italy's best female player, Morace made her international and Women's Serie A debut at the age of only 14. She went on to win 12 league titles with eight different clubs and scored more than 500 goals. A lethal finisher, Morace was twice a runner-up with Italy in the European Championships. After retiring in 1999, she became the first female coach of an Italian men's professional team, Viterbese in Serie C. She later became the coach of the Italian women's national team.

▲ *Ruud Gullit shoots against England at Euro '88.*

RUUD GULLIT
Netherlands, born 1962
Caps: 66 Goals: 17

In 1978 the dreadlocked Gullit started out as a sweeper for Dutch team Haarlem. He possessed great attacking flair, stamina, a tough tackle, and a powerful pass. He was the subject of feverish transfer activity, moving to Feyenoord, PSV Eindhoven, and AC Milan, with whom he won European Cups in 1989 and 1990. After a season at Sampdoria, he moved to Chelsea, and in 1996 he was appointed the player-coach of the London club. By winning the 1997 FA Cup, he became the first non-British coach to obtain a major domestic trophy in England.

KENNY DALGLISH
Scotland, born 1951
Caps: 102 Goals: 30

The only player to have scored more than 100 goals for both English and Scottish top-division clubs, Dalglish gave defenders nightmares. He became a legend at Celtic—where he won four league titles and four Scottish Cups—thanks to a quicksilver turn and an icy coolness in front of the goal. In 1977 Liverpool signed Dalglish as a replacement for Kevin Keegan. He became Liverpool's player-coach in 1985, winning three league titles. He won a fourth in 1995 with Blackburn Rovers, becoming one of the few coaches to win the English league with different clubs.

DIEGO MARADONA
Argentina, born 1960
Caps: 91 Goals: 34

Diego Armando Maradona was a phenomenal soccer player. Stocky and with a low center of gravity, he made mesmerizing, weaving runs through the tightest defenses, lightning turns that left opposition players kicking at thin air, and sublime shots, chips, and flicks. Maradona debuted at the age of 15 for Argentinos Juniors. Calls for his inclusion on the 1978 World Cup team were ignored by Argentina's coach, Cesar Luis Menotti, but he would appear at the next four tournaments. Mardona's finest hour came in 1986, when he was the player of the tournament as he led an unremarkable team to World Cup victory (see pages 56–57). Maradona captained Argentina at the 1990 World Cup, where he reached the final, but the following year he failed a drug test and was banned for 15 months. A further failed test during the 1994 World Cup saw him sent home after playing the first two games. His international career was over. Since then Maradona has battled with drug addiction, but in 2000 he was the joint winner of FIFA's Footballer of the Century award with Pelé.

FACT FILE Diego Maradona's moves to Barcelona in 1982 (for $7.98 million) and then to Napoli in 1984 (for $9.66 million) were both world-record transfers. After nine years at Napoli and a stint at Sevilla, he returned to Argentina with Newell's Old Boys and Boca Juniors.

▼ *The magical Maradona brings the ball under control at the 1986 World Cup.*

ALFREDO DI STEFANO
Spain, born 1926
Caps: 31 Goals: 23

To many people, Di Stefano was the "complete" player, years ahead of his time. His astonishing energy helped him play all over the field—defending, tackling, unselfishly distributing the ball, and creating chances for others as well as for himself. Born in a poor suburb of Buenos Aires, he played for his father's old club, River Plate, in a relentless forward line known as *La Máquina* ("The Machine"). A move to Europe in 1953 saw him become part of the legendary Real Madrid team that dominated Europe in the 1950s and early 1960s. Di Stefano formed a deadly partnership with Ferenc Puskas, scoring in five European Cup finals in a row. Real Madrid player and coach Miguel Muñoz explained: "The greatness of Di Stefano was that with him on your side, you had two players in every position."

▲ *As well as appearing for Real Madrid (pictured) and Spain, Di Stefano also played seven unofficial games for Argentina and four for Colombia.*

JÜRGEN KLINSMANN
**West Germany/Germany,
born 1964 Caps: 108 Goals: 47**

Sharp and athletic around the penalty area
and an outstanding goal poacher, Klinsmann
was German Footballer of the Year in his first
stint at VfB Stuttgart. He then moved to
Internazionale, where he won the 1989 Serie
A title. He was part of West Germany's 1990
World-Cup-winning team, scored five goals
in the 1994 competition, and captained the
team at the 1998 tournament. Klinsmann
enjoyed stints with Monaco and, in 1994, the
first of two stints with Tottenham Hotspur. The
British media and some supporters were
suspicious of a player who had a reputation
for diving to win free kicks and penalties. But
in his first Premiership season Klinsmann's
performances and 29 goals won the support
of many fans, and in 1995 he was voted
England's Footballer of the Year. The striker
moved to Bayern Munich, Sampdoria, and
Tottenham Hotspur once again before retiring
in 1998. In 2004 he was appointed Germany's
manager and coached an exciting team to
third place at the 2006 World Cup.

▲ Jürgen Klinsmann
surges forward
with the ball during
Germany's Euro '96
qualifying campaign.

FACT FILE Luigi
Riva had such a fearsome
shot that he once broke
the arm of a spectator.

EUSEBIO
**Portugal, born 1942
Caps: 64 Goals: 41**

Eusebio da Silva Ferreira was the first
African soccer superstar.
Lethal in the air and
equipped with a power-
packed right-foot shot,
he scored an incredible
727 goals in 715
professional games.
Eusebio played his early
soccer for Sporting
Lourenço Marques in his home
country of Mozambique—a
Portugese colony at the time. The striker was
at the center of one of the fiercest transfer
disputes when he arrived in Portugal. He was
virtually kidnapped by Benfica in order to keep
him away from rivals Sporting Lisbon.
Benfica's $21,000 purchase proved to be one
of the buys of the century. Over a 15-year
career with Benfica, Eusebio scored at an
awe-inspiring ratio of more than one goal per
game. He was the Portuguese league's
top goal scorer seven times, twice the
leading goal scorer in all of Europe,
and the 1966 World Cup's top scorer,
with nine goals for Portugal.

LUIGI RIVA
**Italy, born 1944
Caps: 42 Goals: 35**

Luigi Riva started his career with Italy's
Legnano before moving in 1963 to
second-division team Cagliari, where he
spent the rest of his career. He helped the
Sardinian team gain promotion to Serie A
and then win the 1970 league title. Riva was
Serie A's leading scorer three times (1967,
1969, and 1970). He was part of the Italian
team that won Euro '68 and was the
national team's leading goal scorer at the
1970 World Cup. Riva then suffered a
broken leg that kept him out of action for
six months, but he returned in 1971 to
score his 170th league goal. Two
years later he turned down what
would have been the world's biggest
transfer—for $3.6 million to Juventus.
After playing in the 1974 World Cup,
Riva announced his retirement.

▲ Benfica's Eusebio (right) competes for
the ball with Cesare Maldini of AC Milan
during the 1963 European Cup final.

GEORGE WEAH
**Liberia, born 1966
Caps: 61 Goals: 22**

In 1988 the Monaco coach, Arsène Wenger
(now at Arsenal), shrewdly plucked the
young, raw Weah from Cameroon team
Tonnerre Yaoundé. Weah exploded onto the
European scene, winning the French league
with Monaco in 1991 and Paris Saint Germain
in 1994 before moving to AC Milan. A truly
devastating finisher, Weah scored many
spectacular goals to help AC Milan win
two Serie A titles. He was voted African
Footballer of the Year four times and also
won European and World Player of the Year
awards in 1995 and FIFA's Fair Play Award
the following year. He had short stints at
Chelsea, Manchester City, and in the United
Arab Emirates late in his career before
retiring in 2002. A UNICEF ambassador
since 1997, Weah has invested a lot of time
and money helping build schools and clinics
in his war-torn home country of Liberia.

FACT FILE In 1996 George
Weah paid for his teammates' uniforms
and expenses so that Liberia could
enter the African Nations Cup.

RONALDO
Brazil, born 1976
Caps: 97 Goals: 62

Ronaldo Luis Nazario de Lima became a hot commodity as an 18 year old by scoring 58 goals in 60 games for Brazil's Cruzeiro. Still in his teens, Ronaldo moved to PSV Eindhoven and then to Barcelona, where his close ball control and devastating bursts of speed helped him become Europe's top scorer in the 1996–1997 season, with 34 goals. He was sold to Internazionale and was its top scorer in his first season. However, he then endured four injury-ravaged years, playing only one fourth of Inter's games. After a disappointing performance in the 1998 World Cup final, many doubted his ability to perform at the highest level, but he bounced back in 2002 as the tournament's top scorer. One month later, Real Madrid paid $56 million for the Brazilian. In 2006, he became the highest scorer in World Cup history, with a tally of 15 goals.

FACT FILE
Ronaldo's ex-wife, Milene Domingues, broke the world record for keeping a soccer ball off the ground in 1995. She kept the ball in the air for nine hours and six minutes, making 55,187 touches in the process.

▼ Ronaldo shows his speed against Italy. In 2002 he won his third FIFA World Player of the Year award.

MIA HAMM
U.S., born 1972
Caps: 276
Goals: 158

Born with a partial club foot that had to be corrected by casts, Mia Hamm went on to become the world's most famous female soccer player. She was the youngest-ever player for the U.S. women's team when she debuted against China at the age of 15 and the youngest member of the U.S. team that won the 1991 World Cup. Hamm played in three more World Cups, as well as winning two Olympic gold medals and one silver. A phenomenal all-around player with an icy-cool finish, she is the leading scorer in the history of women's international soccer. Hamm was also a founding member of WUSA, playing for the Washington Freedom when the league began in 2001.

HENRIK LARSSON
Sweden, born 1971
Caps: 93 Goals: 36

A goal-scoring predator, Larsson played in Sweden before being signed by Feyenoord coach Wim Jansen in 1993. Four years later Jansen, by then the manager of Celtic, signed him again. Larsson became the Scottish Premier League's most feared striker, with 28 or more goals in five of his seven seasons. He retired from internationals in 2002, but he changed his mind to help Sweden qualify for Euro 2004. Larsson then moved to Barcelona. In his final match for the Spanish team, the 2006 Champions League final, he came on as a substitute to play a key role in Barcelona's win. The striker returned to his former team, Helsingborg, before moving to Manchester United on loan in 2007.

◄ The legendary Mia Hamm playing for the U.S. at the Women's Gold Cup in 2002. In the final against Canada her "golden goal" in extra time secured the trophy.

MARIO KEMPES
Argentina, born 1954
Caps: 43 Goals: 20

Kempes was a powerful center-forward who bristled with goal-scoring intent. Having played for Instituto Córdoba and Rosario Central in his home country, Kempes moved to Spanish team Valencia in 1976 and was twice the top scorer in La Liga. The winner of the Golden Boot award and the player of the tournament at the 1978 World Cup, he was the only European-based player on the Argentinian team who won the title. His second goal in the final against the Netherlands showed his flair as he made a surging run past three defenders. Returning to Argentina in 1981, he played for River Plate and for the national team at the 1982 World Cup before embarking on a coaching career.

◄ Barcelona's Henrik Larsson battles for the ball during a 2004 friendly against Japan's Kashima Antlers. Barcelona won 5-0.

PELÉ
Brazil, born 1940
Caps: 92 Goals: 77

Edson Arantes do Nascimento simply had it all. Considered the greatest soccer player of all time, Pelé was a masterful attacker with seemingly limitless skills, creativity, and vision. He was magnificent in the air, lethal on the ground, could dribble, pass, and take swerving free kicks, and saw passes and opportunities that other players could not. His father had been a striker for Fluminense, and at 11 years old Pelé was spotted by a former Brazil player, Waldemar de Brito, who took him to Clube Atletico Bauru. Four years later, Pelé trained at Santos, for whom he made his debut at age 15. He would play for the São Paulo team for the next 18 years. Pelé was only 17 when he appeared at the 1958 World Cup, scoring a hat trick in the semifinal and two superb goals in the final as Brazil won its first World Cup. A pulled muscle cut short Pelé's involvement in the 1962 competition, and he had to be content with winning the World Club Cup for Santos. Injured by brutal tackling in the 1966 World Cup, Pelé was outstanding at the 1970 tournament. He retired from international soccer in 1971— in front of around 180,000 fans at

the Maracana Stadium—and from club soccer in 1974. In tribute, Santos removed the number ten shirt from its team lineup.

Pelé later came out of retirement to play in a star-studded lineup for the New York Cosmos. He went on to become Brazil's minister of sports and a United Nations (UN) ambassador. He remains one of the most respected figures in world soccer, and in 1999 he was voted Athlete of the Century by the International Olympic Committee.

▲ Pelé bounds away in delight after scoring at the 1970 World Cup.

FACT FILE
Pelé's father once scored five headed goals in one game, a feat Pelé never achieved. However, his header in the 1970 World Cup final was Brazil's 100th World Cup goal.

GAME ACTION

Against Uruguay in the 1970 World Cup semifinal, Pelé came close to scoring what would have been one of the greatest goals ever seen. A through pass from Gerson saw Pelé and the Uruguayan goalie, Ladislao Mazurkiewicz, racing for the ball just outside of the penalty area. Pelé made an outrageous dummy to the left, letting the ball run to the other side of the bewildered goalkeeper. The striker sprinted to collect the ball and hit a first-time shot from a tight angle. The ball sped past Uruguayan defender Atilio Ancheta, only to flash mere inches wide of the left post.

▲ Germany's Birgit Prinz uses her agility to avoid the tackle of Norway's Lise Klaveness in 2003.

BIRGIT PRINZ
Germany, born 1977
Caps: 154 Goals: 100

Germany's best female soccer player, Prinz is a tall center-forward, imposing in the air but just as strong on the ground. With FFC Frankfurt, she won the Women's Bundesliga title, the German Cup, and, in 2002, the first UEFA Women's Cup. She then moved to the U.S. to play for the Carolina Courage, scoring 12 goals in 15 games to help win the WUSA league title. With Germany, she has won the European Championships three times, and in 2003 she scored seven goals to propel her team to World Cup glory, finishing as the top scorer in the tournament. That year she bacame FIFA World Women's Footballer of the Year, a title she retained in 2004 and 2005.

Pelé 2

Ancheta

Mazurkiewicz   Pelé 1

GABRIEL BATISTUTA
Argentina, born 1969
Caps: 77 Goals: 56

Batistuta played one season for each of his home country's three biggest clubs—Newell's Old Boys, River Plate, and Boca Juniors—before moving to Italy in 1991, the year of his international debut. In nine seasons and 269 games at Fiorentina the striker was rarely not at his best, netting 168 goals. He even stayed with the club after relegation, helping them win promotion back into Serie A. In 2000 he joined Roma for the huge fee of $36 million. There, Batistuta finally won the Serie A title in 2001. A winner of two Copa Americas, Batistuta scored five goals at the 1998 World Cup as Argentina made the quarterfinals. The 2003–2004 season saw him make a lucrative move to Qatar, where he played for Al-Arabi.

MARCO VAN BASTEN
Netherlands, born 1964
Caps: 58 Goals: 24

One of the steadiest finishers in world soccer was only 29 when an ankle injury in the 1993 European Cup final effectively ended his playing career—although he struggled on until 1995. Renowned for spectacular goals in crucial games, Van Basten was European Footballer of the Year three times (1988, 1989, and 1992), and in 1988 he hit the headlines as the Netherlands won the European Championships. He scored a hat trick against England in the quarterfinal, the semifinal winning goal versus Germany, and a breathtaking volley from the tightest of angles in the final against the Soviet Union. With Ajax, he won three league titles, scoring 128 goals. He then moved to AC Milan, scoring 90 goals in 147 games and winning three Serie A titles and two European Cups.

▶ Marco van Basten on the rampage in the Netherlands' 3-1 win over England at Euro '88.

▲ Denis Law unleashes a shot during a 1974 World Cup game against Zaire.

LEADING INTERNATIONAL GOAL SCORERS (TO JANUARY 2007)

PLAYER	COUNTRY	CAPS	GOALS
Ali Daei	Iran	149	109
Ferenc Puskas	Hungary	84	83
Pelé	Brazil	92	77
Sandor Kocsis	Hungary	68	75
Bashar Abdullah	Kuwait	132	74
Hassam Hossan	Egypt	170	69
Gerd Müller	West Germany	62	68
Stern John	Trinidad & Tobago	100	67
Majed Abdullah	Saudi Arabia	139	67
Kiatisuk Senamuang	Thailand	117	64
Jassem al-Houwaidi	Kuwait	74	63
Ronaldo	Brazil	97	62

▲ Argentina's all-time top scorer, Batistuta began the 1994–1995 season by scoring in each of Fiorentina's first 11 games, a Serie A record.

HUGO SANCHEZ
Mexico, born 1958
Caps: 57 Goals: 26

Mexico's most famous player, Sanchez spent the peak of his playing career in Spain, scoring more than 230 goals for Atlético Madrid and Real Madrid. He formed a lethal partnership with Emilio Butragueno at Real as they won five league titles in a row. Sanchez was La Liga's top scorer in five different seasons, and in 1990 he won the European Golden Boot award for a record 38 goals in one season. Sadly, his commitments to European soccer and frequent problems with Mexican soccer officials meant that he appeared in only a fraction of the international games played by his home country. He had a disappointing finish at the 1986 World Cup on home soil, scoring only one goal.

FACT FILE Playing for Manchester City in 1974, Denis Law scored a spunky back-heeled goal but did not celebrate—because the goal relegated his former team, Manchester United.

DENIS LAW
Scotland, born 1940
Caps: 55 Goals: 30

In 1962 Manchester United paid $322,000—a world record at the time—to bring the former Huddersfield Town, Manchester City, and Torino striker Denis Law to Old Trafford. The money was well spent, as the quick-witted Scotsman formed a magnificent forward line with Bobby Charlton and George Best, scoring 160 goals in 222 games for the club. Fast over the ground and brave in the air, Law won the 1964 European Footballer of the Year award, as well as league titles and the European Cup with Manchester United, before moving to Manchester City and then retiring in 1974.

MARADONA'S WORLD CUP

Diego Maradona, the Argentinian striker with magical balance and touch, ended the 1986 World Cup with his hands on the trophy and a highly impressive five goals and five assists. Yet these statistics do not tell the story of his true impact, for Mexico '86 was Maradona's tournament. He roused a fairly ordinary Argentinian team into recapturing soccer's biggest prize (the South Americans had won the trophy on home soil in 1978) and wiped out the memory of a disappointing tournament in 1982.

In a tense quarterfinal against England controversy raged over Maradona's infamous "hand of God" goal (see right), but his second and winning goal was pure genius. The Argentinian collected the ball in his own half and then dribbled, twisted, and turned through the English defense to score what was later voted the goal of the century. He would score a goal of similar brilliance in the semifinal versus Belgium. At this point, at the age of only 25, Maradona was without a doubt the greatest soccer player on the planet.

▲ Maradona deliberately handles the ball past England goalkeeper Peter Shilton to score Argentina's first goal in a 2-1 victory.

Diego Maradona, clutching the World Cup after his team's epic 3-2 victory over West Germany in the 1986 final, is carried around the Azteca Stadium on the shoulders of ecstatic Argentinian fans.

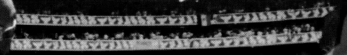

THE BRAIN GAME

Soccer is a sport that calls for speed, power, stamina, and skill, but it also demands mental agility. Players with the ability to think one step ahead of the opposition are highly prized, and these skills can win a game for their team. The same applies to managers and coaches. In the run-up to a game they have several key decisions to make. They must decide who to select, which formation to play, and must choose the tactics they will use in their bid to outwit the opposition.

TEAM SELECTION

To a casual spectator, team selection appears simple—just pick the team's best 11 players. With large teams of players, the truth is much more complex. Teams need flair, skill, composure, aggression, sound defensive skills, and goal-scoring abilities—all in the right quantities. Some players, despite being soccer superstars, may not play well with each other or work with the rest of the team, while other, less famous players may actually perform a more effective job in a particular game. The way that the opposition plays can dictate which players are selected, as can the fitness and performances of individuals. Star players, who would normally be first on the team sheet, may not be picked if they are recovering from injuries or suffering from a lack of confidence. Both young, talented players emerging from the reserve team and experienced veterans at the end of their careers will have strong cases for a place on the team. It all adds up to a complex puzzle

that coaches must solve. As the legendary Ajax and Netherlands coach Rinus Michels said, "It is an art in itself to compose a starting team, finding the balance between creative players and those with destructive powers and between defense, construction, and attack—never forgetting the quality of the opposition and the specific pressures of each game."

PICKING AND PLAYING

Picking the right players for the game ahead can be a tricky task. Coaches are often criticized by fans for dropping a favorite player or not playing them in their favored position. But they have to hold their nerve and go with what they feel is their best team for a particular game. Cesar Luis Menotti, for example, was attacked by the Argentinian public and media for refusing to include the teenage prodigy Maradona on his 1978 World Cup team, fielding veteran striker Mario Kempes instead. But Menotti proved himself to be a strong-willed and clever coach, who surprised opponents with an exciting, attacking game, and his team went on to win the tournament by beating the Netherlands in the final.

With large teams, coaches at the top teams often rotate and rest key players. In games against a supposedly weaker opposition they might field an understrength team. While resting your best players and giving young players first-team experience can bring benefits, it is a risky tactic. Liverpool coach Rafael Benitez discovered this in 2005, when his understrength team was knocked out of the FA Cup by Burnley.

▲ In 2000–2001 Liverpool's 28-man team played 61 games. No player appeared in all of the games. In 1983–1884 their league and European-Cup-winning team (above) played 66 games with a team of only 16. Bruce Grobbelaar, Alan Kennedy, Sammy Lee, and Alan Hansen appeared in every game.

▼ West Germany coach Josef "Sepp" Herberger (right) is chaired off the field as his team wins the 1954 World Cup. Early in the competition he sent out a weakened team that lost to favorite Hungary. Having already beaten Turkey, Herberger's gamble meant that his team got an easier opponent, meeting Turkey again in a play-off that the Germans won 7-2.

FACT FILE FIFA changed its rules on substitutions in international friendlies in 2004, limiting a team to six subs. The move was prompted, in part, by the mass substitutions of England coach Sven-Goran Eriksson. In 2003 he made 11 substitutions during a game that Australia won 3-1.

SUBSTITUTIONS

Although they were allowed in some friendly games, substitutes were not a feature of competitive games until the 1960s. Before this time the lack of subs resulted in all kinds of heroics, from outfield players going in the goal to players persevering in spite of a serious injury. One of the most famous examples is that of Manchester City's

German goalkeeper Bert Trautmann, who continued playing in the 1956 FA Cup final even though he had broken his neck. Today's coaches have the chance to alter their team selection and tactics by making up to three substitutions in most competitions (more in friendly games). The timing and choice of substitutes can be crucial. They can bolster a winning team's momentum, help a defense hold onto a lead, or turn a losing team's fortunes around. In the 2006 World Cup, for example, Australia were losing 1-0 to Japan. Coach Guus Hiddink brought on two substitutes, Tim Cahill and John Aloisi, who scored three goals between them in the last six minutes of the game to secure a 3-1 victory.

◄ Danish striker Jon Dahl Tomasson was often used as a substitute by AC Milan. During the 2002–2003 Champions League (which Milan won), he came off the bench in the quarterfinal against Ajax to score the injury-time winner.

▼ With Manchester United losing 1-0 to Bayern Munich in the 1999 Champions League final, Alex Ferguson brought on Norwegian striker Ole Gunnar Solskjaer in the 81st minute. After another substitute, Teddy Sheringham, had tied the game, Solskjaer scored this memorable winning goal in injury time.

▲ After leading South Korea to the semifinals of the 2002 World Cup, Dutchman Guus Hiddink— a firm believer in attacking tactics—was made an honorary citizen of South Korea.

FORMATIONS

The way in which a team lines up on the field is known as its formation. The first international soccer game, in 1872, saw two teams field heavily attacking formations. Scotland began playing in a 2-2-6 formation, with two backs, two halfbacks (similar to midfielders), and six attackers. England went even farther, playing 1-1-8 (eight forwards), but crowded goal areas saw the game end 0-0.

EVOLVING TACTICS

Although England's eight forwards quickly became a thing of the past, attacker-heavy formations, such as 2-3-5, persisted for more than 50 years. A change to the offside law in 1925 (see page 19) reduced the number of players needed between an attacker and the goal from three to two. It gave attackers more scoring chances and forced a rapid rethink for coaches. None was quicker than Arsenal's Herbert Chapman, who, two days after a 7-0 loss to Newcastle, debuted his W-M formation (named for the shapes that the two groups of five players made). The change resulted in a 4-0 win over West Ham. The W-M formation was effectively 3-2-2-3 and was adopted by many teams. Other teams played the *metodo* formation, devised by World-Cup-winning Italian coach Vittorio Pozzo. It was also based on 2-3-5 but was actually 2-3-2-3, with two of the forwards pulled back to link between midfield and attack and to defend against breaks by the opposition.

FOUR AT THE BACK

The arrival of four defenders at the back sounds like a negative formation, but it was first unveiled by the amazing attacking Brazil team that won the 1958 World Cup. The Brazilian formation was actually 4-2-4, with two wingers up front feeding two central strikers. By the next World Cup, Brazil and many other teams were opting for a slightly less attacking 4-3-3, with an extra player to stop the midfield from being overrun. This formation can work with a single winger who switches flanks at will, or it can feature two genuine wingers feeding a single striker. England won the 1966 World Cup playing 4-4-2 with no out-and-out wingers, but they had midfielders with the energy and stamina to add width to an attack, as well as defending when necessary. This formation is still widely used today. In the late 1980s and 1990s AC

◄ German wingback Philipp Lahm holds off Portugal's Cristiano Ronaldo at the 2006 World Cup. Wingbacks play on the flanks. They act like fullbacks in defense and also make attacking runs up the field.

Milan and Italy coach Arrigo Sacchi had success playing a modified 4-4-2 with the line of four defenders high upfield. In this "pressing game" the defense tried to catch the opposition offside while the midfield closed down space. Juventus was one of several Italian teams to copy this formation; playing it, they won Serie A and several European competitions.

◄ Italy coach Arrigo Sacchi issues instructions to his players during a training session at the 1996 European Championships.

▲ The Serbia and Montenegro international Sinisa Mihajlovic enjoyed six glorious seasons at Lazio as a powerful sweeper, strong in defense but with an eye for the goal, especially from set pieces.

SWEEPING UP

In many teams around the world—and especially in Italian soccer—a different system is used at the back, with a sweeper (also known as a *libero* or "free man") in the center of defense. Sweepers tend to play behind the main line of defenders, literally sweeping up loose balls and acting as a last line of defense if an opposition attack breaks through. In some formations a sweeper can be too negative. This was seen as the case with the *catenaccio* system, invented by Padova coach Nereo Rocco in the early 1950s and popularized by Helenio Herrera's Internazionale team of the 1960s.

▲ Barcelona coach Ronald Koeman (left) and Ajax coach Frank Rijkaard shake hands before a game. The pair played in the Dutch team that won Euro '88, playing a brand of total soccer.

Effectively a 1-4-3-2 or 1-4-4-1 system, *catenaccio* aimed to stifle attacks with large numbers of defenders, relying on counterattacks by a few forwards. Italy has produced a long line of world-class sweepers, including Giovanni Facchetti, Gaetano Scirea, and Franco Baresi. But it took a German, Franz Beckenbauer, to show

▲ A team often alters its formation after a sending off. This team has lost its left midfielder (shown by the red arrow) and switches from a 3-2-3-2 system with wingbacks to a 4-3-1-1 formation with a flat back four, three in midfield, and split strikers up front.

a different side to the sweeper's art. Beckenbauer linked play going forward and would often surge ahead of his defense,

> **FACT FILE** Ronald Koeman is one of the highest-scoring defenders of all time. Playing mostly as a sweeper, he enjoyed great success with AC Milan, Barcelona, and the Netherlands, scoring an incredible 193 goals in 533 games.

creating an extra player in attack and opening up the game. Since Beckenbauer's time players such as Ronald Koeman, Ciriaco Sforza of Switzerland, and Lothar Matthäus have mastered the position, while Traianos Dellas successfully operated as a sweeper on Greece's winning team at the 2004 European Championships.

TOTAL SOCCER

"Total soccer" was never completely formation-free soccer, but it did involve players switching positions and roles within the team with amazing frequency. Under Rinus Michels, defenders would crop up in attack, strikers in midfield, and midfielders just about everywhere. It proved a hard system to defend against, but few teams could boast the quality of player to make it work since it relied on excellent ball skills and very high energy levels. Today players switch positions with remarkable ease and regularity, so much so that a person might wonder why "total soccer" caused such a stir. Formations in the past were more rigid, however, with fullbacks staying in their half and strikers staying upfield throughout the game. While this gave a team a shape and structure, it could also make it easier for opponents to mark dangerous players and defend.

FORMATIONS

A formation is the way in which a team lines up for a game. This is usually shown in terms of the numbers of outfield players from the defense forward. In reality, soccer is a dynamic game, and players move around the field. Sometimes they are drawn out of position by an opposition attack. At other times players choose to move out of position. For example, a central striker may drift out wide or drop back to find space.

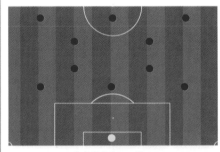

3-2-2-3 formation

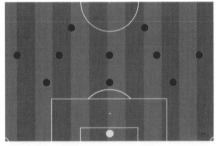

3-5-2 formation

4-4-2 formation

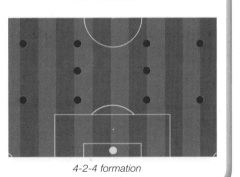

4-2-4 formation

TACTICS

Teams may start off a game in one of several common formations, but there can be great variations in how they play within that formation and in the tactics that they use. For example, a team that lines up as 4-4-2 may choose to play defensively, with midfielders helping out, or aggressively, with one or more midfielders joining the strikers in attack.

TAILORING TACTICS

Coaches start a game with what they feel are the best tactics for the players available and the opposition that they face. They closely watch how a game unfolds, knowing that they can change tactics at any time in order to exploit an opponent's weakness or to fix problems in their own team's play. Most top players can play in several positions. A coach may switch formations using the same players or may bring on a substitute with different attributes and skills. In the 2004–2005 Champions League epic game between Chelsea and Barcelona, Chelsea coach José Mourinho started with one striker up front, and the other helped out behind in order to harass Barcelona's playmaker, Xavi. This tactic led directly to Chelsea's first goal. Later in the game Mourinho removed the second striker in favor of a central defender to close out the game, which Chelsea won 4-2.

TACTICS IN DEFENSE

Teams have several choices about how they defend. Some coaches prefer defenders to patrol areas of space that overlap, a system known as zonal marking. This tactic is often used by Argentinian clubs and many national teams. It requires good communication between defenders. Alternatively, each defender marks an individual player, tracking their opponent's attacking runs throughout the game. Greece used this system, known as man marking, with good effects at Euro 2004. It man marked both French strikers, David Trezeguet and Thierry Henry, for example—a tactic that contributed to the team's 1-0 victory. When an opposing team features a dangerous playmaker positioned behind the strikers, a team may nominate a midfield player to man mark him or her.

▲ Michael Essien of Ghana is put under pressure by Italy's Daniele de Rossi during a 2006 World Cup group game. Dynamic midfielders such as Essien are in great demand, as they can play the role of midfield anchor, breaking up opposition attacks and launching attacks of their own.

▶ The offside trap is a defensive tactic in which the back three or four players move upfield in a straight line in order to catch an opponent offside. It can be very effective but may be beaten by a player dribbling through the line or by a well-timed through pass combined with an attacking run.

GAME ACTION

One goal down and under pressure from a Danish attack down its right wing, Senegal scored a superb counterattacking goal at the 2002 World Cup. Senegal's Henri Camara made a firm tackle on Martin Jorgensen and played a quick pass down the wing to El Hadji Diouf. Diouf, closely marked by Jan Heintze, spotted Salif Diao's run and back heeled the ball into his path. Diao hit a perfect pass to Khalilou Fadiga, who was sprinting into the center circle. As Diao continued his run, Fadiga took the ball into the Danish half before playing a perfectly timed through pass. Racing between two defenders, Diao latched onto the ball and coolly sent it into the corner of the goal.

LONG OR SHORT

All teams seek to pass and move the ball into the attacking one third of the field, where goal-scoring chances can be made. The way in which they get the ball there can vary greatly. For many decades British teams favored a direct style with few passes. Coaches believed that hitting long balls toward tall target strikers in the opponent's penalty area created more goal chances, often through a defensive mistake. In continental Europe and elsewhere a shorter, passing-and-moving game was often preferred, with teams keeping possession for fairly long periods of time as they looked for an opening in the opposition defense. Another tactic, originally favored by many Central and South American teams, is to rely on precise passing and skillful dribbling to get into the opposition penalty area. Some teams play a counterattacking game, defending in large numbers and soaking up the pressure. When they retrieve the ball, they move it rapidly out of defense with a long pass or by running with the ball. Fast, accurate counterattacking can catch the opposition off guard and outnumbered but requires players with good speed and awareness. Many coaches alternate their passing and movement tactics—if their team is behind with only minutes to go, for example, they may switch to a direct style, pushing extra players up into the opposition penalty area to look for headers and knockdowns.

◄ Portugal's Cristiano Ronaldo practices free kicks at a training camp ahead of Euro 2004. He is watched by teammates Deco Souza (left) and Rui Costa (right), as well as coach Luiz Felipe Scolari.

HIT THE NET

www.thecoachingcorner.com/soccer/index/
A thorough grounding in the laws of the game and its key tactics.

www.pags.org/coaches/articles/43768.html
A short article on the main ways in which a player or team can attack without falling foul of the offside trap.

http://sportsvl.com/soccer/general/training.html
Links to soccer sites, with many covering training, tactics, and formations.

FACT FILE With half an hour to go in a 1957 English league game, Charlton Athletic was down to ten men and losing 5–1 to Huddersfield Town. But an astonishing comeback, featuring four goals from Johnny Summers, saw the team triumph 7–6.

▶ Bayer Leverkusen defender Boris Zivkovic (left) challenges Ruud van Nistelrooy of Manchester United. The Croatian-born Zivkovic often plays as a man marker, sticking close to the opposition team's most threatening attacker.

THE COACH'S ROLE

A successful team needs more than great tactics. It needs to be prepared, instructed, and inspired in order to produce a great performance. Motivating players, directing them, and giving them the confidence to perform is all part of a coach's job. Crucially, coaches can determine the tone, style, and attitude of their team through the players they hire and send out onto the field, as well as through their work during training.

THE TEAM BEHIND THE TEAM

Behind the players on a major team is a large team of staff. At the forefront is the coach and his or her assistants, some of whom may specialize in training goalkeepers or strikers or may specifically work with younger players and youth teams. A top club will also include a fitness coach, a dietician, and one or more physiotherapists and medical staff to help with players' preparation and recovery from injury. Videos

▲ José Mourinho (second left) became the Chelsea coach in 2004. Here, he unveils his coaching team. Assistant coach Steve Clarke (second right) was the only survivor from the coaching setup of former coach Claudio Ranieri.

of games that interest the management are studied in detail, while scouts are employed to check out and report on forthcoming opposition teams and to watch potential transfer targets in action. Many teams also arrange visits from temporary personnel such as sports psychologists, balance and coordination specialists, as well as inspirational figures from other sports.

INS AND OUTS

With soccer teams becoming increasingly big businesses, a coach's ability to deal profitably and successfully in the transfer market is essential. Some coaches are highly prized for their ability to hire players cheaply and sell them for profit or to put together a team on a limited budget that can seriously challenge anyone. European-Cup-winning coach Brian Clough was famous for working wonders with bargain buys. Scottish legend Archie Gemmill cost Clough's Derby team around $100,000, while striker Gary Birtles was bought by Clough at Nottingham Forest for $4,000 in 1978 and sold to Manchester United two years later for almost $3 million. Many modern coaches and teams also have an eye for a bargain. Porto bought relatively unknown striker Mario Jardel from Gremio in Brazil in the 1996–1997 season. The South American scored a staggering 130 goals

▶ Italian team Lecce paid only around $19,000 for young Bulgarian striker Valeri Bojinov (left) in 2002. It proved to be a smart move—three years later they sold him to Fiorentina for around $16 million.

FACT FILE Irishman Tony Cascarino was sold in 1982 by Crockenhill FC to Gillingham for a new team uniform and some corrugated iron to patch up the ground. The total cost was said to be around $340.

in 125 appearances for the Portuguese team. Arsenal coach Arsène Wenger bought Nicolas Anelka in 1997 for $850,000; two years later he was sold to Real Madrid for $40 million. Other coaches are noted for their ability to bring promising young players through from their youth teams or to attract good players who are loaned from other teams to help strengthen their own.

UNDER PRESSURE

Few people in sports are under as much pressure as the coach of a major club or national team. Coaches stand or fall by their results. In the past some coaches stayed at teams for season after season. Miguel Muñoz, for example, managed Real Madrid for 417 games during the 1960s. At the top level today few coaches stay in charge of the best teams for more than a handful of seasons.

In the English league, on average, around one third of the managers are fired or resign every season. In 2005–2006 eight of the 18 Bundesliga managers had left their posts by the halfway point of the season. Even recent success does not guarantee a long stay. Bobby Robson had taken Sporting Lisbon to the top of the Portuguese league when a shock loss to Casino Salzburg in the UEFA Cup saw him fired in December 1993. Real Madrid's Vicente del Bosque had delivered two Spanish league titles, two Champions League trophies, and other cups to the Spanish giants in only four years, but he was dismissed in June 2003. In such an unforgiving climate, Alex Ferguson's record of more than 1,000 games in charge of Manchester United is remarkable.

▲ Ronaldo celebrates with the European Cup Winners' Cup alongside Barcelona coach Bobby Robson. Robson has had a highly successful career as a coach since 1967.

◄ Bora Milutinovic led five different countries to successive World Cups—a unique feat in soccer coaching. In late 2006 he was appointed the coach of Jamaica.

MANAGERIAL MIGRATIONS

Like modern players, top coaches often move overseas in order to further develop their coaching careers. Portugal are one of the few top national teams to have a foreign coach (Luiz Felipe Scolari), but many countries below the highest tier rely on the experience of foreign talent. In the past British coaches were influential overseas. Willy Garbutt helped shape Genoa into a powerful team, while Fred Pentland coached Athletic Bilbao to Spanish league success in 1930 and 1931. Jimmy Hogan, who used pass-and-move tactics years ahead of his time, worked with Austrian coaching legend Hugo Miesl to set up the Vienna school of soccer. This created the Austrian *Wunderteam* that remained unbeaten in 14 internationals and narrowly missed out on glory at the 1934 World Cup and 1936 Olympics. Today managers and coaches

switch countries and continents frequently. Argentina's Hector Cuper coached Internazionale, Brazilian legend Zico has coached in Japan, and Italian coach Cesare Maldini assisted Paraguay at the 2002 World Cup. Few globe-trotting coaches can compete with the Serbian Bora Milutinovic, however. He has taken five countries to World Cups (Mexico in 1986, Costa Rica in 1990, the U.S. in 1994, Nigeria in 1998, and China in 2002).

▼ Most national team bosses have had managerial experience at club level. Jürgen Klinsmann (right), Germany's coach at the 2006 World Cup, is an exception. He had never coached a major club team before his appointment in 2004.

FACT FILE In a 1999 Spanish second division game Leganes coach Enrique Martin ran onto the field to run down an opposition player who was clean through on goal. Martin received a ten-game ban.

▲ Globe-trotting Frenchman Philippe Troussier has successfully coached Nigeria, South Africa, and Japan, as well as coaching teams in Europe.

GREAT COACHES

There have been dozens of truly great managers and coaches in soccer. Some have been masters at discovering new talents and putting together successful teams on tight budgets; others are soccer visionaries who have helped improve the skills and playing of the world's biggest stars. Below are profiles of eight of the finest coaches in the history of soccer.

HERBERT CHAPMAN
1878-1934

Only four teams have won the English league three seasons in a row, and Chapman created two of them. After arriving at Huddersfield Town in 1921, he won the league in 1924 and 1925. By the time Huddersfield made it three in a row, Chapman had left for Arsenal. They were in 20th place when he took over but finished the season second, right behind his former team. Arsenal went on to win a hat trick of league titles, the first two under Chapman. The Englishman took tactics very seriously, and his W-M formation (see page 60) was used by many teams. He pioneered large-scale youth coaching, undersoil heating, top-class medical facilities, and professional training regimes. Some of his proposals, such as numbered shirts and playing regular evening games under floodlights, were only adopted long after his death.

GIOVANNI TRAPATTONI
Born 1939

Trapattoni's coaching career got off to a flying start, winning the 1973 European Cup Winners' Cup as caretaker coach of AC Milan, for whom he had played as a fearsome center-back. After moving to Milan's great rivals Juventus, he enjoyed an unmatched run of success, winning six Serie A league titles, two UEFA Cups, and, in 1985, a European Cup. The backbone of his team contained many of the players who won the 1982 World Cup, from goalie Dino Zoff to striker Paolo Rossi. Trapattoni won a further Serie A title with Internazionale in 1989 before moving to Bayern Munich in the 1990s, where he became the first foreign coach to win the Bundesliga. His teams were based on strong defenses, usually with three central defenders linked to exciting attackers who were often hired from overseas. He was finally given a chance to coach the Italian national side at 63 years of age, but the team fell short at the 2002 World Cup and Euro 2004, after which Trapattoni had stints at Benfica, Stuttgart, and Salzburg.

▲ *Trapattoni argues with the officials during Italy's game against Bulgaria at Euro 2004.*

BELA GUTTMANN
1900-1981

The only coach to have won the top club trophy in both South America and Europe, Guttmann is a coaching legend. He was a gifted amateur player for MTK Budapest and appeared at the 1924 Olympics for Hungary. After retiring in 1935, he embarked on a 40-year-long coaching career that took him to Switzerland, Uruguay, Greece, Portugal, Brazil, Romania, Italy, and Austria. He won national league titles in five different countries, including the 1955 Serie A title with AC Milan; he won the European Cup twice as the coach of Benfica and also lifted the Copa Libertadores with Peñarol. He was a big influence on Gusztav Sebes, the coach of the magical Hungarian teams of the 1950s, and his forward-thinking 4-2-4 formation and styles of play are believed to have inspired Brazil to become the great attacking force of the late 1950s onward.

JOCK STEIN
1922-1985

Jock Stein began his coaching career as the assistant coach at Celtic. In 1960 he moved to Dunfermline and beat his old team in the following season to win the Scottish Cup. In 1962 Dunfermline caused a major upset, knocking out top Spanish team Valencia from the Inter-Cities Fairs Cup. Stein moved on to Hibernian for one season before being appointed as the coach of Celtic. He quickly built one of British soccer's finest and most entertaining teams. Under Stein, Celtic won 11 Scottish league titles and, in 1967, overturned the mighty Internazionale to become the first British team to lift the European Cup. The "Big Man" left Celtic in 1977 for an ill-fated stint at Leeds United but later became Scotland's coach, guiding them to the 1982 and 1986 World Cup tournaments.

◀ *Herbert Chapman (right) watches an Arsenal game in 1932 alongside trainer Tom Whittaker (left) and star player Alex James.*

FACT FILE In the 1970s two coaching legends, Jock Stein and Brian Clough, both had stints at Leeds United that lasted only 44 days.

ALEX FERGUSON
Born 1941

As European soccer's longest-serving top-class manager, Sir Alex Ferguson has taken Manchester United to a record eight Premiership titles and the 1999 Champions League crown. A ruthless and highly driven player, Ferguson carried those attributes into his coaching career, first with East Stirling and then at St. Mirren and Aberdeen. With limited resources at Aberdeen, he broke the monopoly of Celtic and Rangers to win three Scottish league titles; in 1983 his team defeated Real Madrid to lift the European Cup Winners' Cup. Ferguson also served as the assistant Scotland coach under Jock Stein, taking over in 1985 when Stein died. At Manchester United, Ferguson developed young talents such as David Beckham, Ryan Giggs, and Paul Scholes and proved to be a masterful player of mind games with rival coaches. His transfer dealings have not always been successful, but he has made some excellent purchases, including Eric Cantona for around $1.8 million and Peter Schmeichel for around $825,000.

FACT FILE Alex Ferguson has only been fired once, in 1978, when Scottish club St. Mirren dismissed him for a range of offenses that included "unpardonable swearing at a lady."

RINUS MICHELS
1928-2005

The man behind "total soccer," which revolutionized both Ajax and the Dutch national team, Marinus "Rinus" Michels had been a center-forward as a player, winning five caps for the Netherlands in the 1950s. As the coach of Ajax in the mid-1960s, he gave 17-year-old Johan Cruyff his debut. Michels later coached Cruyff at Spanish giants Barcelona and on the Dutch team that finished runner-up at the 1974 World Cup. Michels returned to Ajax in 1975 and became the coach of German team Cologne five years later. He rejoined the Dutch national team in 1984 and, with a star-studded team, won the 1988 European Championships—the Netherlands' first major trophy. Michels' achievements were acknowledged in 1989, when he was named FIFA's Coach of the Century.

VALERY LOBANOVSKY
1939-2002

A gifted mathematician, Valery Lobanovsky viewed soccer as a science and was one of the first coaches to analyze the performances of teams and players. His management style was strict, yet it enabled creative talents such as Oleg Blokhin and Andriy Shevchenko to flourish. After four years in charge of Dnipro Dnipropetrovsk, he was appointed the coach of Dynamo Kiev, guiding them to five Soviet league titles between 1974 and 1981 and two European Cup Winners' Cup victories (1975 and 1986). He also coached the Soviet Union three times, reaching the 1988 European Championships final, only to be defeated by Rinus Michels' Dutch team. After stints with the United Arab Emirates and Kuwait, he returned to Kiev in 1996, taking them to five Ukrainian league titles in a row (1997–2001) and reaching the semifinals of the Champions League in 1999.

▶ Rinus Michels with Johan Cruyff during their time at Barcelona.

HELENIO HERRERA
1917-1997

The well-traveled Argentinian Helenio Herrera was a tough coach who liked to control almost every aspect of a team. At Spain's Atlético Madrid, he won consecutive league titles. After stints with Malaga, Valladolid, and Sevilla, he joined Barcelona. Under his management, they won two Spanish titles and two Inter-Cities Fairs Cups. Internazionale liked what they saw and hired him in 1960. Herrera's reign and his use of catenaccio tactics (see page 60) coincided with Inter's most glorious era, in which they won three Serie A titles, two European Cups, and two World Club Cups. Herrera was also in charge of the Italian national team during qualification for the 1962 World Cup, but by the time the tournament began, he was the coach of Spain.

◀ In November 2004 Alex Ferguson celebrated his 1,000th game in charge of Manchester United by beating Lyon in the Champions League.

▶ Helenio Herrera poses with two soccer balls in 1971, while the coach of Italian team Roma.

Lothar Emmerich of West Germany fires a shot past England's George Cohen (far left) and Martin Peters during the epic 1966 World Cup final at Wembley.

SNAPSHOT
THE WINGLESS WONDERS

The tactics of England coach Alf Ramsey caused a lot of debate at the 1966 World Cup. His midfield had no wingers but did include a striker, Bobby Charlton, and the tough-tackling defender Nobby Stiles. The English defense was in top form, and the "Wingless Wonders," as Ramsey's team was nicknamed, cruised to the final against West Germany. It was, therefore, a shock when England fell behind to a Helmut Haller strike in the 12th minute. Stirred into action, England went 2-1 up with goals from Geoff Hurst and Martin Peters, only for Wolfgang Weber to tie in the dying seconds of the game. In a World Cup first the final went into extra time, and two events passed into soccer folklore. First was the controversial goal awarded to Geoff Hurst in the 101st minute—even today, it is unclear if the ball crossed the line. Then came Hurst's third goal, which left no one in any doubt. His thumping shot into the roof of the net secured England an historic 4-2 win and made Hurst the only player to score a hat trick in the final of the World Cup.

GREAT TEAMS

What makes a team special? Great players, playing with spirit and supported by passionate crowds—with the help of excellent coaches—often win. Yet assembling a team of superstars does not guarantee success. Sometimes unheralded players gel together to win against the odds. In the last ten years Nigeria, Japan, Cameroon, and South Korea have lit up world soccer by beating more powerful countries. Similar upsets occur at club level—provincial team Toluca's rise to win the Mexican league, for

example. This chapter looks at some of the world's great national and club teams over the years. The key word is "some"; there are dozens of other successful teams, from Argentina's Independiente—the most frequent winner of the Copa Libertadores—to Olympiakos, who won their seventh Greek league title in a row in 2003. The focus in this section is on teams that at one point in their history were especially exciting, revolutionary, or dominant in the soccer competitions in which they played.

NATIONAL TEAMS

▶ Hungarian goalkeeper Gyula Grosics gathers the ball under pressure from England's Stan Mortensen. Hungary's 6-3 win condemned England to its first home defeat to a team from Europe.

FACT FILE The team was still at its peak when the Soviet Union invaded Hungary in 1956. Many of its star players were on tour with their club, Honved, and chose not to return home. Puskas signed for Real Madrid, while Kocsis and Czibor joined Real's great rivals, Barcelona.

HUNGARY
Founded: 1901

The Hungarian national team of the 1950s was exceptional and was one of the few teams at club or international level to change the way that soccer is played. Organized at the back by the dependable Jozsef Bozsik, Hungary brimmed with attacking talent thanks to Zoltan Czibor, Sandor Kocsis, Nandor Hidegkuti, and Ferenc Puskas. At a time when almost every team played the W-M formation (see page 60), coach Gusztav Sebes devised a simple but devastating alternative. Hidegkuti was the team's center-forward, but he played very deep, allowing Puskas, Kocsis, and other teammates to raid forward into space. Opposition teams simply did not know how to play against a team that swept all before it, winning the 1952 Olympics and scoring 220 goals in 51 games during the first half of the decade. In 1953 the team earned its nickname—the "Magnificent Magyars"—by beating a stunned England 6-3 at Wembley Stadium. That memorable win was followed by a 7-1 knockout of the English team in Budapest. From June 1950 to November 1955, Hungary's international record read: played 50, won 42, tied seven, lost one. The defeat was heartbreaking, however, as it came in the final of the 1954 World Cup. After taking a 2-0 lead against a West German team that they had thrashed 8-3 in the group stages, Hungary—fielding an unwell Puskas—lost 3-2. That single defeat should not detract from one of the finest teams ever to grace the international stage.

WEST GERMANY
Founded: 1900

West Germany staged a major shock when they courageously toppled the favorite, Hungary, to win the 1954 World Cup thanks to two goals from Helmut Rahn. Its team of the mid-1960s finished runner-up at the 1966 tournament and third in 1970. Coach Helmut Schön then rebuilt the team shrewdly, keeping the superb Sepp Maier

in the goal and moving Franz Beckenbauer from midfield into defense, where he played alongside Hans-Georg Schwarzenbeck and one of the best fullbacks of the 1970s, Paul Breitner. Schön incorporated the talented Günter Netzer into midfield and often played a 4-3-3 formation, with Uli Hoeness in attack alongside goal machine Gerd Müller. West Germany's players had a very strong team spirit because they came almost exclusively from just two clubs—Bayern Munich and Borussia Mönchengladbach. Their self-confidence was evident as they powered to the 1972 European Championships title and then went one step further, winning the 1974 World Cup on home soil. By this time the talented but outspoken Netzer had been replaced by Wolfgang Overath, while midfielder Rainer Bonhof had also played his way onto the team. A defeat to Czechoslovakia in the 1976 European Championships final signaled the end of a remarkable period in which West Germany had become the first team to hold the European and World crowns at the same time.

◄ *West German defender Berti Vogts holds the World Cup up in 1974, with Hans-Georg Schwarzenbeck (number four) and Rainer Bonhof (16) to his left.*

UNITED STATES (WOMEN)
First international game: 1985

Women's international soccer came of age during the 1990s with the arrival of World Cup and Olympic competitions. The decade's most successful nation was undoubtedly the U.S. With a team built around a core of players who have played together throughout the 1990s and into the 2000s, the U.S. has won two out of a possible three Olympic titles (1996 and 2004) and two out of four Women's World Cups (1991 and 1999). Their record in World Cup games is remarkable, with 20 wins, two ties, and only two defeats. Four players appeared for the American team in all four World Cups: Joy Fawcett, Julie Foudy, Mia Hamm, and Kristine Lilly. Hamm was considered the world's finest female striker, while in 2000 Lilly became the first player of either sex to pass 200 international caps.

For a number of the U.S. women's team, 2004 proved a successful swan song, with victory over Brazil to win Olympic gold.

◄ *American winger Kristine Lilly (13) fights for the ball against Australia's Dianne Alagich at the 2004 Olympics. The United States remained unbeaten throughout the tournament.*

FRANCE
Founded: 1919

France has a long and illustrious soccer pedigree. It has produced several superb teams, especially in the late 1950s—the era of Raymond Kopa and Just Fontaine—and in the early 1980s, with an impressive team led by Michel Platini. But it was the team of the late 1990s that finally translated great promise into World Cup success (see pages 92–93). As world champion, France entered Euro 2000 with the majority of its key players still at their peak, including flamboyant goalie Fabien Barthez and strong, skilled defenders Marcel Desailly, Lilian Thuram, and Bixente Lizarazu. In midfield a blend of flair and dynamism was headed by the world's best attacking midfielder, Zinedine Zidane. Up front, young players such as Sylvain Wiltord and Thierry Henry were intent on making their marks. Five players scored two or more goals in their six-game Euro 2000 campaign, which ended with France beating Italy 2-1 to become the second team (after West Germany in 1974) to hold European and World titles at the same time.

▲ France celebrates its Euro 2000 triumph after a "golden goal" from David Trezeguet (center, with Fabien Barthez's hand on his head) sealed victory.

SOUTH KOREA
Founded: 1928

At the 2002 World Cup, cohost South Korea was given little chance of success by many people. In truth, the country boasted an improving team and had qualified for the previous three World Cups. Under the guidance of Guus Hiddink—a former Real Madrid and Netherlands coach—the South Koreans beat Poland 2-0 to record their country's first win at the World Cup. After a 1-1 tie with the U.S., South Korea knocked a strong Portugal team out of the tournament thanks to Park Ji-Sung's goal. An extraordinary second-round game versus Italy saw South Korea miss a penalty and then fall behind, only to tie two minutes before the final whistle. Urged on by an entire country, the hardworking team defended resolutely and attacked with energy, skill, and surprise. A "golden goal" three minutes before the end of extra time knocked Italy out of the tournament and sent the country into raptures. The drama was not over, however. A tense quarterfinal against Spain ended in a thrilling penalty shoot-out, with goalie Lee Woon-Jae pulling off a magnificent save from Joaquin before captain Hong Myung-Bo took home the winning penalty. A narrow 1-0 defeat to Germany in the semifinals did not dampen the cohost nation's enthusiasm, and attendances at club level rocketed in the following seasons.

FACT FILE Ahn Jung-Hwan struck the goal that knocked Italy out of the World Cup. Ahn played for Italian team Perugia, whose president was so enraged that he terminated the South Korean midfielder's contract.

HIT THE NET

www.fifa.com/en/organisation/na/index.html
A list of the 205 national associations affiliated with FIFA, together with the dates of their formation, team uniforms, and links to the Web sites of most of these associations.

www.expertfootball.com/history/dream_teams.php
This Web site contains profiles of some of soccer's greatest teams, including the Brazilian World Cup team from 1962 and the Ajax team of the early 1970s.

www.womensoccer.com/refs/usabios.shtml
A site containing biographies and achievement records of more than 35 members of the U.S. women's team from the late 1980s to the present day.

▲ South Korea's Lee Chun-Soo (number 14), Choi Jin-Cheul (4), Hwang Sun-Hong (18), and Park Ji-Sung (21) celebrate their team's penalty shoot-out victory over Spain in the quarterfinals of the 2002 World Cup.

NIGERIA
Founded: 1945

In 1985 Nigeria's young players captured the World Under-17 Championship to become the first African nation to win a world tournament. Eleven years later the "Super Eagles," as the team is nicknamed, were the stars of the Atlanta Olympics thanks to their attacking energy, team spirit, and will to win. Featuring talented players like Celestine Babayaro, Emmanuel Amunike, and Daniel Amokachi, Nigeria beat Hungary 1-0 and Japan 2-0 before losing to Brazil 1-0 in the group stages. The team then beat Mexico 2-0 in the quarterfinals, setting up a second meeting with Brazil. That game is considered to be the finest in Olympic history. With only 13 minutes to go, Nigeria was losing 3-1. But the Africans pulled back one goal before their captain, Nwankwo Kanu, scored a last-gasp goal to tie. In a frenetic period of extra time Kanu struck again to seal a 4-3 victory. Another great comeback in the final saw Nigeria win gold by defeating Argentina 3-2 thanks to an 89th-minute goal by Amunike.

◄ *Daniel Amokachi scored the second of Nigeria's three goals against Argentina in the 1996 Olympic final.*

ITALY
Founded: 1898

Italy and Uruguay emerged as the leading teams during the first decade of the World Cup. The Italians chose not to enter the first tournament, in 1930, but were the hosts of the second, where they were coached by Vittorio Pozzo, who was nicknamed the "Old Maestro." Pozzo deployed several *oriundi*—Argentinians of Italian descent—including Raimundo Orsi and the captain, Luisito Monti. His team also included one of the world's finest attackers of the interwar years, Giuseppe Meazza. Italy won the 1934 World Cup under Pozzo's leadership and also triumphed at the 1936 Olympics. Recognizing the fact that his team was aging, the wily Pozzo introduced more and more young players so that by the time of the 1938 World Cup, only two members of the 1934 team,

Meazza and Giovanni Ferrari, remained. Pozzo's overhaul of the team proved to be a triumph, as Italy beat the popular French, Brazilian, and Hungarian teams to reclaim the trophy and make Pozzo the only coach in history to have won two World Cups.

▲ *Italy's national team, including star striker Giuseppe Meazza (front row, center), poses before the 1938 World Cup. The Italians comfortably beat Hungary 4-2 in the final.*

FACT FILE In the semifinal of the 1938 World Cup the string on Giuseppe Meazza's shorts broke, and they fell to the ground just as he went to take a penalty shot. Holding his shorts up with one hand, Meazza calmly hit the penalty home past the bemused Brazilian goalkeeper, Valter.

ENGLAND
Founded: 1863

As an England player, Alf Ramsey's last game had been the 6-3 demolition by Hungary in 1953—the game that punctured English belief in its soccer superiority. After coaching Ipswich Town from the lowly Third Division South to the league championship in 1962, Ramsey was named the England coach later that year. By the 1966 World Cup, he had assembled a powerful team with a strong backbone—Gordon Banks in goal, Jackie Charlton and Bobby Moore in central defense, Bobby Charlton in midfield, and, up front, Roger Hunt and the free-scoring Jimmy Greaves (who was injured during the tournament and replaced by Geoff Hurst). Propelled by goals mostly from Hunt and Bobby Charlton and by a prudent defense that did not concede a goal until the semifinal, England beat Mexico, France, Argentina, and Portugal. In the final at Wembley a memorable hat trick by Geoff Hurst and a goal from Martin Peters saw England beat West Germany 4-2 to win the trophy (see pages 68–69). After reaching the semifinals of the 1968 European Championships, England was one of the favorites for the 1970 World Cup. In the quarterfinal they were leading 2-0 with only 20 minutes left to play before West Germany struck back to win 3-2.

▲ *England's captain, Bobby Moore (left), and goalie Gordon Banks hold up the World Cup at Wembley.*

◄ *Gao Hong makes a save during training before the final of the 1999 Women's World Cup between China and the U.S.*

SAUDI ARABIA
Founded: 1959

Saudi Arabia began to take soccer seriously in the 1970s, luring foreign coaches and developing its leading clubs such as Al-Ahly, Al-Hilal, and Al-Ittihad. In the 1980s the national team won two Asian Cups and the World Under-16 Youth Cup. At the 1994 World Cup the Saudis lost narrowly to the Netherlands before beating Morocco 2-1 in the first all-Arab nation tie at the World Cup final. In their next game, against Belgium, Saeed Owairan scored the goal of the tournament. Picking up the ball deep in his own half, he sped upfield, skipping a number of tackles before kicking the ball home past Michel Preud'homme. The goal took the Saudis into the final 16 of the World Cup for the first time, where they lost to Sweden. Two years later they won the Asian Cup and almost defended their title in 2000, reaching the final but losing 1-0 to Japan.

◄ *Saeed Owairan at the 1994 World Cup.*

CHINA (WOMEN)
First international game: 1983

While the U.S., Norway, and, more recently, Germany have vied for the title of the leading team in women's international soccer, all contenders for the crown have had to overcome the considerable and consistent threat of the Chinese. Dubbed the "Steel Roses," China has dominated women's soccer in its own continent, winning seven consecutive Asian Women's Championship titles from 1986 onward. In 1997 the Chinese recorded their biggest-ever victory, crushing the Philippines 16-0. At the heart of the team throughout most of the 1990s were world-class players such as goalkeeper Gao Hong, dynamic midfielder Liu Ailing, and the high-scoring Sun Wen. On the world stage the Steel Roses have endured agonizingly close defeats, losing the 1996 Olympic final by a single goal and the 1999 World Cup final in a penalty shoot-out, both to the U.S. In the latter tournament China reached the final thanks to an unbeaten group record and a 5-0 mauling of the World Cup holder, Norway.

▶ Johan Neeskens evades the tackle of Argentina's Americo Gallego during the 1978 World Cup final.

NETHERLANDS
Founded: 1889

Rinus Michels, a former center-forward for the Netherlands, masterminded a revolution in Dutch soccer in the mid-1960s. First at club team Ajax and then with the national team he developed a system in which all of his players were comfortable on the ball and would switch positions, often with devastating results. Called "total football" (see page 61), the system revolved around such world-class talents as Johan Cruyff, Johan Neeskens, and Ruud Krol. With Michels at the helm, the Dutch powered to the 1974 World Cup final, scoring 14 goals and conceding only one in qualifying. They soared through the rounds, demolishing Argentina 4-0 and beating Brazil 2-0 on the way to the final against West Germany. Despite taking a one-goal lead within 80 seconds, the Netherlands suffered heartbreak, losing 2-1. Two years later they reached the semifinals of the 1976 European Championships, losing to the eventual winner, Czechoslovakia, in extra time. The Dutch entered the 1978 World Cup without Cruyff but could still call on many of the 1974 team, including Neeskens, Krol, and strikers Johnny Rep and Robbie Rensenbrink. They reached the final again, this time losing 3-1 to Argentina. Considered the most talented team to *never* win the World Cup, the Dutch enthralled millions of fans with their exploits and flair.

MEXICO
Founded: 1927

Having reached the quarterfinals of the two World Cups it has hosted (1970 and 1986), the soccer-crazy nation of Mexico had much to cheer about in the 1990s, when its national team dominated the continental

FACT FILE At the 1998 World Cup Mexican striker Cuauhtemoc Blanco amazed spectators and bewildered defenders with the trick of jumping over tackles with the ball clenched between his feet.

championships, the CONCACAF Gold Cup. In the inaugural competition of 1991 Mexico lost to the U.S. at the semifinal stage, but in the next three competitions it was unbeatable. It was rampant in 1993, beating Canada 8-0 and Jamaica 6-1 before humbling the U.S. 4-0 in the final. At the 1996 Gold Cup it defeated invited guests Brazil to win the title and, four years later, beat the U.S. again to secure a hat trick of wins. At the heart of Mexico's authoritative displays was the defender Claudio Suarez, nicknamed the "Emperor" for his commanding performances. Suarez made his national debut in 1992 and notched up his 172nd cap in the 2004 Copa America game against Ecuador. Mexico's success was also underpinned by a succession of great attackers, including Hugo Sanchez, Luis Garcia, Carlos Hermosillo, and Luis Hernandez.

▶ Mexico's Luis Hernandez is tackled by Dietmar Hamann of Germany at the 1998 World Cup. Hernandez and Carlos Hermosillo are the joint top scorers for Mexico, with 35 goals each.

BRAZIL
Founded: 1914

The 1958 World Cup signaled the arrival of Pelé and the start of a magnificent era for Brazil, who enchanted fans of the "beautiful game" as the team won three out of four World Cups. The team that claimed the 1970 World Cup is considered by many people to be international soccer's greatest team. In attack, few nations before or since have been able to field a team so blessed with flair, composure, and skill with the ball, as well as superb vision and movement. Opposition teams sometimes tried to mark Pelé out of the game, but this would only give space and opportunities to marvelous players such as center-forward Tostao, the bustling Roberto Rivelino (who had one of the most fearsome shots in world soccer), the midfielder Gerson, or the powerful winger Jairzinho. At the back, top-class players such as Carlos Alberto and center-back Wilson Piazza maintained a solid defense, but this team was all about the attack. After going one goal down to Czechoslovakia in its first game at the 1970 World Cup, Brazil responded by scoring four times. It scored three to beat Uruguay in the semifinal and four in the final, in which it beat a strong Italian team with one of the greatest-ever displays of attacking soccer. Brazil dazzled with its wit and inventiveness, and the 4-1 scorecard was completed by a fantastic team move ending in a thunderous shot by Carlos Alberto (see below). In his last game for

▲ Brazil's team that beat England at the 1970 World Cup. Back row, left to right: Carlos Alberto, Brito, Wilson Piazza, Félix, Clodoaldo, Everaldo, Mario Zagalo (coach); front row: Jairzinho, Roberto Rivelino, Tostao, Pelé, Paulo Cesar.

Brazil, Pelé was chaired off the field by his teammates owing to his part in the victory. The departure of other members of the team meant that by the time of the 1974 World Cup, only Rivelino and Jairzinho remained from the team that had captured the imagination of millions.

> **FACT FILE** In 1970 Brazil's coach, Mario Zagalo, became the first person to have both played in and coached a World-Cup-winning team. He had played in Brazil's 1958 and 1962 World Cup triumphs.

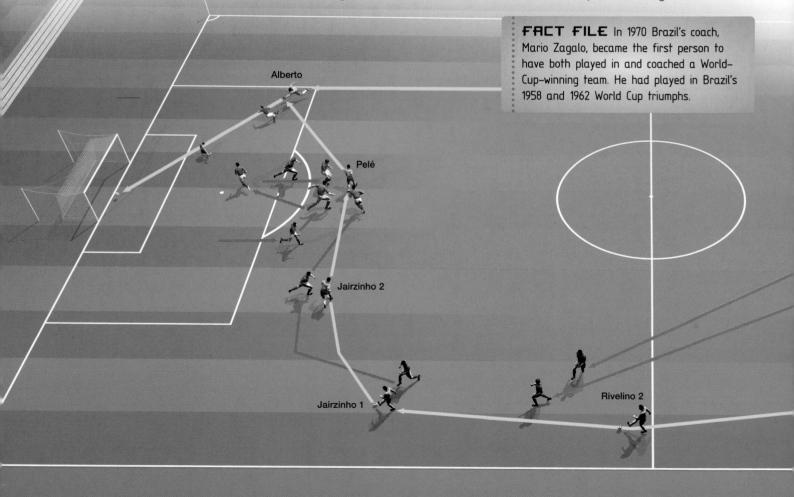

Alberto

Pelé

Jairzinho 2

Jairzinho 1

Rivelino 2

FACT FILE Idriss Carlos Kameni was only 16 when he was the goalkeeper for Cameroon in the 2000 Olympic final. He was a hero as early as the fifth minute when he saved a Spanish penalty. Cameroon went on to win gold in a penalty shoot-out, making the coach, Jean-Paul Akono, the first African coach to win a major world soccer competition.

▶ *Roger Milla runs past Colombian keeper Jose Higuita on his way to scoring during Cameroon's 2–1 victory in the second round of the 1990 World Cup. Cameroon was the talk of the tournament, defeating World Cup holders Argentina in the group stage.*

GAME ACTION

In the 1970 World Cup final against Italy right-back Carlos Alberto scored one of the best-ever team goals. The move started in the Brazilian half with a series of passes and some highly skilled dribbling by defender Clodoaldo. He released Roberto Rivelino, who fired a pass down the touchline. Jairzinho controlled the ball instantly and cut infield, shielding the ball from Italian defenders before feeding Pelé. Pelé spotted a run by a teammate on his right and nonchalantly rolled the ball diagonally into the penalty area. Marauding down the right flank, Carlos Alberto met the pass with a booming right-foot shot that sent the ball crashing low into the corner of the net.

FACT FILE Brazil's first international game was in July 1914 when it played English league team Exeter City. In 2004 the 1994 Brazilian World-Cup-winning team played a rematch against Exeter, winning the game 1–0.

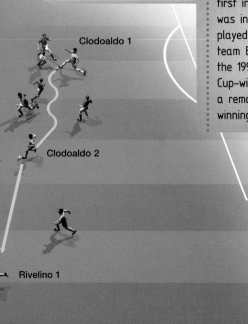

Clodoaldo 1

Clodoaldo 2

Rivelino 1

CAMEROON
Founded: 1960

Cameroon threatened a major shock at the 1982 World Cup, tying against Italy (the eventual winner) and Poland, yet narrowly failing to reach the second round. In 1990 a team led by Roger Milla lit up the tournament, winning a tough group containing the Soviet Union, Argentina, and Romania, beating Colombia in round two, and taking England to extra time before losing 3-2. Recently many of Cameroon's players have played for Europe's top clubs—Geremi at Real Madrid, Samuel Eto'o at Barcelona, and Salomon Olembe at Marseille, for example. After a disappointing 1998 World Cup, Cameroon roared back in 2000. It won the African Nations Cup, beating Nigeria. The team then triumphed at the Olympics, stunning Brazil in the quarterfinals, Chile in the semis, and Spain in the final to win gold.

LONGEST UNBEATEN INTERNATIONAL RUNS (IN GAMES)

36	Brazil 1993–1996	25	Italy 2004–2006
31	Argentina 1991–1993	24	Brazil 1975–1978
	Spain 1994–1998		Ghana 1981–1983
30	France 1994–1996	23	Brazil 1981–1982, 1997–1998
	Hungary 1950–1954		Czechoslovakia 1974–1976
29	Brazil 1970–1973		West Germany 1978–1981
27	Colombia 1992–1994		

CLUB TEAMS

BARCELONA
Spain
Founded: 1899
Stadium: Nou Camp

With its own bank, radio station, and one of the most impressive stadiums in the world, Barcelona can easily claim to be one of the world's largest soccer clubs. Despite being overshadowed in Europe by fierce rivals Real Madrid, Barcelona's domestic achievements are impressive—its sixth-place finish in the Spanish league, La Liga, in 2003 was its worst since 1942. The club has won 18 league titles, finished runner-up 21 times, and tops the list of Spanish Cup winners, with 24 victories. It has also won the European Cup Winners' Cup four times—more than any other team. Barcelona smashed the world transfer record in 1973 when it paid almost $2 million for Dutch maestro Johan Cruyff. Fifteen years later he returned as the club's coach. In his first season Cruyff steered the team to second place in La Liga and to victory over Sampdoria to collect the European Cup-Winners' Cup. Dutchman Ronald Koeman and Denmark's Michael Laudrup were signed to play alongside Spanish stars such as goalie Andoni Zubizarreta and midfielder José Bakero. In 1991 Barcelona won the

▲ Barcelona's captain, Carles Puyol, lifts the trophy after his team's 2–1 victory over Arsenal in the final of the 2006 Champions League.

first of four league titles in a row and one year later won their first European Cup, beating Sampdoria. Their second triumph in the competition came in 2006, capping a wonderful year in which the team also won the Spanish league.

KASHIMA ANTLERS
Japan
Founded: 1991
Stadium: Kashima Soccer Stadium

The former factory team of Sumitomo Metals Industries, the Kashima Antlers were formed in time to enter the inaugural J-League competition in 1993. Their name comes from the literal translation of "Kashima," meaning "deer island." Little was expected of the team, which lacked the pedigree of Japanese teams such as the Yokohama Marinos and Verdy Kawasaki. The Antlers' management team was ambitious, however, recruiting Brazilian World Cup star Zico, first as a player and later as the technical director. Zico's fellow countrymen Mazinho, Jorginho, and Bismarck—along with talented Japanese players such as Atsushi Yanagisawa, Tomoyuki Hirase, and Yasuto Honda—helped take the Antlers to four J-League titles and three Japanese Cups between 1996 and 2002.

▲ Kashima's Yasuto Honda celebrates with the J-League trophy in 2000.

AL-AHLY
Egypt
Founded: 1907
Stadium: Mukhtar El-Tetsh

Cairo-based Al-Ahly is the dominant soccer club in Egypt and one of the most successful teams in North Africa. Having won the first Egyptian league competition in 1949, it held onto the title until 1960, when it lost to fellow Cairo team and fierce rivals Zamalek. The 1980s was especially glorious for Al-Ahly. At home, it won five of the seven Cup of Egypt trophies and seven out of a possible ten league titles between 1980 and 1989. Overseas, Al-Ahly won the African Champions League twice, in 1982 and 1987, and was runner-up in 1983. It also won the African Cup Winners' Cup-three times in a row from 1984 to 1986. Al-Ahly was named the CAF African Club of the 20th Century before going on to win the African Champions League in 2001, 2005, and 2006.

FACT FILE Two of Al-Ahly's youngest stars during the 1990s were the twins Hossam and Ibrahim Hassan, the most capped players in Egyptian soccer. The brothers were idolized as they helped Al-Ahly win four league titles but turned from heroes to villains when they sensationally left the club to join rivals Zamalek in 2000.

FLAMENGO

Brazil
Founded: 1895
Stadiums: Gávea, Maracana

Brazil is full of famous soccer teams, including Vasco da Gama, São Paulo, Botafogo, and Corinthians. Flamengo is the most heavily supported of them all, having recorded 42 attendances of 100,000 or more at their games. Many gifted players have worn the team's distinctive black-and-red striped shirts. One of the greatest was Léonidas da Silva, known as the "Black Diamond" and the star of the 1938 World Cup. After a successful period in the 1950s, when the team won three Rio state league titles and earned the nickname the "Steamroller," Flamengo had to wait more than 25 years for its next great era. Inspired by Zico and his strike partner, Nunes, the team won the Rio Championship (the Carioca) in 1978, 1979, and 1981 and the Brazilian National Championship in 1980, 1982, and 1983. In 1981 it captured the Copa Libertadores and one month later went on to claim the World Club Cup, beating Liverpool 3-0.

▲ Flamengo's Ze Carlos da Silva performs a spectacular overhead kick during the 2003 Brazilian Cup final against Cruzeiro.

MANCHESTER UNITED

England
Founded: 1878
Stadium: Old Trafford

Sir Alex Ferguson, the Premiership's longest-serving and most successful coach, led Manchester United to a unique triple in English soccer when it won the Premiership, the FA Cup, and the Champions League in 1999. Forty years earlier a Manchester United team coached by Sir Matt Busby—another Scotsman who became a knight—had captured the hearts and minds of fans everywhere. The story began in the mid-1950s. Great things were expected of the young "Busby Babes" team that had won two league titles (in 1956 and 1957) and included, among other talents, the young England stars Roger Byrne and Duncan Edwards. But in 1958 a tragic airplane crash in Munich, Germany, killed 23 people on

◄ Bobby Charlton (left) celebrates after scoring the opening goal in Manchester United's defeat of Benfica to win the European Cup in 1968.

board, including eight members of the Manchester United first team. Busby had to build a new team, which contained tough defenders like Nobby Stiles, young midfielders such as Brian Kidd, and two survivors from the Munich crash, Bobby Charlton and central defender Bill Foulkes. Although often playing in midfield, Charlton formed a glittering attacking trio with Denis Law and George Best. Busby's team won the league title in 1965 and 1967, but the pinnacle of its achievements came in the 1968 European Cup. After beating Real Madrid in the semifinals, Manchester United faced Benfica in the final. Two goals from Charlton, one from Best, and one from the 19-year-old Kidd secured a memorable 4-1 victory. The "Red Devils," as the team is nicknamed, had become the first English team to win the European Cup.

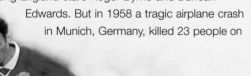

◄ Manchester United winger Ryan Giggs (left) speeds past Bayern Munich's Stefan Effenberg during the 1999 Champions League final.

INTERNAZIONALE (INTER MILAN)

Italy
Founded: 1908
Stadium: Giuseppe Meazza (San Siro)

Also known as Inter Milan, Internazionale was formed by a group of
former AC Milan players. During the rule of dictator Benito Mussolini,
the club was forced to change its name to Ambrosiana-Inter but
changed it back in 1942. Argentinian coach Helenio Herrera joined
Inter in 1960 and pioneered a new tactical system, playing a sweeper
behind a back four and using fast-moving defenders to build attacks.
Known as the *catenaccio* (door bolt) system, it was seen as negative
and defensive by some. Yet with fast, attacking fullbacks such as the
outstanding Giacinto Facchetti, the commanding Spanish midfielder
Luis Suarez, and creative attackers Alessandro Mazzola and Angelo
Domenghini, the team flourished. Inter won Serie A in 1963, 1965,
and 1966 and also triumphed over Real Madrid in
1964 and the mighty Benfica in 1965 to win
the European Cup twice. It added the
World Club Cup to its list of honors in
1964 and 1965, but it did not add to its
European tally until the 1990s, when
it won the UEFA Cup three times.
In 2006 Inter was
controversially awarded
the Italian league title
when Juventus
was stripped of
the trophy.

▲ *Sparta Prague's Radoslav Kovac is challenged by Michael Chrysostomos
of Cypriot team APOEL Nicosia during a Champions League qualifier in 2004.*

SPARTA PRAGUE

Czech Republic
Founded: 1893
Stadium: Letná

One of the grand clubs of eastern European soccer, Sparta has
been known by a series of different names, from Kralovske Vinohrady
(King's Vineyard) to AC Sparta, Spartak Sokolovo, and Sparta
Bratrstvi. The club has dominated the domestic game, winning 23
Czech Cups and 30 league championships. It has also finished as
league runner-up no less than 20 times since the professional Czech
league began in 1925. The first great Sparta team competed
admirably in Europe in the late 1920s and 1930s, winning the Mitropa
Cup (the forerunner of the European Cup) in both 1927 and 1934.
A number of Sparta players also featured on the Czechoslovakia
team that finished runner-up in the 1934 World Cup. These included
star striker Oldrich Nejedly, who was the tournament's leading scorer
with five goals. Sparta had several more great eras, notably in the
early 1960s and the beginning of the 1990s, when it competed in the
first Champions League competition in 1991–1992. Despite
memorable victories over Olympique Marseille, Dynamo Kiev, and
Barcelona, Sparta narrowly failed to qualify for the final.

◄ *Luiz Suarez, Inter Milan's elegant midfielder, on the
ball in 1967. Inter broke the world transfer record to
buy the Spaniard, paying $397,600 in 1961.*

SANTOS
Brazil
Founded: 1912
Stadium: Vila Belmiro

Santos is most famous as being Pelé's club. It had won few honors before he began playing for the team in 1956, aged only 15. During his 19 years at the club Santos won the São Paulo Championship ten times and the Copa Libertadores twice, in 1962 and 1963. It also won the World Club Cup in those years, the first with an extraordinary 5-2 win away at Benfica, which included a sensational hat trick from Pelé. Santos has fared less well in the years since, but a number of bright young stars emerged in this century. The club took a gamble on many of these players in the 2002 Brazilian National Championship, fielding a team with an average age of only 22. With 17-year-old midfielder Diego and 18-year-old striker Robinho especially prominent, Santos rolled back the years and delighted many neutral fans by winning the competition.

▲ *Young Santos striker Robinho (left) skips past the Corinthians' Vampeta during a Brazilian National Championship game in 2002. Robinho is currently one of the hottest commodities in world soccer.*

BOCA JUNIORS
Argentina
Founded: 1905
Stadium: La Bombonera

Best known in Europe as the club for which Diego Maradona played, Boca Juniors was founded by a group of Italian immigrants and an Irishman, Patrick MacCarthy. With its Buenos Aires neighbors, River Plate, they form one of the fiercest rivalries in world soccer. Boca has the edge in the derby games between the two teams and has won three more Copa Libertadores than River. Boca had a strong resurgence at the end of the 1900s. Beginning in May 1998 it went 40 league games unbeaten, setting an Argentinian record. The run helped the team win the Clausura and Apertura league titles in 1999, a feat that was followed by three Copa Libertadores triumphs—in 2000, 2001, and 2003. Boca also won the World Club Cup in 2000 and 2003.

DICK, KERR LADIES
England
Founded: 1917
No stadium

W. B. Dick and John Kerr owned a railroad and tram equipment-making factory in Preston in northwest England. During World War I women began to work in factories, taking the jobs of the men serving in the war. In 1917 the women at Dick, Kerr challenged their male coworkers to a game of soccer and went on to organize games against male and female opponents to raise money for war charities. By 1920, Dick, Kerr Ladies was playing games to sell-out crowds. One game against St. Helen's Ladies attracted 53,000 spectators to Everton's Goodison Park. In 1921, at the peak of its popularity, Dick, Kerr Ladies played 67 games, and a tour of the U.S. the following year saw the team win three and tie three out of nine games against male teams. The Football Association felt threatened by a team that, in some cases, was attracting bigger crowds than the men's game. In 1921 the FA banned all women from playing soccer on the fields of its member clubs. Incredibly, the ban remained in force for 50 years. As a result, support for women's soccer dwindled, and by 1926, Dick, Kerr Ladies had disbanded. Yet the team left an important legacy by showing that women could play soccer in a competitive, entertaining way.

◀ *The Dick, Kerr Ladies attack the penalty area during a floodlit game against Heys of Bradford in 1919.*

AC MILAN
Italy
Founded: 1899
Stadium: Giuseppe Meazza (San Siro)

AC Milan's first period of notable success came in the 1950s when a trio of Swedish stars— Gunnar Gren, Nils Liedholm, and Gunnar Nordahl—followed by Uruguayan striker Juan Alberto Schiaffino helped them win four Serie A titles. Nordahl remains the club's highest scorer, with an amazing 210 goals in 257 games. The 1960s saw AC Milan emerge as one of the leading clubs in Europe, winning two European Cups and a Cup Winners' Cup trophy. A period of decline followed, which included an enforced relegation in 1980 as a result of a betting scandal. Milan's fortunes were revived by the arrival of a new chairman, Silvio Berlusconi, in 1986. The wealthy media tycoon and future Italian prime minister appointed Arrigo Sacchi as the coach the following year. An exciting team was assembled, which included the superb Dutch trio of Ruud Gullit, Marco van Basten, and Frank Rijkaard alongside the homegrown talents of Franco Baresi, Roberto Donadoni, and Paolo Maldini. Milan won Serie A in 1988 and went on to win it five times during the 1990s. Starting in 1991, Milan went unbeaten in Serie A for an incredible 58 games, a run that included annihilations of Foggia (8-2) and Fiorentina (7-3).

▲ *George Weah scores for AC Milan during a 1997 derby game against Internazionale. Weah was bought as a replacement for Marco van Basten.*

The team also put five goals past Sampdoria, Lazio, Pescara, and Napoli (twice). In Europe, Milan beat Real Madrid 5-0 and then Steaua Bucharest 4-0 in the final to collect the European Cup in 1989—a competition that it won again in 1990, 1994, and 2003, and in which they were runners-up in 1993, 1995, and 2005. Domestically, Milan claimed the Serie A title for the 17th time in 2004.

RIVER PLATE
Argentina
Founded: 1901
Stadium: Monumental

River Plate is one of Argentina's leading teams. In the late 1930s it moved to a wealthy suburb of Buenos Aires, which, along with a team of expensive players, led to its nickname, the "Millionaires." River is renowned for its attacking style. In the late 1940s its powerful forward line became known as *La Máquina* ("The Machine"), and the club has produced a succession of world-class attackers, including Omar Sivori, Mario Kempes, Hernan Crespo, Javier Saviola, and the legendary Alfredo di Stefano. River Plate has won a total of 32 Argentinian league titles, yet it was not until 1986 that it triumphed at the Copa Libertadores. The team had made the final twice previously (in 1966 and 1976) before a team featuring Norberto Alonso, Juan Gilberto Funes, and the great Uruguayan striker Enzo Francescoli beat America Cali of Colombia. River continued its habit of making the Copa Libertadores final in years ending in six with their second win, again versus America Cali, in 1996.

◄ *Paraguayan striker Nelson Cuevas (left) is congratulated by Gaston Fernandez after scoring River Plate's first goal in a 3-2 victory over Colón in 2004.*

KAIZER CHIEFS
South Africa
Founded: 1970
Stadium: Johannesburg Athletics Stadium

Kaizer Motaung played for South Africa's oldest and most famous club for black players, the Soweto-based Orlando Pirates. In 1968 he moved to the U.S. to play for the Atlanta Chiefs in the newly formed NASL. After returning to South Africa, he founded the Kaizer Chiefs (named after Motaung and his former U.S. team) with ex-Orlando Pirates teammates Zero Johnson, Ratha Mokgoatlheng, Msomi Khoza, and Ewert Nene. Featuring a mixture of promising young players and experienced veterans, the Chiefs soon made their mark. The team won the Life Cup in 1971 and 1972 and the BP Top Eight Cup in 1974. In the same year it claimed its first South African league title. Tragedy struck in 1976 with the death of captain Ariel Kgongoane in the Soweto uprising and the killing of Ewert Nene, but the Chiefs went on to win the league in 1977 and 1979.

▲ Patrick Mabedi (left) of the Kaizer Chiefs tackles Vikash Dhorasoo of Olympique Lyonnais during the 2003 Peace Cup competition, held in South Korea.

▼ Eluding Red Star Belgrade's Miodrag Belodedic (left), Jean-Pierre Papin of Marseille powers upfield during the 1991 European Cup final.

MOST CONSECUTIVE LEAGUE CHAMPIONSHIPS

14	Skonto Riga (Latvia)	1991–2004
13	Al-Faisaly (Jordan)	1959–1966, 1970–1974
13	Rosenborg (Norway)	1992–2004
12	Tafea FC (Vanuatu)	1994–2005
11	Al-Ansar (Lebanon)	1988, 1990–1999
10	BFC Dynamo (East Germany)	1979–1988
10	Dinamo Tblisi (Georgia)	1990–1999
10	Taipower (Taiwan)	1995–2004

OLYMPIQUE MARSEILLE
France
Founded: 1899
Stadium: Vélodrome

Arguably the best known French club team, Olympique Marseille boasts an intensely passionate fan base. After a flurry of league titles at the start of the 1970s (helped by Yugoslavian striker Josip Skoblar, who scored a record 44 goals in the 1970–1971 season), Marseille found success hard to come by. New chairman Bernard Tapie arrived in 1985 and invested heavily, bringing in expensive stars

such as Enzo Francescoli, Jean-Pierre Papin, Didier Deschamps, and the Ghanaian midfielder Abedi Pele. Papin had the greatest impact, showing an incredible appetite for goals and becoming the French league's leading scorer for an astonishing five consecutive seasons from 1988 to 1992. The team rampaged through the domestic league, winning five championships in a row from 1989 to 1993. Marseille was agonizingly close to becoming the first French club to win the European Cup, losing out in the semifinals to Benfica in 1990 and losing on penalties in the final to Red Star Belgrade the following year. In 1993 a header by Basile Boli sent Marseille fans into ecstasy as it beat AC Milan 1-0 to win the trophy. Then it all went very wrong, as Marseille was found guilty of game fixing a French league game against Valenciennes. The team was stripped of its 1993 league title and relegated, as well as being denied the right to defend the Champions League trophy the following season. Tapie was eventually imprisoned for corruption. Marseille spent the rest of the 1990s battling to regain its status, with a certain degree of success—in 1999 it was the runner-up in both the French league and the UEFA Cup.

FLUMINENSE
Brazil
Founded: 1902
Stadiums: Laranjeiras, Maracana

Founded in 1902, Fluminense has traditionally been supported by the middle classes, while its fierce Rio de Janiero rivals, Flamengo, drew support from the working class. Derby games between the two always guarantee big crowds. One "Flu v. Fla" derby in 1963 attracted a world-record attendance for a club game, with 177,656 supporters crammed inside the enormous Maracana Stadium. Fluminense also competes in Rio's oldest derby, the *Classico Vovô* ("Grandpa Derby"), with Botafogo, the cofounders of the Rio league. Despite being the home club of a series of Brazilian soccer legends, including Didi during the 1950s and Carlos Alberto and Roberto Rivelino in the 1960s and 1970s, Fluminense has always disappointed on the international stage. It has never won a major South American competition, nor even reached a final. However, it has achieved a lot in Brazil, winning the Rio Championship title 29 times. One of its most impressive runs occurred in the 1980s when the Tricolores—so nicknamed for their traditional green, red, and white colors—won three Rio Championships in a row from 1983 to 1985. With Paraguay's star striker, Julio César Romero, leading the line, Fluminense also won the Brazilian National Championship in 1984.

◀ *Brazilian legend Romario (right), in Fluminense colors, celebrates with his teammates during a league game against Goias in 2004.*

ARSENAL
England
Founded: 1886
Stadium: Highbury (Emirates Stadium from 2006)

First known as Dial Square FC, Arsenal was formed by workers from the Royal Arsenal ammunitions factory in Woolwich in south London—hence its nickname, the "Gunners." After a move to the north of the city in 1913, the club's rise to the top of the English game coincided with the appointment of Herbert Chapman as the coach in 1925. Chapman was highly innovative both on and off the field, and he built a counterattacking team featuring inside-forwards Alex James and David Jack and winger Cliff Bastin, whose 178 goals for the club remained a record for more than 50 years. Arsenal was the league runner-up in Chapman's first season and went on to win the title in 1931 with a point total that would not be beaten for 30 years. Runner- up in 1932, it then claimed three league titles in a row (1933–1935) and two FA Cups (1930 and 1936). Despite a league and FA Cup double in 1971, the

FACT FILE Under Herbert Chapman, "The Arsenal" became just "Arsenal," allegedly to make them appear at the top of an alphabetical list of Division One clubs. Chapman also successfully campaigned for the Gillespie Road subway station, close to the stadium, to be renamed "Arsenal."

▲ *Arsenal players congratulate Thierry Henry after his goal against Fulham. Henry scored 37 goals in all competitions in both 2002–2003 and 2003–2004.*

closest Arsenal has come to its earlier dominance has been under French coach Arsène Wenger. With a team boasting Thierry Henry, Dennis Bergkamp, and Patrick Vieira, it has won three Premiership titles and four FA Cups since 1998. Arsenal was unbeaten through the 2003–2004 league season, eventually recording a total of 49 league games without defeat, a record in English soccer. It reached its first Champions League final in 2006, narrowly losing to Barcelona.

JUVENTUS
Italy
Founded: 1897
Stadium: Delle Alpi

▲ *Alessandro del Piero of Juventus lines up an overhead kick during the 2003 Champions League final against AC Milan.*

Juventus is one of the most famous teams in the world. Formed by a group of high-school students in the city of Turin, they played in pink shirts before a club official visited England in 1903. He was so taken by Notts County's shirt of vertical black-and-white stripes that he took a set of them back to Italy, where they became Juve's official home colors. The team has enjoyed many successful periods, including five consecutive league titles from 1931 to 1935 and a 1980s team that won Serie A four times. Juve beat Liverpool to win the 1985 European Cup, but the victory was overshadowed by the Heysel Stadium tragedy in which 39 fans died. Financed by the extremely wealthy Agnelli family, the owners of the Fiat motor company, Juventus spent lavishly on recruiting world-class players in the 1990s, including Roberto Baggio, Gianluca Vialli, Attilio Lombardo, Fabrizio Ravanelli, Angelo di Livio, Alessandro del Piero, and Christian Vieri. After capturing the UEFA Cup twice in the early 1990s, Juve won an Italian league and cup double in 1995 and beat Ajax to win the Champions League in 1996. The team lost the final of that competition in 1997 and 1998, but its devoted fans could console themselves with Serie A titles in both years. Following a game-fixing scandal in 2006, however, Juventus was stripped of its 2005 and 2006 Serie A titles and relegated to Serie B for the first time in its history.

STEAUA BUCHAREST
Romania
Founded: 1947
Stadium: Ghencea

Formed by the Romanian army, Steaua Bucharest had built a formidable team by the mid-1980s. The team included the superb goalkeeper Helmut Ducadam, Miodrag Belodedici (one of the best sweepers in Europe), goal machine Marius Lacatus in attack, and Romania's greatest player, Gheorghe Hagi. In August 1986 the club began an unbeaten run that is unique in Romanian soccer. It did not suffer a defeat for three league seasons, conceding 63 goals but scoring a staggering 322. The team made history overseas, too, beating Spanish giants Barcelona in the final of the 1986 European Cup to become the first east European club to lift the prestigious trophy. In the early 1990s, after three seasons as runner-up in the Romanian league, Steaua began another incredible run, winning six consecutive domestic titles between 1993 and 1998.

GALATASARAY
Turkey
Founded: 1905
Stadium: Ali Sami Yen

Turkey's three biggest clubs— Galatasaray, Fenerbahçe, and Besiktas—are all based in Istanbul, and their passionate fans are fierce and occasionally violent rivals. Galatasaray has won the league title 16 times (the same number as Fenerbahçe) and the Turkish Cup 14 times (ten more than Fenerbahçe). It is the best-known Turkish club overseas, partly because of its competitive performances in Europe during the 1990s. Visiting foreign teams often encounter an intimidating atmosphere—from "Welcome to Hell" banners displayed at the airport by fans to a stadium that turns into a cauldron of color and noise on game nights. Galatasaray went unbeaten at home in Europe from 1984 to 1994, the year in which they tied 3-3 at Old Trafford to knock Manchester United out of the Champions League. In 2000 the team won its first major European trophy by beating Arsenal to win the UEFA Cup.

▲ *Striker Hakan Sukur has made more than 300 appearances for Galatasaray, scoring almost 200 goals.*

BAYERN MUNICH
Germany
Founded: 1900
Stadium: Allianz Arena

Germany's most famous club was formed in 1900 from rebels who had split from their former club, MTV 1879. The new team beat their old team 7-1 in the first game between the clubs. Although Bayern won a league title in 1932, by the early 1960s it was one of West Germany's less popular clubs and did not achieve a place in the Bundesliga when it was formed in 1963. But it earned promotion soon after and by the late 1960s was a

▶ *Bixente Lizarazu (right) battles Valencia's Gaizka Mendieta in the 2001 Champions League final. Bayern won the title on penalties.*

dominant force in the domestic game. At the forefront were future soccer legends such as Sepp Maier, Franz Beckenbauer, and Gerd Müller, who was the Bundesliga's top scorer in seven seasons (1967, 1969–1970, 1972–1974, and 1978). With that team, Bayern won German Cups in 1966 and 1967 and a European Cup Winners' Cup in 1967. In the early 1970s Bayern's stars were joined by more world-class players such as Paul Breitner and Uli Hoeness. The team won three Bundesliga titles in a row and three consecutive European Cups from 1974 to 1976. In 1976 Bayern's international reputation was sealed when the team won the World Club Cup, beating Belo Horizonte of Brazil. Until 2005, Bayern and TSV 1860 shared the Olympic Stadium in Munich, but both clubs now play at the Allianz Arena, which will hosted games for the 2006 World Cup.

▲ *Werner Roth rounds the Atlético Madrid goalkeeper as Bayern Munich powers to a 4-0 victory to win the 1974 European Cup final replay. Bayern had salvaged a 1-1 tie in the first game with a goal in the last minute of extra time.*

BENFICA
Portugal
Founded: 1904
Stadium: Estadio da Luz

Benfica remains Portugal's most famous and successful club, despite the long periods of glory enjoyed by rivals Porto and Sporting Lisbon. Its greatest era was undoubtedly the 1960s, which began under the management of Hungarian Bela Guttmann. The team played with a mix of speed, power, and skill, typified by the midfielder Mario Coluna and the brilliant Eusebio. Benfica began the decade by defeating Barcelona 3-2 to win the 1961 European Cup. The following year, facing the mighty Real Madrid in the final, the team found themselves 3-1 down to a Ferenc Puskas hat trick but fought back to beat the Spanish giant 5-3. It featured in five European Cup finals during the 1960s and won eight out of ten league championships. Defending another league title in the 1972–1973 season, Benfica went unbeaten through 30 league games, scoring 101 goals in the process.

▲ *Benfica poses before the 1968 European Cup final, having beaten Juventus in the semifinals. Amazingly, their toughest opponents were Northern Irish team Glentoran in the first round—Benfica sneaked through on the away goals rule.*

ASANTE KOTOKO
Ghana
Founded: 1935
Stadium: Kumasi Sports Stadium

Asante Kotoko, nicknamed the "Porcupines," developed out of a team formed in the 1920s by Kwesi Kuma, a taxi driver. In 1967 the club won the first of three consecutive league titles and reached the final of the African Champions League. Despite two ties against Tout Puissant Englebert of Zaire (now the Democratic Republic of the Congo), the Ghanaian club was declared the loser when it refused a play-off to decide the contest. In 1970 the two clubs met again in the final. This time Asante Kotoko secured a 2-1 away win (after a 1-1 tie at home) to become the first Ghanaian team to win the African Champions League. The club was runner-up in the 1971 and 1973 competitions and won the 1972 Ghanaian league title.

NACIONAL
Uruguay
Founded: 1899
Stadium: Centenario

Nacional is engaged in a seesaw battle for supremacy in Uruguayan soccer with Peñarol, the team with which it shares the country's biggest stadium. Since 1991 Nacional has won seven league championships. One of the team's greatest eras, however, was in the late 1960s. Led by Argentinian striker Luis Artime, it won three league titles in a row from 1969 to 1971, made the final of the Copa Libertadores in 1969, and won that competition in 1971. Nacional again claimed South America's biggest club prize in 1980 and 1988 and each time went on to win the World Club Cup.

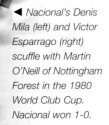

◀ Nacional's Denis Mila (left) and Victor Esparrago (right) scuffle with Martin O'Neill of Nottingham Forest in the 1980 World Club Cup. Nacional won 1-0.

ANDERLECHT
Belgium
Founded: 1908
Stadium: Constant vanden Stock

It took 39 years from the club's formation for Anderlecht to win its first Belgian league championship. Since then the Brussels-based team has made up for lost time, winning a staggering 28 league titles—15 more than the second most successful team in Belgium, Club Brugge. In addition, Anderlecht has been runner-up 18 times. Such consistency has seen the club qualify to play in a major European competition every year from 1964 to 2007. The 1970s were a golden era for Anderlecht. It was the runner-up in the 1970 Inter-Cities Fairs Cup, losing 4-3 over two stages to Arsenal. By the mid-1970s, under the management of Raymond Goethals, Anderlecht's team boasted many high-quality players. A strong midfield, featuring Frankie van der Elst, Ludo Coeck, and Arie Haan, played behind talented attacking duo Benny Nielsen and Robbie Rensenbrink. The club contested three European Cup Winners' Cup finals in a row, beating West Ham 4-2 in 1976 but losing to Hamburg the following year. Anderlecht bounced back to knock the same German team out of the 1977–1978 competition on its way to the final, where the team thrashed Austria Vienna 4-0. The team also added two European Supercups to its trophy cabinet by beating Bayern Munich in 1976 and Liverpool in 1978.

▲ Belgian striker Enzo Scifo on the ball for Anderlecht against PSV Eindhoven—the team for which Luc Nilis, Scifo's World Cup teammate, played.

HIT THE NET

www.soccerlinks.net/pages/index.html
A huge collection of Web links to more than 5,000 official and unofficial club Web sites, searchable by continent and country.

www.mls.net
The official site of Major League Soccer in the U.S., with news, statistics, and information about MLS teams and players.

www.expertfootball.com
A comprehensive soccer Web site, featuring a history of the game, profiles of teams and players, the latest news and transfer rumors, plus a forum for fans.

ESPERANCE SPORTIVE TUNIS
Tunisia
Founded: 1919
Stadium: El-Menzah

With a distinctive uniform that gave the team its nickname— the Blood and Golds—Esperance has long been one of the leading clubs in Tunisia and North Africa. Consecutive Tunisian league wins in 1993 and 1994 paved the way for its 1994 African

▲ *Esperance's Karim Ouji and Ali Zitouni celebrate reaching the semifinals of the 2004 African Champions League.*

Champions League triumph, where, in front of a delirious home crowd, it beat the Egyptian holders, Zamalek, 3-1. In 1997 Esperance began a record-breaking league run. Seeing off the challenge of leading rivals such as Etoile Sportive du Sahel and Club Africain, the team captured an incredible seven straight league championships. Before this feat no Tunisian club had won more than three league titles in a row. Many of the team's most prominent players—including Radhi Jaidi, Brazilian-born José Clayton, and long-serving club captain Khaled Badra—were part of the Tunisian national team that won the 2004 African Nations Cup on home soil.

MOSCOW SPARTAK
Russia
Founded: 1922
Stadium: Lokomotiv

Although Moscow Dynamo is the most famous Russian team outside of the country, its local rival, Moscow Spartak, has claimed more victories, winning 12 Soviet league titles and ten Soviet Cups. The team also made the semifinals of European competitions two times in the early 1990s. Unfortunately, Spartak's greatest team (of the late 1940s and early 1950s) peaked in the days before major European competitions existed. Spartak has dominated the Russian league since its formation in 1992, winning the title nine times in its first ten seasons.

▲ *Spartak Moscow's Senegalese defender Baye Ali Ibra Kebe (right) tackles Liverpool's Jamie Carragher during a Champions League game in 2002.*

▼ *Peñarol players celebrate their winning goal against fierce rivals Nacional to claim the 1999 Uruguayan Championship.*

PEÑAROL
Uruguay
Founded: 1891
Stadium: Centenario

Along with Nacional, Peñarol dominates Uruguayan soccer. Peñarol is marginally more successful, with more than 45 league titles. In head-to-head meetings up until the start of 2007 Peñarol leads its rivals by 176 wins to 154. The club's first golden era came in the 1960s. Led by Ecuadorian striker Pedro Spencer, the team won three Copa Libertadores (1960, 1961, and 1966) and two World Club Cups (against Benfica in 1961 and Real Madrid in 1966). Peñarol's team of the 1980s added to this tally, winning two more Copa Libertadores and, in 1982, beating Aston Villa to win a third World Club Cup. Peñarol holds a number of Copa Libertadores records: the largest win (11-2 against Valencia of Venezuela in 1970), the highest aggregate win (14-1 versus Everest of Ecuador in 1963), and the most consecutive participations in the competition (15 between 1965 and 1979).

AJAX
Netherlands
Founded: 1900
Stadium: Amsterdam ArenA

Coach Rinus Michels arrived at Ajax in the 1964–1965 season, just in time to save it from relegation. (The team finished 13th out of 16). Michels went on to develop the concept of "total soccer" (see page 61), which would have a major impact at both the club and international levels. Signs of a renaissance at Ajax began to show as early as 1966, when the team won the Dutch league and beat Liverpool 5-1 in the European Cup. Three years later Ajax became the first Dutch team to reach the final of that competition, where it lost to AC Milan. Spurred on by Dutch rival Feyenoord winning the European Cup in 1970, Ajax went on to claim the trophy for the next three years with the help of such legends as Johan Cruyff, Arie Haan, Ruud Krol, and Johan Neeskens. Playing an electric style of fluid soccer with the emphasis firmly on the attack, the team was crowned Dutch league champion six times in eight seasons (1966–1968, 1970, 1972–1973) and won the European Supercup and World Club Cup, both in 1972. Ajax also supplied most of the players for the Dutch team that finished runner-up at the 1974 World Cup. By the mid-1970s, however, Neeskens, Cruyff, and

Michels had moved to Spain, and Ajax entered a period of decline. But through a comprehensive and much-copied youth system, the team was eventually able to replace its former stars with several new waves of talent such as Frank Rijkaard, Dennis Bergkamp, and the De Boer brothers, Frank and Ronald.

▼ *Twins Frank and Ronald de Boer, together with strikers Nwankwo Kanu and Finidi George, take a victory lap after Ajax's 1-0 win against AC Milan in the final of the 1995 Champions League.*

LIVERPOOL
England
Founded: 1892
Stadium: Anfield

In 1959 Liverpool was struggling in the English second division and had been knocked out of the third round of the FA Cup by amateur team Worcester City. Then Bill Shankly arrived as the coach.

He was a passionate, no-nonsense Scotsman who went on to build a successful Liverpool team that won the league championship three times and lifted the UEFA Cup in 1973. One year later he resigned, and Bob Paisley—Shankly's assistant for 15 years—was promoted to coach. Paisley's Liverpool won 19 major trophies in nine years, making him the most successful British coach of the 1900s. The club won six league titles and three League Cups owing to a watertight defense, a quick, accurate passing game, and intelligent attacking by players such as Kevin Keegan, Steve Heighway, John Toshack, and Kenny Dalglish. A UEFA Cup win in 1976 was followed by European Cup triumphs in 1977 and 1978, making Liverpool the first British team to successfully defend the trophy.

In 1981 the club beat Real Madrid to win the European Cup for a third time, and a fourth win came (after penalties) in 1984 against Italian team Roma.

FACT FILE
Between January 1978 and January 1981, Liverpool set an all-time record of 85 home games unbeaten in all competitions. Included in this run were an incredible 63 home league games in a row.

◀ *Liverpool's Ray Kennedy (far left), Graeme Souness, and Alan Hansen close down Flamengo star Zico during the 1981 World Club Cup.*

CELTIC
Scotland
Founded: 1888
Stadium: Celtic Park

Celtic, along with its Glasgow-based rival, Rangers, has dominated Scottish soccer for decades. However, Celtic had not won the league title for 11 years before the arrival of Jock Stein as the coach in 1965. Stein developed a homegrown team, all of whom hailed from Glasgow and the surrounding area. The team was full of youth and speed and had an adventurous style of play. These qualities were typified by the ingenious winger Jimmy Johnstone, marauding fullback Tommy Gemmell, prolific strikers Steve Chalmers, Bobby Lennox, and Willy Wallace, and a defensive rock in Billy McNeill, the captain. Celtic began an astonishing run from 1966, winning nine Scottish league championships in a row and achieving a Scottish Cup and league double five times during that period. Yet they contested the 1967 European Cup final in Lisbon, Portugal, as underdog to a powerful Internazionale team that had won two of the previous three European Cups. Against the odds, Celtic recovered from one goal down to beat the Italians 2-1, becoming the first British team to win the biggest club prize in European soccer. The "Lions of Lisbon" narrowly failed to repeat their achievement when they reached the 1970 European Cup final, going down 2-1 to Dutch team Feyenoord. It would be 33 years before the Scottish club reached its next European final, losing 3-2 to Porto in the 2003 UEFA Cup final.

▶ *Winger Jimmy Johnstone (left) scored 130 goals for Celtic on the way to nine league championships, five League Cups, and four Scottish Cups with the club.*

COLO COLO
Chile
Founded: 1925
Stadium: David Arellano

With around 60 percent of the country's soccer fans following the team, Colo Colo is easily the most popular and successful of all of the Chilean club teams. The team has won a record 25 league championships (13 more than fierce rivals Universidad de Chile), as well as the Chilean Cup—the *Campeonato de Copa*—ten times. Under its coach, Arturo Salah, Colo Colo captured league titles in 1986 and 1989 before former Yugoslavia under-20 coach Mirko Jozic became the coach during the 1990 season. The team won a sequence of three league titles in a row in 1991, the same year that it enjoyed fantastic success overseas. In 1973 Colo Colo had been the first Chilean team to contest a final of the top South American club cup competition, the Copa Libertadores. In 1991 the club went one stage further, beating the mighty Argentinian team River Plate in the semifinals and the cup holder, Olimpia, 3-0 on aggregate to win the trophy. Under Jozic, the team would win a further league title in 1993, while one member of the 1991 team, Jaime Pizarro, would go on to coach them to league success in 2002.

▲ *Colo Colo's Rodolfo Madrid moves away from Alfredo Moreno of Argentinian team Boca Juniors during a Copa Libertadores game in 2003.*

DYNAMO KIEV
Ukraine
Founded: 1927
Stadium: National Sport Komplex Olimpiyskiy

Originally the soccer team of the Soviet secret police, Dynamo Kiev was the first club outside of Moscow to win the Soviet league championship. A player on that 1961 team, Valery Lobanovsky, became Kiev's coach 13 years later. He led the club through its greatest era, which began spectacularly with consecutive Soviet league titles. In 1975 Kiev won the Cup Winners' Cup, becoming the first Soviet team to win a European competition. It also beat Bayern Munich 3-1 to win the European Supercup. In total, Lobanovsky (in three separate periods) coached Kiev to win eight league titles, six Soviet Cups, and two European Cup Winners' Cups. In 1991, after the breakup of the Soviet Union, Kiev played in the newly formed Ukrainian league. The team has dominated the competition, winning the title in every year except for 2002 and 2005.

▲ Dynamo Kiev poses with the 2003 Ukrainian Cup after beating the holders— and Kiev's most competitive rivals in Ukrainian soccer—Shakhtar Donetsk.

REAL MADRID
Spain
Founded: 1902
Stadium: Bernabeu

Real Madrid is one of the world's most famous and successful teams. It has won 29 Spanish league titles, 11 more than rivals Barcelona and 20 more than its neighbors, Atlético Madrid. It has also captured 11 European trophies and three World Club Cups. In the 1940s and 1950s Real's president, Santiago Bernabeu, began to transform the club with foreign players and a huge desire to win the newly formed European Cup competition. Real did not disappoint, capturing not only the first European Cup in 1956 but the next four as well. The team included two of the world's outstanding attacking talents in Ferenc Puskas and Alfredo di Stefano, as well as speedy winger Paco Gento, central defenders Marcos Marquitos and Juan Zarraga, and attacking midfielder Hector Rial. From 1957 to 1965, Real remained unbeaten at home in 121 Spanish league games and won five La Liga titles in a row (1961–1965). A transformed team captured the European Cup for a sixth time in 1966.

Today Real is one of the world's richest clubs, with a habit of buying soccer's most famous players such as Zinedine Zidane, Ronaldo, and David Beckham. With these stars, known as *galácticos*, Real won the 2001 and 2003 Spanish league titles and has taken its total of European Cup/Champions League triumphs to nine—more than any other team.

▲ Real Madrid's victorious team poses with the 1960 European Cup after one of the greatest-ever displays of attacking soccer (see pages 14–15).

◄ After wins in 1998 and 2000, Fernando Hierro lifts Real's third Champions League trophy in 2002—adding to the club's total of six European Cups between 1956 and 1966.

SNAPSHOT
THE WORLD CUP COMES HOME

France entered the 1998 World Cup under intense pressure. The tournament was to be held on French soil, they had failed to qualify for the previous World Cup, and critics claimed that the team lacked a striker of true international quality. What they did have, however, was the world's most creative midfielder in Zinedine Zidane, a strong defense, and a group of hard-working midfielders and attackers. France powered through its group, winning all three games. In the second round, veteran defender Laurent Blanc scored the first "golden goal" at the World Cup, to beat Paraguay. Further victories over Italy and Croatia took *Les Bleus* to a final against the mighty Brazil, led by Ronaldo. More famous for his mesmerizing ball skills on the ground, Zidane scored two headed goals against a subdued Brazilian team, and an injury-time strike by Emmanuel Petit completed a 3-0 victory. The World Cup had been the brainchild of a Frenchman back in the 1920s. Now, at last, the cup had come home. *Les Bleus* were on top of the world.

France's Zinedine Zidane (number ten) rises high to score with a header in the 1998 World Cup final.

SOCCER DREAMS

From Beijing to Buenos Aires, Manchester to Mexico City, millions of children, teenagers, and adults play soccer for fun, exercise, and as a sport. Many are content to take part at an amateur level, but for some, the dream of emulating the stars they read about, watch, and worship is a passion.

YOUNG DREAMS

Promising players often emerge at an early age on school and local teams. In most countries young players can play at a regional, county, or state level in organized youth team competitions. Major soccer clubs run youth teams and soccer academies and also send scouts to watch games in the hope of spotting new talent. Young players may be invited to an open day or trial, where scouts and coaches can observe them in action at close hand. A club may then offer a contract or a place in its youth academy to a promising player. Famous academies exist at clubs such as Bayern Munich, Manchester United, and Porto. The most famous is De Toekomst, the youth academy of Dutch team Ajax. It has been responsible for producing truly great players such as Johan Cruyff, Marco van Basten, Dennis Bergkamp, Patrick Kluivert, and, more recently, up-and-coming stars such as Rafael van der Vaart and Wesley Sneijder.

▲ Freddy Adu was born in Ghana but is now a U.S. citizen. Here, aged 14, he shoots past Sierra Leone's goalie at the 2004 Under-17 World Championship.

YOUTH TEAMS AND COMPETITIONS

As young players approach the pinnacle of the game, there are international games for children, as well as under-17 and youth competitions. These reach a peak with FIFA's Under-17 World Championship and the World Youth Championship. The latter competition began in 1977; at the 1991 tournament Portugal swept to the title with a midfield containing teenagers João Pinto, Rui Costa, and Luis Figo. Ten years later Argentina won the trophy thanks to the goals of Javier Saviola. The young striker was the top scorer at the tournament, with 11 goals, ahead of rising Brazilian player Adriano and France's Djibril Cissé. FIFA's Under-17 World Championship

FACT FILE
Internazionale offered $750,000 to sign Freddy Adu in 2000. The offer was rejected by his mother—Adu was only ten years old.

▲ Young Chinese players perform wheelbarrow exercises. They are part of a group of 27 teenagers, known as the 2008 Star Team, who are expected to form the core of China's team at the next Olympics.

has also featured a number of stars. The 1997 competition, for example, showcased the talents of the up-and-coming Ronaldinho, Spanish goalkeeper Iker Casillas, and Germany's Sebastian Deisler. Some young players are thrown into action with the adults on the reserve team or first team at a professional club. One of the youngest was Freddy Adu, who, in 2004, came on as a substitute for U.S. team D.C. United in its game against the San Jose Earthquakes. He was only 14 years old.

HANDLING REJECTION

For millions of hopefuls, the desire to play professional soccer remains just a dream. As players rise through the soccer ranks, their talents are surpassed by others, and they are unable to progress further. Some talented young players are rejected because coaches believe that their slight builds or lack of height would put them at a disadvantage. As young players, Kevin Keegan and Allan Simonsen were rejected by major clubs for being too small, yet both went on to star for their countries and win the coveted European Footballer of the Year award. Other players are turned down because their levels of fitness are not high enough. As a 16 year old, the great

Michel Platini was rejected by French club Metz after medical checks revealed that he had poor breathing and a weak heart.

Rejection is hard to take for many young players, but some are able to use such a setback to spur themselves on and prove their doubters wrong. Young England star Shaun Wright-Phillips was discarded by Nottingham Forest at 15 for being too small and not good enough. He eventually signed to Manchester City, the club that released 14-year-old Ryan Giggs from its academy. The great Dino Zoff tried out at Internazionale, whose coaches were unimpressed. The same thing happened at Juventus, but the young goalie was not discouraged—he worked hard at his game and was eventually signed by Udinese. More than 20 years later he captained Italy to the World Cup trophy.

▼ *Souleymane Maman (right), playing for Belgian team Royal Antwerp, moves away from Mohammed Diallo of Beveren. Maman came on as a substitute for his national team, Togo, in a 2002 World Cup qualifying game against Zambia. He was only 13 years old.*

▶ *In the final of the men's blind soccer tournament at the 2004 Paralympics, held in Greece, Argentina's Oscar Moreno (right) holds off Sandro Soares of Brazil.*

SOCCER FOR ALL

Soccer can be enjoyed in all climates and conditions and by people of all ages and abilities. It is also played competitively by people with disabilities that range from being wheelchair-bound to having impaired hearing. In 2005 Great Britain, Iran, and Germany were the soccer medalists at the Deaflympics, held in Australia. Amputee soccer is played by outfield players using crutches but no artificial leg and by goalkeepers who are single-arm amputees. Since 1984 the Paralympics has included a seven-on-seven soccer competition for people suffering from cerebral palsy and brain injuries. The game is played largely according to FIFA's seven-on-seven rules but with bigger goals, no offsides, and two 30-minute halves. Soccer for blind and visually impaired athletes uses a special ball. It contains tiny ball bearings that make a distinctive sound as the ball moves. Teams consist of four blind outfield players, a goalie who can be partially sighted, and five substitutes. In 2004 the sport made its debut at the Paralympics, with teams from South Korea, France, and Argentina among others. The teams played 50-minute games, with Brazil emerging as the gold medalist after a dramatic penalty shoot-out in the final.

FACT FILE Francesc "Cesc" Fabregas was signed by Arsenal from Barcelona in 2003. He became Arsenal's youngest-ever first-team player at the age of 16 years and 177 days.

▶ *Eric Cantona controls the ball during a beach soccer game. The sport is popular around the globe—in May 2005 spectators flocked to the first beach soccer World Cup in Rio de Janeiro, Brazil.*

A PRO'S LIFE

Viewed from the outside, a professional soccer player's life seems glamorous, exciting, and rewarding. But behind the appearances in top games, on television shows, and at celebrity events lies a lot of hard work and sometimes frustration and disappointment.

MAKING THE FIRST TEAM

Signing as a young player for a big club is every aspiring soccer star's dream, but in truth, a young player in this position is only halfway toward his or her goal. Competition for one of the 11 starting places is intense. Many young players do not make the grade and have to move elsewhere—often down a division or two—to play first-team soccer. "If you're good enough, you're old enough" is a motto used by some coaches who have thrust exceptionally talented young players into first-team action for their team or country. Cameroon striker Samuel Eto'o, for example, first played for his country the day before his 16th birthday. Wayne Rooney made his Premiership debut just months after leading Everton to the final of the FA

Youth Cup. He later became England's youngest international, aged 17 years and 111 days, although his record was beaten in 2006 by Theo Walcott (17 years 75 days). In contrast, most young players have to wait much longer for their first-team debut, often spending several seasons in their club's junior or reserve teams.

LOANED OUT

Increasingly in a number of major leagues, players are loaned out to other clubs to gain experience. Loan stints can be relatively short and to a lower-division club in the same country such as David Beckham's six-week loan to Preston North End when he was a young player at Manchester United. They can also be for longer periods and to a club in a different country such as Tottenham Hotspur's 18-month loan of Egyptian striker Mido from Italian club Roma. Many players who are frustrated by a lack of opportunities seek a loan or permanent move elsewhere to play first-team soccer. This is not only limited to young, inexperienced players. Spanish striker Fernando Morientes has scored more than 20 times for his national team, but he could not get into the Real Madrid first team ahead of Raúl and Ronaldo. He went on loan for the 2003–2004 season to Monaco, where his nine goals helped take the team to the Champions League final. On his return to Real Madrid, however, first-team action was again in short supply, and in 2004 he was moved to Liverpool and then back to Spain with Valencia in 2006.

◀ Fernando Morientes cannot hide his delight as he scores for Monaco. The goal knocked Real Madrid—the team that loaned him—out of the 2003–2004 Champions League.

TRAINING, INJURIES, AND RECOVERY

A typical week for a soccer player involves training, resting, going to team functions, and traveling to one or more games. Training usually involves a mixture of fitness, strength, and flexibility exercises to boost a player's stamina, speed, and alertness. Players also practice skills and tactics—improving their heading or working on free kicks, for example. In continental Europe players have eaten a healthy, scientifically managed diet for years. Great Britain, in contrast, was slow to catch on. Even in the 1970s and 1980s, a pregame meal was often as heavy as a steak and fries.

Injuries occur fairly often in soccer. An English FA study of the 1997–1998 and

> **FACT FILE** Spanish goalkeeper Santiago Canizares missed the 2002 World Cup after dropping a bottle of aftershave on his foot.

▲ Thierry Henry gets away from a defender at Arsenal's training ground before a Champions League game against Rosenborg in 2004.

▲ Gary Neville and Wayne Rooney in training for England. Players train hard and often, following a program devised by their coaches.

▲ *Ronaldo works out in the gym to strengthen his injured knee. Recovery from an operation or a serious injury can be a difficult time, as players miss key games and face a long period of training.*

1998–1999 seasons recorded more than 6,000 injuries, mostly to knee and ankle joints or leg muscles. In December 2006 more than 70 players in Spain's top division were out with an injury, including Barcelona stars Samuel Eto'o and Lionel Messi. In Serie A, that figure was more than 100, including Atalanta's Christian Vieri and 2006 World Cup winners Fabio Grosso (Internazionale) and Simone Perrotta (Roma).

Injured players are treated by a club's doctor and physiotherapist. They are sent to the best consultants to ensure as quick a recovery as possible. This can take weeks or months and usually involves long days in the gym, gentle training, and intensive sessions with the physiotherapist. Injured players are painfully aware that their place in the team has been filled. A young player may have seized the chance, making it even harder for the injured player to return.

A soccer career can be short, with players retiring by their early 30s (although goalies can play into their late 30s). Serious injuries are what pro players most fear. Every year an average of 50 English league players are forced to retire because of injuries.

REWARDS AND RESPONSIBILITIES

Soccer's top players are paid well and are treated as celebrities in a similar way to music and movie stars. Some use their celebrity status to publicize good causes, to help coach and inspire young people, or to visit hospitals, schools, and charities. Just like movie stars, players have to deal with the media. A club may ask players to give interviews for Web site features or to cooperate with newspapers and television companies to promote an upcoming game or new uniform, for example. What can be harder for young players to handle is the way in which the press can

▶ *Goalkeeper Fabien Barthez shields the ball from car-racing legend Michael Schumacher during a charity game in Monte Carlo. The money raised went to a number of children's charities.*

invade their private lives. Photographers and reporters may besiege a player's home and follow their family and friends. Soccer players are seen as important role models for young people, and any wrongdoing, such as being fined for speeding, snubbing autograph hunters, or partying, attracts a lot of negative television and newspaper attention.

FACT FILE In 2004 QPR coach Ian Holloway took his team to train with ballet dancers. The aim was to improve the players' flexibility and balance, helping them avoid injuries.

◀ *Top players are constantly in the public eye. Here, David Beckham signs autographs at an open training session. To attend, each fan donated around $6 to charity.*

FACT FILE Blackburn Olympic spent a week at a health spa before the 1893 FA Cup final. The players' daily diet included a glass of port and two raw eggs for breakfast, a leg of lamb for lunch, and 12 oysters for dinner.

THE PLAYERS' STAGE

Without stadiums, soccer would still be played, but games would be much quieter and less passionate and exciting affairs. Stadiums spring into life on game days, when they are transformed from empty, silent steel and concrete structures into a seething sea of noise and color.

GREAT STADIUMS

England and Scotland boasted the world's first great stadiums. Glasgow's Hampden Park was built in 1903; in 1937 almost 150,000 spectators were admitted to watch an international game between Scotland and England. The biggest crowd at London's Wembley Stadium—which was built in only 300 days—was its first, for the 1923 FA Cup final. More than 200,000 people crammed inside, spilling onto the field and forcing the kickoff to be delayed.

The mighty Maracana Stadium in Rio de Janiero, Brazil, is almost completely round. It holds the official world record for a soccer crowd—in 1950 around 199,850 people watched a World Cup game there between Brazil and Uruguay. Mexico City's Azteca

▲ A staggering 114,000 spectators, all standing, cram into London's Crystal Palace to watch the 1901 FA Cup final between Tottenham Hotspur and Sheffield United.

is the only stadium to have hosted two World Cup finals (1970 and 1986). Many of the world's biggest soccer arenas were built to host the World Cup or European Championships—from the Centenario in Uruguay, the location for the first World Cup in 1930, to Portugal's new Estadio da Luz, which hosted the final of Euro 2004. The 2002 World Cup saw the most locations ever used for the tournament, with ten stadiums in South Korea and ten in Japan providing venues for the 32 teams.

BEHIND THE SCENES

The forgotten people of soccer are often the staff who run a stadium and ensure that a game day goes smoothly. We tend to think of them only when there is a problem such as crowd trouble or a field that is unfit for play. The team or stadium owner liaises with police and local authorities and employs stewards to prevent field invasions, violence, and other problems. Box office staff do their best to ensure that tickets are sold and distributed correctly, while turnstile operators, program sellers, and food and drink vendors all work at a stadium

▼ At Euro 2004 Fabien Barthez saves a David Beckham penalty in the Estadio da Luz in Lisbon, Portugal. The 65,000-capacity arena is Benfica's home ground.

▶ Ground staff in traditional dress prepare the goal nets at the National Stadium in Lagos, Nigeria, before the opening game of the 1999 World Youth Championship.

on a game day. At the 2006 World Cup tickets contained tiny microchips that could be read by scanners, easing crowd congestion and helping prevent ticket fraud.

The ground staff are in charge of the goals, the field, and its markings. They work especially hard when the field is in poor condition because of bad weather—clearing snow, thawing out the field, or soaking up excess moisture. On the day of the game—or sometimes earlier—the game referee examines the field carefully and talks to the ground staff before deciding whether the game can go ahead.

▲ A groundskeeper gives the field a close cut at Newcastle United's St. James Park stadium. Field care is vital at all top-level stadiums.

STADIUM INNOVATION

Stadium tragedies have occurred all over the world (see pages 104–105), prompting many governments and soccer authorities to bring in much stricter rules for stadium design, capacities, and crowd control. In the past 30 years new safety laws and innovations in architecture have led to major changes in the design of soccer stadiums. Despite fans feeling a strong emotional attachment to a stadium, dozens of teams have abandoned their old stadiums in or near the center of a town or city. The money raised from the sale of the land is used to build a new stadium on the outskirts. Many of these stadiums form part of a hotel, entertainment, or shopping complex. A famous example is the Stade de

FACT FILE Azerbaijan's national stadium is named after Tofik Bakhramov, the official who famously awarded England's controversial third goal in the 1966 World Cup final.

FACT FILE At the 1986 World Cup eagle-eyed officials spotted that the field markings at the edge of the penalty area for the France-Hungary game were in the wrong place. They had to be quickly repainted.

France in Paris, which was built to host the final of the 1998 World Cup. It features 17 stores and 43 cafés and restaurants for its 80,000 spectators.

Notably, the U.S. staged the first indoor World Cup qualifier (at the Seattle Kingdome) and the first indoor World Cup final game (at the Pontiac Silverdome). Stadiums with a sliding roof have become more and more popular, allowing the venue to host music concerts and other indoor events. The Amsterdam ArenA was opened in 1996 as Ajax's new stadium. The first European stadium with a retractable roof, it seats 51,859 spectators. The Millennium Stadium in Cardiff, Wales, and the Oita "Big Eye" Stadium in Japan also have sliding roofs. Inside a new stadium fans may find a removable field, corporate boxes for business entertaining, and giant screens that replay action from the game. Germany's Arena Auf Schalke, opened in 2001, has 540 video screens throughout the stadium and a giant video cube suspended from the roof. With four 387.5 sq. ft. (36m²) video screens, it is the first of its type in Europe.

TOP-TEN LARGEST SOCCER STADIUMS

POPULAR NAME	LOCATION	CAPACITY
Saltlake	Kolkata (Calcutta), India	120,000
Azteca	Mexico City, Mexico	106,000
Azadi	Tehran, Iran	100,000
Nou Camp	Barcelona, Spain	98,600
Maracana	Rio de Janeiro, Brazil	95,095
San Siro	Milan, Italy	85,700
Soccer City	Soweto, South Africa	85,000
Olimpiyskiy	Kiev, Ukraine	83,160
Olimpico	Rome, Italy	82,556
Mineiro	Belo Horizonte, Brazil	81,897

▲ Munich's Allianz Arena was constructed for the 2006 World Cup. The 66,000-seat stadium has a see-through roof and walls. Lights enable the color of the stadium to change, depending on which team is playing.

FANS AND TEAMS

Dreams are not only held by players and coaches. Everyone connected to a club or national team dreams that their team will achieve glory and success, and this especially includes the most loyal, passionate, and vocal group of all—the fans.

FOLLOWING A TEAM

For millions of fans, following their club or national team is a lifelong passion. Fans may chant for a coach to leave or be unhappy with certain players or the team's current ranking, but their love of the team tends to remain. Dedicated fans go to great lengths to follow their team, putting up with poor weather and long hours of traveling to away games. Many fans spend a lot of their income every season on getting to as many games as possible and buying jerseys and other merchandise—from T-shirts and scarfs to team-branded toothpaste and credit cards. Do these supporters get a fair deal for their time, effort, and expenditure? To many casual or nonfans, the answer appears to be "no." Entertainment and the "right" result are never guaranteed, and ticket prices have soared, sometimes pricing

▼ Mascots are a feature at many soccer games. These British mascots are taking part in the 2002 Mascot Grand National, which was won by Oldham Athletic's Chaddy the Owl.

ordinary fans out of the game. Yet being a loyal soccer fan is rarely a decision made with the head. It is all about the heart and emotions. Every loyal fan loves to feel the rush of excitement as they approach their home ground, chant with the crowd, and witness the start of a game. What comes next is a 90-minute roller coaster ride of highs and lows, ending at the final whistle and followed by a postgame discussion of what went right and wrong, before hope and expectancy build up for the next game.

◄ Face-painted Greek fans celebrate their team's surprise triumph at the 2004 European Championships.

HIT THE NET

www.stadiumguide.com
Information on the leading soccer stadiums in Europe and elsewhere, including the venues for Euro 2008.

http://fifaworldcup.yahoo.com/06/en/p/cs/index.html
Profiles of the world's most famous stadiums, including the Azteca, the San Siro, and Munich's Olympic Stadium.

FACT FILE With a Dutch mother and a Belgian father, fan Raymond Brul had a problem at Euro 2000. In the end, he showed his support for both nations by painting half his car in Dutch team colors and half in Belgian colors.

FANS AND THE MEDIA

Few stadiums hold more than 60,000 spectators, but the rise of television coverage has opened up the game to millions of new fans. Some fans, however, criticize TV for concentrating on the top teams and moving games to different days and new starting times. TV companies spend a fortune on buying the rights to show live games and highlights from the top leagues. Back in the studio, famous ex-players and coaches comment on the action, while reporters and

▲ *Pelé's 1970 World Cup shirt was auctioned in 2002 for around $237,000, beating the sum paid for Geoff Hurst's 1966 World Cup shirt by almost $100,000.*

statisticians provide interviews and highly detailed analysis of games.

Coverage of soccer in other media has boomed too. Fans coach their own teams in computer simulations or fantasy soccer leagues, while scores, news, and video clips are sent to their cell phones. They can read about their teams in books, magazines, and fanzines. More recently, the rise of radio phone-ins and online message boards has allowed fans to voice their opinions on games, players, coaches, and referees.

MORE THAN A GAME

Fans look forward to certain games in particular—a clash between two teams at the top of the league standings, for example. In a knockout cup competition a game between a small club and a top team allows fans to dream of a famous giant-killing victory. Sometimes even a tie in these games goes down in history such as Latvia's 0-0 result against Germany at Euro 2004.

The most anticipated and passionate of all games tend to be derby games between two neighboring teams. Most clubs have some

▶ *Fans of Turkish club Galatasaray drum up a fearsomely loud atmosphere before their team's 2002 Champions League game against Barcelona.*

form of derby, but certain rivalries have passed into soccer folklore. Among them are the Buenos Aires games between Boca Juniors and River Plate, the Peñarol-Nacional clash in Uruguay, the Milan derby between Internazionale and AC Milan, and, in Greece, the battle between Olympiakos and Panathinaikos. The most intense derby in Great Britain is between the two Scottish "Old Firm" teams—Rangers and Celtic. For some fans, beating their rivals in a derby can be even more important than league or cup success.

Some of the biggest derbies are not between neighboring teams but between the top clubs in the country. Spain's *Superclassico*, for example, is contested by two teams that are 300 mi. (500km) apart—Real Madrid in the heart of the country and Barcelona on the east coast.

WHEN FANS TURN BAD

Sometimes the passion of fans at a game can turn violent. Fighting between fans has occurred since soccer's early days, but it became known as the "English disease" in the 1960s and 1970s as "hooliganism" flared up around the country. In 1995 a game between England and the Republic of Ireland had to be abandoned after 27 minutes when English fans rioted. At the 1998 World Cup and Euro 2000 England fans fought running battles with other nationalities. More recently, fan problems at English clubs have declined dramatically thanks to CCTV cameras, undercover police operations, all-seater stadiums, and police forces working with clubs to identify, ban, and even jail troublemakers. These techniques are being adopted in other countries where fan violence is a problem. In 2000 two Leeds United fans were stabbed to death in Turkey by Galatasaray fans, while in 2002 two men died when Russian fans went on the rampage in Moscow after a World Cup defeat to Japan. The final of the 2000 African Women's Championship was abandoned when South African fans rioted after a controversial Nigerian goal. Yet, for all the incidents reported in the media, the large majority of soccer fans never cause trouble.

◀ *AC Milan goalie Dida is struck by a flare thrown by Internazionale fans during a Champions League quarterfinal in 2005. Referee Markus Merk abandoned the game, and AC Milan was awarded a 3-0 win.*

THE SOCCER INDUSTRY

Soccer is an extremely big business. The world's largest teams are valued in hundreds of millions of dollars and generate around $100 million per year in income. But the pressure to achieve success has seen many teams fall deeply into debt, with some facing the threat of going out of business.

BIG BUSINESS

The leagues of Germany, Italy, England, Spain, and France are the wealthiest in the world, generating more than $8 billion in income during 2005–2006. But within these leagues there are huge differences in spending power. In the summer of 2006, for example, Real Madrid spent more than $100 million on new players, while fellow La Liga team spent less than $1 million. Money is no guarantee of success, however. Manchester United and Real Madrid are the richest clubs in the world, yet neither won a league or Champions League title between 2003 and 2006. Some other big spenders in recent years have also won relatively little— Serie A teams Internazionale, Sampdoria, and Lazio, for example.

Less wealthy clubs can still succeed in soccer. In 1997 Spain's Villareal was at the bottom of the second division, had only three members of staff, and a stadium that held 3,500 fans. The club, based in a small town with only 40,000 people, has since reached the Spanish first division and the semifinals of the 2004 UEFA Cup and 2006

> **FACT FILE**
> In 1991 Manchester United was valued at around $24 million. In 2005, to buy control of the club, American businessman Malcolm Glazer had to spend $1.5 billion.

Champions League. Porto do not figure in the list of the world's top-20 richest clubs, but in 2004 it won the biggest club prize in Europe, the Champions League.

MONEY MATTERS

In the past soccer teams received almost all of their money from selling programs, tickets, food and drinks. Today these items often contribute less than one third of all the money that a team generates in one year. Sales of merchandise and deals with advertisers may make up around one third of a team's income (sometimes more for the biggest teams). The largest part of a team's income comes from the sale of broadcasting rights to television in particular but also to radio and the Internet. In 2002–2003, 55 percent of the money earned by Serie A clubs came from the sale of media rights.

Some teams have succeeded through the backing of a wealthy company or individual who spends millions on the team. In less than four seasons Roman Abramovich has spent around $500 million buying players for Chelsea, while the

> **FACT FILE** In 1999 Romanian club Nitramonia Fagaras was so cash-strapped that it could not pay a $22,000 gas bill. The team had to transfer two players, Gabor Balazs and Ioan Fatu, to Gazmetan Medias (the gas company's soccer team) as payment.

▲ *In 2006 Carlos Tevez (above) and Javier Mascherano made surprise moves from Corinthians of Brazil to West Ham United. The unusual deal was set up by MSI, a company that owned the rights to the two Argentinian players.*

TRANSFER MILESTONES

YEAR	FEE	PLAYER
1905	$4,870	Alf Common (Sunderland to Middlesbrough)
1929	$48,200	David Jack (Bolton to Arsenal)
1952	$145,600	Hans Jeppson (amateur to Napoli)
1961	$397,600	Luis Suarez (Barcelona to Internazionale)
1968	$1.2m	Pietro Anastasi (Varses to Juventus)
1975	$2.88m	Giuseppe Savoldi (Bologna to Napoli)
1985	$5m	Diego Maradona (Barcelona to Napoli)
1992	$18m	Jean-Pierre Papin (Marseille to AC Milan)
1996	$22.5m	Alan Shearer (Blackburn Rovers to Newcastle United)
1998	$33.6m	Denilson (São Paolo to Real Betis)
1999	$51.2m	Christian Vieri (Lazio to Internazionale)
2001	$68.43m	Zinedine Zidane (Juventus to Real Madrid)

▲ *Fans survey the wide range of merchandise for sale at the Nihondaira Stadium, one of the two homes of Japanese J-League team Shimizu S-Pulse.*

Agnelli family—the owners of car maker Fiat—has financed Juventus for many years. Some clubs sell shares in the company that runs them, with mixed success. Share prices are sensitive to a team's performance. When Borussia Dortmund was knocked out of the Champions League in 2003–2004, for example, the value of the club fell by more than 15 percent. In 2006 this famous club was recovering from near-bankruptcy.

Many teams, big and small, have huge debts owing to excessive transfer fees and wages, the collapse of TV deals, or poor management. The entire debt of the Bundesliga clubs is valued at more than $600 million. In Spain the debt of Real Madrid alone is believed to be more than $240 million. Some clubs, such as Colo Colo and River Plate, have been forced to sell their best players. Others have dropped down the leagues or, like Fiorentina or Czech team Bohemians, have gone bankrupt. Fans of smaller teams have sometimes banded together to buy their teams and try to turn them around.

▶ *Real Madrid bought Luis Figo, David Beckham, and Zinedine Zidane for around $150 million—almost one million times the $300 it cost Bolton Wanderers to put together their entire 1958 FA-Cup-winning team.*

FACT FILE
In 2006 Ronaldinho's salary at Barcelona was believed to be $31 million.

PLAYER MOVEMENT

Players have always moved from team to team, and for 100 years the best players have often cost a transfer fee. In the 2006–2007 season Chelsea could field a starting 11 that cost more than $300 million in transfer fees. Fees spiraled from the mid-1980s, reaching a peak with the sale of Zinedine Zidane for more than $65 million in 2001. Since then transfers have tended to drop in value. Part of the reason is that many teams now face growing debts and lower incomes from media rights and other sources, making them unwilling to spend beyond their means. In 1995 a ruling by the European Court of Justice—the Bosman ruling—made it easier for players to move from team to team at the end of their contracts through a free transfer. This has pushed up players' salaries, as many top players choose to see out their time at one team and leave for nothing in order to gain a big sign-on fee or higher salaries elsewhere.

RICH REWARDS?

More of a soccer team's money is spent on buying and paying players than on any other expenditure. In 2003–2004 Chelsea spent $230 million on salaries, more than any other Premiership team. The yearly salary of a player in the English top division averages more than $1 million. The rewards for top players are similar in the world's richest leagues, which are all in Europe. Players employ agents to handle transfer moves, from which they may receive five percent or more of the overall fee plus a sign-on bonus. Advertising and endorsing products, sponsorship deals, and writing books and newspaper columns can greatly boost the income of a player. In 2005 David Beckham, for example, was believed to be earning almost $28 million per year in endorsements. But in the lower divisions of the top leagues and in smaller leagues around the world the rewards are much smaller, and job security for players can be weak.

◀ *Walter Strutz, the chairman of Mainz, despairs as his team misses out on promotion to the German Bundesliga. For teams everywhere, playing in the top division—where the financial rewards are the greatest—is a major goal.*

SOCCER NIGHTMARES

Soccer has a dark side. With passions running high on and off the field and with so much at stake at big games, the sport has sometimes lurched into a nightmare world of cheating, abuse, violence, and even death.

CUT OFF IN THEIR PRIME

A number of players have died suddenly owing to on-field collisions or because of a medical problem. In 1973 Pedro Berruezo died of heart failure while playing for Sevilla. Thirty years later, during a Confederations Cup game against Colombia, Cameroon's 28-year-old midfielder, Marc-Vivien Foe, collapsed and died shortly afterward. One year later, in 2004, Hungarian international Miklós Fehér suffered a fatal heart attack while playing for Benfica.

Plane crashes have killed entire soccer teams, including Bolivia's most popular team, The Strongest, in 1969, the Soviet (now Uzbek) team of Pakhtakor Tashkent in 1979, and 18 members of the Zambian national team in 1993. Other airplane crashes have devastated club teams such as the 1958 Munich disaster that killed eight Manchester United players and 11 officials and journalists.

▲ In the 1940s Torino won four league titles in a row. When their aircraft crashed in 1949, 18 players died, comprising most of the Italian national team.

GAME FIXING AND CHEATING

In 1909 George Parsonage was banned for life after asking for a $240 sign-on fee when he joined Chesterfield (the maximum allowed was around $48). This looks tiny compared to today's examples of corruption, bribery, and game fixing. In 1999 the former head coach of Romania's Dynamo Bucharest, Vasile Ianul, was sentenced to

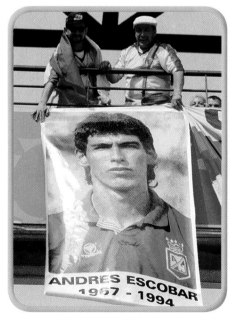

▲ Fans pay tribute to Colombian defender Andres Escobar. The scorer of an own goal in a 2-1 loss to the U.S. at the 1994 World Cup, Escobar was murdered in his home country ten days later, shot 12 times by an unknown gunman.

FACT FILE
In 1999 the owner of Doncaster Rovers, Ken Richardson, was sent to prison for four years for conspiring to burn down the team's main stand.

12 years in prison for stealing more than $2.5 million from the team, while Marseille president Bernard Tapie was jailed in 1997 for bribing players and officials. German soccer was rocked in 2004 when referee Robert Hoyzer admitted to fixing games. He was sentenced to more than two years in prison. But Germany is far from alone—in 2006, after a game-rigging scandal, Italian giants Juventus were relegated to Serie B, while AC Milan, Lazio, Fiorentina, and Reggina Calcio were fined, removed from European competitions, and had league points deducted. An attempt to fix a game on the field occurred when Chile was being outplayed by Brazil in a 1989 World Cup qualifier. Goalkeeper Roberto Rojas cut himself with a razor blade hidden in his glove and pretended to have been injured by an object thrown from the crowd. The game was abandoned, but video footage proved Rojas' cheating. He was banned, and Chile was prevented from qualifying for the 1994 World Cup.

STADIUM DISASTERS

Crumbling stadiums, overcrowding, poor safety rules, and weak crowd control have caused many stadium disasters. The worst-ever soccer tragedy occurred in Lima, Peru, in 1964 when more than 300 fans were killed and more than 500 injured in panic stampedes and riots. In a 1982 European

▲ Emergency workers tend to a victim of a tragedy at South Africa's Ellis Park in 2001. Four major stadium disasters occurred in Africa in that year. Altogether, they took the lives of more than 200 people.

◀ Newcastle United players and Aston Villa's Gareth Barry try to separate brawling teammates Kieron Dyer and Lee Bowyer in April 2005. Both players had been in trouble with the authorities before and have been criticized as poor role models for children.

FACT FILE In November 2004 the mother of Brazilian star Robinho was kidnapped and released 41 days later. The mothers of two more Brazilian star players were kidnapped shortly afterward.

Cup game in Moscow 340 people died, most by crushing, when police tried to force fans out of a crowded section of the stadium and down an icy staircase. Two major disasters occurred in 1985—a wooden stand at Bradford City's ground caught on fire, killing 56 people, while the European Cup final also ended in tragedy. A wall collapsed at the Heysel Stadium in Belgium, and a riot flared when some Liverpool fans charged at Juventus supporters. One Belgian and 38 Italian spectators died as a result.

POOR ROLE MODELS?

Soccer players are highly esteemed as role models to the young, but some have abused their positions and have been convicted of crimes. In 2004 English striker Lee Hughes was jailed for six years for causing death by dangerous driving. Other players have behaved violently on and off the field. In November 2005 a huge fight begun by Turkish players in a World Cup qualifier against Switzerland led to the country having

▲ At Liverpool's Anfield stadium fans lay tributes to the 96 people who died during the 1989 FA Cup semifinal at Hillsborough Stadium.

to play its next six home games in other countries. Players have also fought with fans. Manchester United's Eric Cantona, for example, kicked a Crystal Palace fan in 1995; and in March 2005 Malaga's Paulo Wanchope scuffled with his club's fans.

Like athletes in other sports, soccer players are tested for illegal drug use. In 2003 Rio Ferdinand received an eight-month ban for failing to attend a drug test, while one year later Adrian Mutu tested positive for cocaine. Diego Maradona remains soccer's

most notorious drug cheat. He was sent home from the 1994 World Cup after testing positive for the stimulant ephedrine; in recent years Maradona has fought against an addiction to cocaine. Many other players have battled against alcohol addiction, from former England captain Tony Adams to George Best and Brazilian legend Garrincha.

RACISM AND INTIMIDATION

Some fans, players, and coaches have been found guilty of racially insulting or abusing opponents. Racism in soccer was thought to be declining, with nonwhite players making up one fifth or more of the total number of players in many European leagues. Antiracism campaign work has been carried out by many clubs, governments, and groups such as FARE (Football Against Racism in Europe). However, the racist chanting aimed at England's black players at the Bernabeu Stadium during a 2004 Spain-England game and similar incidents of racial abuse in Italy, Spain, England, and eastern Europe prove that a lot of work still needs to be done. Violence and intimidation can occur on and off the field; sometimes referees are the target. In 2000 a French first division game between Metz and Strasbourg was abandoned after an assistant referee was hit by a firecracker. In 2005 referee Luiz Carlos Silva was drawn into a fistfight after being attacked on the field by a fan during the Brazilian derby between America MG and Atlético Mineiro.

▲ Referee Anders Frisk was hit by an object thrown by Roma fans during a 2004 Champions League game against Dynamo Kiev. Frisk abandoned the game at halftime, and UEFA awarded Kiev a 3-0 victory. In 2005 Frisk retired from refereeing after he and his family received death threats.

GREECE WINS EURO 2004

Greece began Euro 2004 as the complete outsider, never having won a game in the final of the European Championships. Short on superstars yet superbly managed by their 65-year-old German coach, Otto Rehhagel, the Greeks made their mark at once. They beat the hosts, Portugal, 2-1 in the opening game of the tournament. Greece stuttered through its next two group games before springing more surprises in the knockout phase. First the team defeated the holders, France, by a single goal and then beat the highly qualified Czech Republic by a "silver goal" in extra time. Meeting Portugal in the final at Lisbon's Estadio da Luz, the Greeks were indebted to their goalkeeper, Antonis Nikopolidis, who made a string of crucial saves to ensure that Angelos Charisteas' goal, a header in the 57th minute, would take them to glory.

Portuguese defenders look on in disbelief as Angelos Charisteas scores the header that would win Greece the Euro 2004 title. It was Charisteas' third strike of the championships.

THE WORLD CUP

Friendlies or charity games are entertaining, but for a soccer game to have meaning, it has to be part of a bigger competition. Soccer has spawned hundreds of different competitions, but none can compete in global interest and prestige with the World Cup. From small beginnings with 13 competing countries, it has grown to the point where 197 nations attempted to qualify for the 2006 competition.

▼ Sepp Blatter and Franz Beckenbauer

HOPING TO HOST

Six nations expressed an interest in hosting the first World Cup, held in 1930. Until Japan and South Korea hosted it in 2002, the tournament had always been staged in Europe or the Americas, but the competition now moves around the globe—in 2010 the World Cup will be held in Africa for the first time. In July 2000 Germany was awarded the 2006 World Cup location, six years after making its bid. Bidding countries must prepare in great detail, making presentations and receiving official inspections from FIFA before a decision is made.

▲ Argentina's goalkeeper, Juan Botasso, makes a desperate dive but fails to stop Hector Castro from scoring Uruguay's fourth goal in the 1930 final.

URUGUAY 1930

Final
Uruguay 4 • Argentina 2
Semifinals
Uruguay 6 • Yugoslavia 1
Argentina 6 • U.S. 1
Games 18 **Goals** 70
Goals per game 3.89

It took 19 minutes for France's Lucien Laurent to write his name in the record books as the scorer of the first World Cup goal. France beat Mexico 4-1, but it was its only victory and, like Belgium and Romania, the team went out at the group stage. Four European teams made the long trip to South America by boat, but only Yugoslavia reached the semifinals. It and the U.S. were thrashed in the semis by Uruguay and Argentina respectively. Argentina boasted the best forward of the competition, Guillermo Stabile, but Uruguay—on home ground and as reigning Olympic champion—was the firm favorite. In the final the team came back strongly after Argentina had taken a 2-1 lead to become the first World Cup winner.

ITALY 1934

Final
Italy 2 • Czechoslovakia 1
Semifinals
Italy 1 • Austria 0
Czechoslovakia 3 • Germany 1
Games 17 **Goals** 70
Goals per game 4.12

In 1934 the South American teams had not forgotten the lack of European entrants for the first World Cup. As a result, world champion Uruguay chose not to defend its title, while Brazil and Argentina sent understrength teams to Italy. Yet 32 nations, mostly European, were eager to enter the competition. With 16 places available, qualification games began in June 1933. Italy's 4-0 win over Greece marked the first and only time that a World Cup host has had to play a qualifier in order to get into the finals. Egypt was the first nation outside of the Americas or Europe to qualify, but following one round of knockout games, the eight remaining teams were all European. After a 7-1 thrashing of the U.S., Italy's goals dried up, and the team only just sneaked past Spain and Austria on its way to the final. In that game Italy's Luisito Monti (formerly of Argentina) became the only player to have appeared in a World Cup final for different countries. Against a battling Czech team, a goal five minutes into extra time from Italy's Angelo Schiavio secured the Jules Rimet trophy for the hosts.

▼ Coach Vittorio Pozzo is carried by triumphant Italian players after masterminding their 1934 World Cup campaign.

FRANCE 1938

Final

Italy 4 • Hungary 2

Semifinals

Italy 2 • Brazil 1

Hungary 5 • Sweden 1

Games 18 **Goals** 84

Goals per game 4.67

With the threat of war looming over Europe, Spain and Austria were forced to pull out of the tournament. But the 1938 World Cup did feature the first team from Asia, the Dutch East Indies (now Indonesia), as well as a Cuban team that sprang a major shock by beating Romania in a replay. Sweden thrashed Cuba 8-0 but was then on the receiving end of a 5-1 semifinal mauling by the first great Hungarian team. The other semifinal saw one of the great managerial blunders when the Brazil coach, Adhemar Pimenta, either because of arrogance or owing to injury fears, rested his star player, Léonidas da Silva. Léonidas had lit up the tournament, most notably in an epic 6-5 thriller against Poland in which he became the first player to score four goals in a World Cup final game, only for Poland's Ernest Wilimowski to do the same five minutes later. Without the tournament's top scorer, Brazil crashed to defeat against Italy, who went on to become the champion for the second time.

▶ *Léonidas da Silva twists and turns at the 1938 World Cup. An amazingly skilled attacker, the Brazilian was one of the first players to master the overhead kick.*

FACT FILE Dr. Ottorino Barassi, the vice president of the Italian FA, smuggled the World Cup out of a bank in Rome and hid it to prevent the Nazis from stealing the trophy. For most of World War II, soccer's greatest prize lay in a shoe box underneath Barassi's bed.

BRAZIL 1950

Final pool

Uruguay 5 pts. • Brazil 4 pts.

Sweden 2 pts. • Spain 1 pt.

Games 22 **Goals** 88

Goals per game 4.00

The only World Cup to feature a final pool of four instead of a final, the 1950 tournament started poorly. Scotland and Turkey withdrew, only 13 nations attended, and the mighty Maracana Stadium was not ready to host the first game. But the competition grew in excitement and drama as the goals flowed, often from the cleats of the hosts who, after topping their group, ran rampant in the final pool stages, scoring seven against Sweden and six against Spain. Before that point, there had been several notable shocks, including the U.S.'s 1-0 defeat of a highly qualified England team. The final pool format could have been a letdown, but the outcome went down to the last game, with Uruguay and Brazil separated by one point and playing in front of around 199,850 fans. Despite falling one goal behind to the favorite, Uruguay won the game 2-1 to lift the World Cup once again.

▲ *Brazilian goalie Moacir Barbosa gathers the ball during a 1950 group game against Yugoslavia. The game, watched by more than 142,000 spectators in the Maracana, ended in a 2-0 victory for Brazil.*

FACT FILE At the 1930 World Cup not one of the 18 games was tied. Neither was there a play-off game to decide third place.

WORLD CUP "GOLDEN BOOT" WINNERS

1930	Guillermo Stabile, Argentina (8 goals)
1934	Oldrich Nejedly, Czechoslovakia (5)
1938	Léonidas da Silva, Brazil (8)
1950	Ademir Menezes, Brazil (9)
1954	Sandor Kocsis, Hungary (11)
1958	Just Fontaine, France (13)
1962	Garrincha, Brazil; Vava, Brazil; Valentin Ivanov, U.S.S.R.; Leonel Sanchez, Chile; Florian Albert, Hungary; Drazan Jerkovic, Yugoslavia (4)
1966	Eusebio, Portugal (9)
1970	Gerd Müller, West Germany (10)
1974	Gregorz Lato, Poland (7)
1978	Mario Kempes, Argentina (6)
1982	Paolo Rossi, Italy (6)
1986	Gary Lineker, England (6)
1990	Salvatore Schillaci, Italy (6)
1994	Hristo Stoichkov, Bulgaria; Oleg Salenko, Russia (6)
1998	Davor Suker, Croatia (6)
2002	Ronaldo, Brazil (8)
2006	Miroslav Klose, Germany (5)

SWITZERLAND 1954

Final

West Germany 3 • Hungary 2

Semifinals

West Germany 6 • Austria 1

Hungary 4 • Uruguay 2

Games 26 **Goals** 140

Goals per game 5.38

As the home of the headquarters of FIFA, which was celebrating its 50th birthday, Switzerland was an obvious host for the 1954 tournament. It featured newcomers such as Turkey, South Korea, and the western half of a divided Germany (which had been barred from the 1950 competition). The fans saw plenty of drama and goals, none more than in Austria's 7-5 defeat of Switzerland (the highest-scoring game in the history of the World Cup finals). Hungary, boasting the incredible talents of Ferenc Puskas, Sandor Kocsis, and Nandor Hidegkuti, was the most menacing team, scoring an incredible 27 goals in only five games. At their third World Cup, Uruguay thrashed Scotland 7-0 and beat England 4-2 to reach the semifinals. It was the only team to have never been beaten in the World Cup until it came up against Hungary, who won 4-2 and went into the final as the favorite. West Germany, however, overturned the odds to record a highly emotional victory.

◄ *Pelé chases the ball during Brazil's exciting semifinal against France. The score was poised at 2-1 to Brazil before Pelé scored three goals in 21 minutes.*

FACT FILE Vava's goal in the 1962 final (to add to his pair of goals in the 1958 final) made him the only player to have scored in the finals of successive World Cups.

SWEDEN 1958

Final

Brazil 5 • Sweden 2

Semifinals

Brazil 5 • France 2

Sweden 3 • West Germany 1

Games 35 **Goals** 126

Goals per game 3.60

Fifty-five countries entered the 1958 qualifying tournament, and some big names, including Italy, the Netherlands, Spain, and Uruguay, failed to qualify. All four U.K. home nations (Scotland, England, Northern Ireland, and Wales) reached the finals—the only time that this has ever happened. England had lost key players in the Munich airplane crash (see page 79) but was the only team to hold a rampant Brazilian team to a tie and to stop Brazil from scoring. It was the

World Cup's first-ever 0-0 tie. Yet it was the two smaller British nations, Wales and Northern Ireland, who qualified for the quarterfinals, with the Irish sensationally beating a strong Czechoslovakian team. Free-scoring France and Brazil quickly emerged as the favorites, and their semifinal clash was an epic in which the 17-year-old Pelé blasted a hat trick toward Brazil's victory. France had to be content with a 6-3 mauling of West Germany to secure third place. Just Fontaine's four goals in that game propelled him to the "Golden Boot" with 13 goals in total, a record to this day. The hosts, Sweden, had quietly and efficiently seen off some very strong teams—including Hungary, the Soviet Union, and West Germany—to reach the final, but the team was no match for Brazil. In a rematch of the pair's third-place play-off at the 1938 World Cup, Brazil triumphed 5-2 to win the tournament for the first time.

◄ *Hungary's Zoltan Czibor outjumps Ottmar Walter of West Germany in the 1954 final. Czibor scored to put Hungary 2-0 up but found himself on the losing team after a heroic comeback by the Germans.*

▲ *Argentina's Jorge Albrecht (left) and Uwe Seeler of West Germany struggle for the ball in 1966. Seeler played in each of the four World Cups sandwiched between West Germany's victories in 1954 and 1974.*

CHILE 1962

Final

Brazil 3 • Czechoslovakia 1

Semifinals

Brazil 4 • Chile 2

Czechoslovakia 3 • Yugoslavia 1

Games 32 **Goals** 89

Goals per game 2.78

Chile was a controversial choice to host the World Cup, with its small population and its infrastructure damaged by an earthquake in 1960. As it turned out, most of the problems happened on the field. A series of bad-tempered games occurred in the first round, including the infamous "Battle of Santiago," during which armed police invaded the field three times in order to split up warring Chilean and Italian players. Chile made it through to a semifinal against Brazil by beating the Soviet Union, while two strong eastern European teams, Yugoslavia and Czechoslovakia, battled it out in the other semifinal. The Brazilians lost Pelé to injury after only two games, but in Garrincha and Vava they had two of the best players of the tournament. Brazil efficiently won the final with a team featuring eight World Cup winners from the 1958 tournament.

ENGLAND 1966

Final

England 4 • West Germany 2

Semifinals

England 2 • Portugal 1

West Germany 2 • Soviet Union 1

Games 32 **Goals** 89

Goals per game 2.78

The 1966 World Cup was a well-organized tournament and the first to feature a mascot (World Cup Willie). West Germany and Portugal were the most free-scoring teams in a competition characterized by defensive play. Two huge shocks occurred early on—Brazil was eliminated by Portugal, and newcomer North Korea knocked out Italy with a stunning 1-0 victory. The North Koreans won the support of many neutral fans, and the team's quarterfinal meeting with Portugal was a classic. North Korea was 3-0 up within 20 minutes before Portugal, inspired by the tournament's eventual top

▲ *Portugal's star striker, Eusebio, walks off in tears after his team is eliminated from the 1966 World Cup following a 2-1 defeat by England.*

scorer, Eusebio, hit back to win 5-3. In the semifinal Eusebio's 82nd-minute strike could not stop England from going through to meet West Germany in what proved to be an epic final. The Germans went ahead, and then England scored twice to lead until a surprise last-minute German goal took the game into extra time. Geoff Hurst scored two more goals to secure a dramatic victory for the host nation (see pages 68–69).

> **FACT FILE** Two pairs of brothers have played on winning teams in a World Cup final— Fritz and Otmar Walter of West Germany (1954) and England's Jack and Bobby Charlton (1966).

MEXICO 1970

Final

Brazil 4 • Italy 1

Semifinals

Brazil 3 • Uruguay 1

Italy 4 • West Germany 3

Games 32 **Goals** 95

Goals per game 2.97

For many seasoned soccer observers, the 1970 World Cup remains the best. Most of the brutal, physical play seen in the 1962 and 1966 tournaments was absent. In its place were fascinating tactical and skillful contests between the world's greatest teams. Although the tournament was the first to feature red and yellow cards, no player was sent off, and some of the games have passed into soccer legend. These include a chesslike battle between Brazil and England that the South Americans narrowly won 1-0; Italy's 4-1 defeat of Mexico; and the Italians' amazing 4-3 victory against West Germany in the semifinal. But the final tops the list. Brazil had powered through the rounds, with star players such as Jairzinho (who set a record by scoring in all six of Brazil's games), Pelé, and Rivelino exhibiting great attacking flair. In the final Brazil was unstoppable, recording its third World Cup win and claiming the Jules Rimet trophy in recognition of the team's unique feat.

▼ *Brazilian striker Tostao holds off Italy's Roberto Rosato during the 1970 World Cup final. Tostao suffered a freak eye injury before the tournament, and only last-minute surgery enabled him to play.*

WEST GERMANY 1974

Final

West Germany 2 • Netherlands 1

Third-place play-off Poland 1 • Brazil 0

Games 38 **Goals** 97

Goals per game 2.55

Ninety-nine nations attempted to qualify for the 1974 tournament, which would see the winners lift a new trophy—the FIFA World Cup. Spain, France, and England all failed to reach the tournament, while Zaire, Haiti, East Germany, and Australia made their debuts. Changes to the competition format meant that there would be no semifinal games. Instead the winners of the two second-round groups would contest the final, and the group runners-up would play for third place. The Netherlands, exhibiting its brand of "total football," swept aside Bulgaria (4-1), Uruguay (2-0), Brazil (2-0), and Argentina (4-0) to top Group A and reach the final. Poland was the surprise team of the tournament. Propelled in part by the goals of striker Gregorz Lato, it finished second in Group B after narrowly losing 1-0 to West Germany. The West Germans had taken time to reach full speed, but with Franz Beckenbauer pulling the strings and the prolific Gerd Müller in fine form, the team made the final. There, it overcame the setback of a first-minute Dutch goal from a penalty to win the World Cup for a second time.

FACT FILE On June 14, 1974 Carlos Caszely of Chile became the first player to receive a red card in a World Cup tournament.

▼ Peru's Teofilo Cubillas (center) runs at Argentina's defense during his team's controversial 6-0 defeat. Cubillas scored five goals at the 1978 World Cup, matching his total at the 1970 competition.

ARGENTINA 1978

Final

Argentina 3 • Netherlands 1

Third-place play-off Brazil 2 • Italy 1

Games 38 **Goals** 102

Goals per game 2.68

A colorful and at times controversial tournament, the 1978 World Cup may have lacked some stand-out stars, but it was rarely short of soccer drama. The host found itself in the toughest of groups with France, Hungary, and a young Italian team that beat it, but Argentina made it through to the second group stage. Tunisia caused a shock by tying with holder West Germany and beating Mexico 3-1 to become the first African team to win a World Cup finals game. Austria, with its star striker Hans Krankl, played strongly in the early stages, beating Spain, Sweden, and West Germany. But it was crushed 5-1 by a Dutch team that lacked Johan Cruyff, who had pulled out of the tournament for family reasons. Scotland's campaign held promise but went askew when it failed to beat Iran and lost to Peru. Then the team roused itself, however, to beat the Netherlands 3-2. In the second group stage Italy, Argentina, Brazil, and the Netherlands emerged as the frontrunners. A lot of controversy centered around the Argentina-Peru game. The last game in Group B, it would determine whether Argentina or Brazil reached the final. Peru had played well in the early stages of the tournament, winning its group ahead of the Netherlands. The team's 6-0 loss to Argentina was suspicious and meant that Brazil was knocked out without having suffered a defeat, while Argentina progressed to the final, in which it beat the Netherlands.

◀ Germany's defense, marshaled by legendary goalkeeper Sepp Maier and the incomparable Franz Beckenbauer (far right), holds firm against a Dutch attack in the 1974 World Cup final.

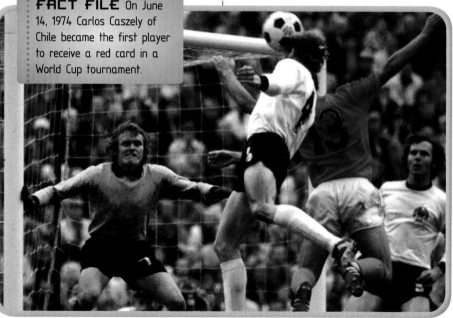

SPAIN 1982

Final

Italy 3 • West Germany 1

Semifinals

Italy 2 • Poland 0

West Germany 3 • France 3 (5-4 penalties)

Games 52 **Goals** 146

Goals per game 2.81

In 1982 the format of the tournament changed again so that 24 countries would appear at the finals. Teams played in six groups of four, with the top 12 teams playing in four groups of three in order to determine the semifinalists. Belgium surprised the holder, Argentina, beating it and El Salvador to win its group, while England topped its group ahead of France. The two surprise teams were Northern Ireland, who beat Spain to reach the second round, and Algeria, who had stunned fans by winning its game against West Germany. Poland made the semifinals, but the host went out after winning only one game. The toughest second-round group, containing Brazil, Argentina, and Italy, saw the Italians go through, beating Brazil in a 3-2 thriller. At the semifinal stage West Germany beat France in an equally exciting encounter but could not stop the Italians from winning their third World Cup.

▶ *In 1982 an Algerian fan waves money in protest as West Germany and Austria conspire to achieve a result that took both European teams through at the expense of Algeria. All final group games are now played simultaneously to give teams an equal chance.*

MEXICO 1986

Final

Argentina 3 • West Germany 2

Semifinals

Argentina 2 • Belgium 0

West Germany 2 • France 0

Games 52 **Goals** 132

Goals per game 2.54

Colombia had been due to host the 1986 World Cup, but troubles in that country meant that it had to withdraw. When Mexico stepped in, it became the first nation to host the tournament twice. More than 120 nations battled for the 24 places in the finals, in which Canada and Iraq both made their debuts. Morocco became the first African nation to reach the second round when it won a group that

FACT FILE The fastest sending off in World Cup history occurred in 1986 when Uruguay's José Batista was dismissed against Scotland after only 55 seconds.

contained Portugal, Poland, and England. Denmark looked promising until it was thrashed 5-1 by Spain, while Belgium squeezed past the Soviet Union 4-3 in one of the best games of the tournament. The quarterfinals were extremely close games. Three went to penalty shoot-outs, while the fourth game saw England face Argentina. Maradona arrived at the World Cup as the world's most expensive player and a heavily marked man. His incredible dribbling and scoring skills made him the best player of the tournament. In the quarterfinal his two goals (one a deliberate handball, the other a magnificent solo effort—see pages 56–57) sank England, and he repeated the feat against Belgium in the semifinal. In the final West Germany went 2-0 down, rallied to 2-2, but was beaten by an 88th-minute goal from Argentinian midfielder Burruchaga.

▲ *Marco Tardelli (left) charges away after scoring Italy's second goal in the 1982 World Cup final against West Germany. Teammates Claudio Gentile and Gabriele Oriali are just as jubilant.*

◀ *Argentina's Diego Maradona is in ecstasy as the team that he both captained and inspired triumphs over West Germany in the 1986 final.*

ITALY 1990

Final

West Germany 1 • Argentina 0

Semifinals

West Germany 1 • England 1 (4-3 penalties)

Argentina 1 • Italy 1 (4-3 penalties)

Games 52 **Goals** 115

Goals per game 2.21

This well-organized and attended World Cup is remembered for moments of great drama, from veteran Cameroon striker Roger Milla's dance at the corner flag to Costa Rica's joy at defeating both Scotland and Sweden to qualify for the second round. Sadly, the tournament also saw a lot of negative soccer and a record number of bookings (164), as well as 16 send-offs. Every previous winner of the World Cup made it through the group stages, with Cameroon the talk of the tournament after its defeat of Romania and Colombia set up a quarterfinal against England. Cameroon went 2-0 up, but two Gary Lineker penalties and a third England goal in extra time saw every neutral's favorite team go out. The Netherlands arrived as European Champion but failed to win a game, while Brazil and the Soviet Union had similarly disappointing tournaments. Both semifinals were tense games that went to penalty shoot-outs, but the final was forgettable. West Germany beat Argentina thanks to an 85th-minute penalty, while Pedro Monzon was the first of two send-offs for Argentina and the first player to be red carded in a World Cup final.

▼ Italian goalkeeper Walter Zenga concedes a headed goal to Argentina's Claudio Caniggia in the 1990 semifinal.

◄ Bulgaria's Iordan Letchkov (left) beats Germany's Thomas Hassler to score a spectacular diving header at the 1994 World Cup.

UNITED STATES 1994

Final

Brazil 0 • Italy 0 (3-2 penalties)

Semifinals

Brazil 1 • Sweden 0

Italy 2 • Bulgaria 1

Games 52 **Goals** 141

Goals per game 2.71

Some feared the crowds at the 1994 World Cup would be small in a country where male soccer is not a dominant sport. But they were proven wrong by a tournament attended by an average of 70,000 fans per game. Attacking play was encouraged by the adoption of both the back-pass rule (see page 24) and three instead of two points for a win during the group-stage games. Despite losing many players since the breakup of the Soviet Union, Russia recorded the biggest win, 6-1 against Cameroon, with Oleg Salenko scoring five goals—the most by one player in a single World Cup game. Maradona exited the tournament when he failed a drug test, but plenty of other stars were there. The Republic of Ireland caused the biggest shock of the group stages by beating Italy 1-0, but Saudi Arabia's win against

Belgium and Bulgaria's defeat of Argentina came close. Bulgaria had a great tournament, knocking out Germany and finishing fourth. European teams dominated the quarterfinals, taking seven out of the eight spots, but Brazil beat the Netherlands, Italy, Sweden, and took the trophy for a record fourth time.

WORLD CUP PENALTY SHOOT-OUTS

YEAR	TEAMS	PENS.
1982	West Germany – France	5-4
1986	West Germany – Mexico	4-1
1986	France – Brazil	4-3
1986	Belgium – Spain	5-4
1990	Rep. Ireland – Romania	5-4
1990	Argentina – Yugoslavia	3-2
1990	Argentina – Italy	4-3
1990	West Germany – England	4-3
1994	Bulgaria – Mexico	3-1
1994	Sweden – Romania	5-4
1994	Brazil – Italy	3-2
1998	Argentina – England	4-3
1998	France – Italy	4-3
1998	Brazil – Netherlands	4-2
2002	Spain – Rep. Ireland	3-2
2002	South Korea – Spain	5-3
2006	Ukraine – Switzerland	3-0
2006	Germany – Argentina	4-2
2006	Portugal – England	3-1
2006	Italy – France	5-3

FRANCE 1998

Final

France 3 • Brazil 0

Semifinals

France 2 • Croatia 1

Brazil 1 • Netherlands 1 (4-2 penalties)

Games 64   **Goals** 171

Goals per game 2.67

More countries from outside of Europe and South America attended the last World Cup of the 20th century, as the number of places was raised from 24 to 32. Newcomers included Jamaica, Japan, and South Africa. Iran caused a shock in its first World Cup for 20 years by beating the U.S. Nigeria upset the odds with a 3-2 defeat of Spain that effectively knocked out the European team. Despite 22 red cards, the competition was enthralling, with teams including Croatia, Denmark, Brazil, France, and the Netherlands playing attacking soccer. England narrowly went out, losing on penalties to Argentina in one of the best games of the tournament. Croatia was the dark horse, progressing quietly and then beating Germany 3–0 in the quarterfinal. For the second World Cup in a row, Italy was knocked out on penalties, this time to France at the quarterfinal stage. A France-Brazil final was an exciting prospect, but Ronaldo was sick before the game and was extremely subdued, as were his teammates. France won with relative ease, aided by two goals from Zinedine Zidane (see pages 92-93).

SOUTH KOREA AND JAPAN 2002

Final

Brazil 2 • Germany 0

Semifinals

Brazil 1 • Turkey 0

Germany 1 • South Korea 0

Games 64   **Goals** 161

Goals per game 2.52

The 2002 competition was the first to be held in Asia and the first to be hosted by two nations. An amazing 193 countries attempted to qualify for the 32 available places, and there were surprise failures to reach the finals by the Netherlands, Yugoslavia, Uruguay, and Colombia, while China appeared at its first tournament. The shocks began in the opening game when France—the World Cup holder and European Champion—was sensationally beaten 1-0 by Senegal. France then lost to

▶ *Turkey's Hakan Sukur (right) tangles with South Korea's Lee Min-Sung during the 2002 third-place playoff.*

Denmark and went out of the World Cup with only one point. The team was joined by Russia and also by European heavyweights Poland and Portugal, who finished in the bottom two places of Group D behind the U.S. and South Korea. Cheered on by passionate home crowds, the South Koreans were the story of the tournament, knocking out Italy, Spain, and Portugal on the way to the semifinals. The U.S. beat Mexico to make it to the quarterfinals, as did Senegal, who beat Sweden before losing to Turkey. The Turks narrowly lost to Brazil in the semifinal but claimed third place overall. In the final Brazilian striker Ronaldo put memories of 1998 behind him, scoring two goals against Germany and winning the "Golden Boot."

▶ *England's David Beckham is shocked to receive a red card for aiming a kick at Argentinian captain Diego Simeone, who had fouled Beckham moments earlier. Argentina won this 1998 second-round match on penalties.*

GERMANY 2006

Final
Italy 1 • France 1 (5-3 penalties)
Semi-finals
Italy 2 • Germany 0 (after extra time)
France 1 • Portugal 0
Games 62 **Goals** 147
Goals per game 2.3

The opening match was a thriller—Germany beating Costa Rica 4-2—and set the scene for an enthusiastically hosted tournament. On the field things were not as friendly, with a record card count (345 yellow and 28 red) and games in which defenses tended to dominate, especially in the knockout stages.

Africa had five teams at the tournament for the first time, although only Ghana progressed from the group stage, with wins over the U.S. and the Czech Republic. Ivory Coast was desperately unlucky, narrowly losing to Argentina and the Netherlands in an ultratough group. Oceania's first representative for many years, Australia, was a surprise, qualifying from a group featuring Brazil, Japan, and Croatia, and only losing to Italy via a controversial last-gasp penalty.

France scraped through the group stage, but their aging team then beat Spain, Brazil, and Portugal to reach the final. There France

▲ Fabio Grosso, scorer of Italy's winning penalty in the final against France, kisses the World Cup.

faced Italy and a defense led by Fabio Cannavaro that had only conceded a single goal, an own goal, during the competition. Italy had beaten an attack-minded German team, the tournament's top scorers, in a high-quality semifinal.

The first all-European final since 1982 was all about two men, Zinedine Zidane—playing in his last competitive game—and Italian defender Marco Materazzi. Zidane scored a penalty, only for Materazzi to equalize from a corner. Both men tussled during extra time, and Zidane was sent off for headbutting the Italian in the chest. During the tense penalty shoot-out, David Trezeguet, who had scored the golden goal that beat Italy in the final of Euro 2000, missed, as Italy won their fourth World Cup.

▶ French midfield star Franck Ribéry (left) challenges Fabio Cannavaro during the final of the 2006 World Cup.

HIT THE NET

www.fifaworldcup.yahoo.com/06/en
Watch video highlights, read game reviews, and find all the statistics from the 2006 World Cup on this FIFA site.

www.worldcup-history.com
An in-depth statistical guide to every World Cup, searchable by player, team, or tournament.

www.planetworldcup.com
Find out about World Cup tournaments, with results, statistics, and stories.

WORLD CUP QUALIFICATION

For the teams that contested the first World Cup qualifying campaign in 1933–1934, it was all or nothing—a single knockout game determined who made it to the finals. Since then, the number of countries aiming for World Cup glory has risen considerably, and qualifying campaigns have grown much longer. To qualify for the 1998 World Cup, Jamaica played a grueling 20 games. For the 2006 World Cup, there were 847 qualifying games. Each soccer confederation organizes its own qualifying contests to fill the places that it is given at the World Cup. For the 2010 tournament, the number of places awarded are: Europe (13), Africa (6), Asia (4.5), South America (4.5), CONCACAF members (3.5), and Oceania (0.5). The half places will be decided by a pair of home and away play-off games between teams from different confederations for the right to appear at the World Cup.

Qualifying is highly competitive, and coaches rarely survive not qualifying for a World Cup. England fans still wince at their team's failure to reach the 1974, 1978, and 1994 tournaments, while the Netherlands failed to qualify for six World Cups in a row before 1974 and also missed out in 2002. Before the 2006 tournament, Portugal had only managed to reach three World Cups (1966, 1986, and 2002). Brazil is the only country to have qualified for and attended every single World Cup tournament.

were all knocked out in the quarterfinals, leaving the U.S., Norway, Sweden, and Germany in the semifinals. Around 65,000 spectators watched the final, in which the U.S. beat Norway with a goal from Michelle Akers just three minutes from full time.

◀ *Sisleide do Amor Lima, better known as Sissi, brings the ball down for Brazil. At the 1999 Women's World Cup, the veteran midfielder tied with China's Sun Wen for the Golden Boot award.*

SWEDEN 1995

Final Norway 2 • Germany 0

The 1995 tournament started with a shock, as an up-and-coming Brazilian women's team beat the host, Sweden, in the opening game. The 25 games that followed saw many goals. Brazil was thrashed 6-1 by Germany, who then lost a 3-2 thriller to Sweden. The U.S. and China shared the spoils in an epic 3-3 encounter, and Norway powered through their group, putting 17 goals past Canada, England, and Nigeria before knocking out the U.S. at the semifinal stage. In the other semifinal Germany beat China in a close game. Sweden's Ingrid Jonsson became the first woman to referee a FIFA final, in which Norway scored two first-half goals to secure the world crown.

UNITED STATES 1999

Final U.S. 0 • China 0 (5-4 penalties)

The 1999 Women's World Cup—featuring 16 teams and 32 games—was a huge success, with large crowds and heavy media coverage. Nigeria, propelled by their star player Mercy Akide, became the first African nation to reach the quarterfinals, where it narrowly lost to Brazil in extra time. The U.S., with Mia Hamm, Brandi Chastain, and Tiffeny Milbrett all playing superbly, had to come from behind against a strong

German team before overcoming Brazil in the semifinals. In contrast, China cruised to the final—its 5-0 mauling of cup holders Norway was an awesome spectacle. The final, played in front of more than 90,000 fans at the Rose Bowl in Pasadena, California, was a very tense affair. Like the 1994 men's final at the same venue, the game went to penalties, with Briana Scurry saving Ying Liu's spot kick to see the U.S. win the shoot-out 5-4.

UNITED STATES 2003

Final Germany 2 • Sweden 1

An epidemic of the SARS virus prevented China from hosting the World Cup for a second time, and the tournament was moved to the U.S. at the last minute. China was compensated by retaining its automatic qualification to the 2003 competition as the host nation, and it hosted the 2007 tournament. The 2003 World Cup was predicted to be a successful swan song for many of the U.S.'s veteran players. However, a vibrant, attacking German team—headed by the tournament's leading scorer, Birgit Prinz—knocked them out at the semifinal stage. In a memorable final a "golden goal" by subsitute Nia Kuenzer secured Germany their first Women's World Cup.

▲ *Germany's captain, Bettina Wiegmann, holds up the 2003 Women's World Cup. Germany was by far the best team at the competition, scoring 25 goals (11 more than any other team) on the way to their first World Cup triumph.*

THE WOMEN'S WORLD CUP

After plenty of lobbying from the women's soccer associations, the FIFA Women's World Cup was launched in China in 1991. Since then interest in the women's game has boomed, with tournaments attracting millions of television viewers.

CHINA 1991

Final U.S. 2 • Norway 1

Although there were several mismatches at the tournament (especially Sweden's 8-0 thrashing of Japan), the first Women's World Cup was a great success and proved that women's soccer had a major global audience. China, Denmark, Chinese Taipei, and Italy

THE EUROPEAN CHAMPIONSHIPS

The European Championships started life in 1958 as the UEFA European Nations Cup but struggled to find enough nations to compete. Today, however, the competition is the largest international soccer competition behind the World Cup. Like that tournament, it is held every four years.

HUMBLE BEGINNINGS

Henri Delaunay, the secretary of the French FA and the first general secretary of UEFA, had suggested a European tournament in 1927. Regionalized European competitions, such as the Balkan Cup and the Home Internationals for the four countries that comprise the U.K., took place, but a complete European-wide competition did not begin until 1958, with the final held in France in 1960. The early tournaments saw teams play a series of qualifying rounds, with the four winners progressing to play a mini tournament consisting of semifinals and a final. The stand-out game in the first competition was the semifinal between France and Yugoslavia. France was ahead 4-2 when Yugoslavia scored in the 75th, 78th, and 79th minutes to win 5-4. The Yugoslavs lost to the Soviet Union in the final and also lost to Italy in the 1968 final. Strong teams from eastern Europe dominated the early competitions—the Soviet Union reached the semifinals or final of every tournament between 1960 and 1972, while Hungary, Yugoslavia, and Czechoslovakia also performed well. The Czechs had a sparkling 1976 competition. In only a matter of days they beat the two 1974 World Cup finalists, West Germany and the Netherlands, to win the title.

FACT FILE
Midfielder Michel Platini holds the record for the most goals scored in a European Championships. He scored nine of France's 14 goals in the 1984 competition.

CHANGING FORMATS

From 1968, qualifying took place in groups rather than rounds of knockout games; the format of the competition has continued to change since then. By the time of the 1980 tournament in Italy, eight teams were taking part in the finals. Belgium was the story of that competition, winning a very tough group containing England, Italy, and Spain before losing narrowly to West Germany in the final. The 1980s saw two highly gifted and entertaining teams, France and the Netherlands, win the European Championships. Throughout the 1980s and early 1990s, however, many top teams failed to reach the finals, which dented the competition's prestige. England, the Netherlands, and Italy all failed to make the 1984 tournament; France failed to qualify for the 1988 Championships; and neither Italy nor Spain were present in 1992. With the countries of eastern Europe dividing into smaller states in the early 1990s, the numbers of competing teams boomed, and UEFA expanded the format so that 16 teams contested the finals of Euro '96.

▶ Slavisa Jokanovic (left) of Yugoslavia tangles with Spain's Alfonso during a truly epic encounter at Euro 2000. Alfonso scored in injury time to secure Spain a 4-3 victory after they had been 3-2 down with only moments left to play.

HOSTS AND WINNERS

YEAR	HOST	FINAL
1964	Spain	Spain 2-1 U.S.S.R.
1968	Italy	Italy 2-0 Yugoslavia (after replay)
1972	Belgium	West Germany 3-0 U.S.S.R.
1976	Yugoslavia	Czechoslovakia 2-2 West Germany (5-3 penalties)
1980	Italy	West Germany 2-1 Belgium
1984	France	France 2-0 Spain
1988	West Germany	Netherlands 2-0 U.S.S.R.
1992	Sweden	Denmark 2-0 Germany
1996	England	Germany 2-1 Czech Republic
2000	Belgium/ Nether.	France 2-1 Italy
2004	Portugal	Greece 1-0 Portugal
2008	Austria/Switzerland	Spain 1-0 Germany

EURO '92

The 1990s began in a colorful way for the Championships, as the Faroe Islands recorded a shock 2-0 victory over Austria in a qualifying game. The 1992 tournament saw perhaps the biggest surprise win in the competition's history. Denmark had failed to qualify, most of its players were on vacation, and the team's coach was decorating his kitchen when news emerged of Yugoslavia's disqualification and Denmark's invitation to join. Inspired by Brian Laudrup, Flemming Povlsen, and Peter Schmeichel in goal, the Danes set about their task with relish, beating France to qualify from Group A. In a dramatic semifinal against the Netherlands a heroic penalty save by Schmeichel saw them through to the final, where they beat Germany to win the most unlikely of crowns.

EURO '96 AND 2000

Euro '96 got off to a strong start, with Paul Gascoigne scoring the goal of the tournament against Scotland, the Czech Republic stunning Italy with a 2-1 win, and Croatia effectively knocking the holder, Denmark, out of the competition. England then sprang a surprise, beating the popular Dutch team 4-1 before losing a semifinal penalty shoot-out to Germany. In the final Germany defeated the Czech Republic with a "golden goal," the first to decide a major soccer competition. Euro 2000 was cohosted by the Netherlands and Belgium—the first time that two countries had jointly held the competition. The Dutch team scored the highest number of goals in a finals game, thrashing Yugoslavia 6-1. The Yugoslavs' two other games were among the most entertaining in the tournament—a 3-3 tie with Slovenia and a 4-3 defeat to Spain. The Spanish impressed but fell to the eventual winners, France, in the semifinal.

▶ England's Paul Gascoigne celebrates at Euro '96, held high by Gary Neville. Gascoigne had just scored the goal of the tournament—a superb volley against Scotland.

▲ Denmark's players line up before their Euro '92 game against Sweden, which they lost 1-0. The underprepared Danes rallied, however, qualifying from their group and winning the title.

> **FACT FILE** Spanish leader General Franco, a critic of communism, refused the Soviet team entry into Spain to play its qualifying game for the 1960 competition. The Soviets were awarded a win.

EURO 2004

Euro 2004 began with 50 nations taking part in the qualifying competition. The first round produced a series of surprises as Spain and Italy were knocked out; the same fate overcame Germany, who tied with Latvia in its group. In Group A, Russia beat Greece thanks to a Dmitri Kirichenko goal scored after only 67 seconds— the fastest in the history of the European Championships. The Czech Republic and France topped their groups unbeaten, but both were knocked out by a hardworking, well-organized Greek team, as was Spain. The Greeks also beat Portugal twice (in the first and last games of the competition) to win the trophy. The 2008 European Championships, to be held in Austria and Switzerland, are likely to conjure up just as many surprises and moments of drama as previous tournaments have.

▲ Czech Republic striker Milan Baros was the top scorer at Euro 2004, with five goals.

▶ Zlatan Ibrahimovic of Sweden lays off the ball ahead of Italy's Giuseppe Favalli in a 1-1 tie at Euro 2004. Italy failed to reach the quarterfinals despite beating Bulgaria in its next group game.

THE OLYMPICS

Until the emergence of the World Cup, the Olympics provided soccer's leading world competition. Soccer appeared in the 1896 Games as an exhibition event and became a full Olympic sport 12 years later. With the exception of the 1932 Los Angeles Games, it has featured at every Olympics since. The competition was boosted in the 1990s by the admittance of professional stars and the emergence of African soccer, which produced two Olympic gold medalists in Nigeria and Cameroon.

AMATEURS ONLY

For most of its history, Olympic soccer was played by amateurs only. The rise of professional soccer in the 1920s meant that many of the world's best professionals were unable to appear at the Games. State-run teams from eastern Europe dominated the Olympics after World War II—from 1952 to 1988, every Olympic winner came from eastern Europe with the exception of the 1984 French team, while Hungary remains the only team to have won soccer gold three times. But as the Olympics began to accept professional athletes in other sports, it also changed the rules for soccer.

Professionals who were part of their national under-23 teams appeared at the 1992 Games. In 1996 the rule was relaxed to allow each team to field three professional players over the age of 23. At Sydney 2000 Chile, led by 33-year-old striker Ivan Zamorano, won bronze. Zamorano's six goals made him the top scorer at the Games.

FACT FILE The 1952 Olympics produced three amazing games. Egypt caused a shock by beating Chile 5-4. Luxembourg eclipsed that with a 5-3 win over England. Yugoslavia led the Soviet Union 5-2 with only 14 minutes to go, but the game ended as a thrilling 5-5 tie.

EMERGING PLAYERS

Great professional players have emerged from the Olympics. For example, French midfielder Michel Platini and Mexican legend Hugo Sanchez burst onto the international scene at the 1976 Montreal Games. The 1996 Brazil team included Rivaldo and Ronaldo. The 1952 Olympics in Helsinki, Finland, saw the arrival of an amazingly good Hungarian team. Featuring players such as Ferenc Puskas, Nandor Hidegkuti, and Sandor Kocsis, the Hungarians conceded two goals but scored 20 on their way to the gold medal. These players went on to form the core of the Hungarian team that lit up international soccer throughout the 1950s (see page 70).

▲ Celestine Babayaro of Nigeria in action during the gripping 1996 Olympic semifinal against Brazil. Nigeria won 4-3 and went on to beat Argentina 3-2 in the final to become the first African team to win a major international tournament.

▶ Cameroon celebrates winning a gold medal at the 2000 Olympics. The African team defeated Brazil and Chile to reach the final, where it beat Spain in a penalty shoot-out.

FACT FILE Records of the first games at the 1896 Olympics are vague but appear to have been between two Greek teams and a Denmark team that won 15-0 in the final. One Greek team fielded five British men, all with the last name Whittal.

OLYMPIC WOMEN

Women's soccer finally became part of the Olympics at the 1996 Atlanta Games after many years of lobbying for its inclusion. With no time for a qualifying competition, the top eight nations at the 1995 Women's World Cup were invited to take part, with the exception of England, who was ineligible to compete. The final saw China beaten 2-1 by the U.S. in front of 76,481 spectators, a world record for a women's sports event. The five powerhouse nations of women's soccer—the U.S., Germany, Norway, China, and Brazil—have since won all of the medals between them. But the qualification system that is now in place will ensure that Asia, Africa, and Oceania are all represented at future Olympics.

▲ The U.S. team celebrates winning a gold medal at the 2004 Olympics. Mia Hamm (front row, second from right), the most famous player in women's soccer, announced her retirement shortly after receiving the gold medal.

► Paraguay's Edgar Barreto (left) shields the ball from Cristian Gonzalez during the 2004 Olympic final. Argentina's win secured the team's first Olympic gold medal in any event for more than 50 years.

THE 2004 GAMES

There were plenty of shocks in the men's competition in Athens. Mali beat the host, Greece, 2-0 in the preliminary rounds, while Iraq caused a sensation with a thrilling 4-2 win over Portugal. The Iraqis were knocked out in the semifinals by Paraguay, who managed to defeat Italy, Japan, and South Korea along the way. In a cagey final with only five shots on target Paraguay lost 1-0 to its South American neighbors, Argentina. In the women's competition China was crushed 8-0 by Germany, a women's Olympic record. A young Brazilian team bounced back from a 2-0 loss to the U.S. to defeat Mexico 5-0 and then Greece 7-0. But the aging U.S. team managed to beat Germany first and then Brazil to win Olympic gold for the second time.

OLYMPIC GOLD MEDALISTS

MEN

1908	Great Britain
1912	Great Britain
1920	Belgium
1924	Uruguay
1928	Uruguay
1936	Italy
1948	Sweden
1952	Hungary
1956	Soviet Union
1960	Yugoslavia
1964	Hungary
1968	Hungary
1972	Poland
1976	East Germany
1980	Czechoslovakia
1984	France
1988	Soviet Union
1992	Spain
1996	Nigeria
2000	Cameroon
2004	Argentina

WOMEN

1996	United States
2000	Norway
2004	United States

THE COPA AMERICA

The oldest continental cup competition, the Copa America has been played under a bewildering array of names and formats ever since the first competition, a three-way affair between Argentina, Uruguay, and Chile in 1910. One thing has remained constant—its status as a major soccer prize for the nations of South America.

CUP DOMINATION

The Copa America has had to contend with teams that are reluctant to release players and the increasing popularity of international club competitions. Yet it still maintains a strong appeal. Its largest-ever audience, 170,000 fans, crammed into the Maracana in 1989 to watch Brazil beat Uruguay in the final. There have been 43 Copa America competitions, eight of which have been unofficial but are counted for the records. The tournament has been dominated by the "big three" South American nations of Argentina, Brazil, and Uruguay. Fifteen Copas passed until another country, Peru, won it. Since then Argentina (15 titles) and Uruguay (14) have maintained a strong grip. Brazil has won eight times; Paraguay and Peru have twice been the victors; and Bolivia and Colombia have each won one tournament.

> **FACT FILE** Two players have scored 17 Copa goals—Norberto Mendez (Argentina) and Zizinho (Brazil).

▲ *Brazil's players charge across the field after beating Argentina in a penalty shoot-out to win the 2004 Copa America.*

INVITED GUESTS

In 1993 the Copa was expanded to 12 teams, including two invited teams from the CONCACAF federation, Mexico and the U.S. Mexico has since competed in four further Copa Americas and has proved to be a tough opponent, finishing as runner-up twice (in 1993 and 2001). Costa Rica, Japan, and South Korea have all competed in the Copa America. Another guest, Honduras, caused a sensation at the 2001 competition, knocking out Brazil 2-0 in the quarterfinals, losing to Colombia in the semifinals, but beating Uruguay to claim third place. The 43rd Copa, held in Venezuela in 2007, saw Argentina lose to Brazil 3–0.

◀ *Bolivia's Ruben Tufino fends off David Ferreira of Colombia during the 2004 Copa America. Attempting to defend its 2001 title, Colombia eventually lost to Argentina in the semifinals.*

COPA AMERICA WINNERS

Year	Winner	Year	Winner
1910*	Argentina	1949	Brazil
1916*	Uruguay	1953	Paraguay
1917	Uruguay	1955	Argentina
1919	Brazil	1956*	Uruguay
1920	Uruguay	1957	Argentina
1921	Argentina	1959*	Argentina
1922	Brazil	1959	Uruguay
1923	Uruguay	1963	Bolivia
1924	Uruguay	1967	Uruguay
1925	Argentina	1975	Peru
1926	Uruguay	1979	Paraguay
1927	Argentina	1983	Uruguay
1929	Argentina	1987	Uruguay
1935*	Uruguay	1989	Brazil
1937	Argentina	1991	Argentina
1939	Peru	1993	Argentina
1941*	Argentina	1995	Uruguay
1942	Uruguay	1997	Brazil
1945*	Argentina	1999	Brazil
1946*	Argentina	2001	Colombia
1947	Argentina	2004	Brazil
		2007	Brazil

*unofficial tournament

THE AFRICAN NATIONS CUP

The first African Nations Cup, held in 1957, was played by only three of Africa's nine independent nations at the time—Sudan, Ethiopia, and the eventual winner, Egypt. Since then the number of independent African countries has risen sharply. At the 2002 tournament 48 teams competed to qualify for 16 places at the finals.

AFRICAN NATIONS CUP WINNERS

Year	Winner	Year	Winner
1957	Egypt	1984	Cameroon
1959	Egypt	1986	Egypt
1962	Ethiopia	1988	Cameroon
1963	Ghana	1990	Algeria
1965	Ghana	1992	Ivory Coast
1968	Congo–Kinshasa	1994	Nigeria
1970	Sudan	1996	South Africa
1972	Congo–Brazzaville	1998	Egypt
1974	Zaire	2000	Cameroon
1976	Morocco	2002	Cameroon
1978	Ghana	2004	Tunisia
1980	Nigeria	2006	Egypt
1982	Ghana	2008	Egypt

◀ *Tunisia and Morocco contest the final of the 2004 African Nations Cup.*

FACT FILE In 1998 Egyptian coach Mahmoud al-Gohari became the first person to have won the African Nations Cup as both a player (in 1959) and as a coach.

UPS AND DOWNS

The African Nations Cup has had to endure its ups and downs, with poor playing facilities in some countries, hostilities between nations, and major controversies. These continue into the modern era. Nigeria, one of Africa's top teams, was expelled from the 1998 tournament after it had refused to travel to the 1996 competition. Since the early 1990s the best teams in the competition have relied on calling back as many of their foreign-based stars as possible. In 2006, for example, not one player on the Ivory Coast and Cameroon teams was based in his home country. Six years before, Ivory Coast's goalkeeper, Alain Gouamene, set a record with his seventh African Nations tournament appearance and his 24th game.

WINNERS AND LOSERS

A qualifying stage for the African Nations Cup was introduced in 1968, with eight places up for grabs. This was increased to 12 in 1992 and 16 for the 1998 competition (including the host and the defending champion). Champions have come from around the continent—from Africa's northernmost country, Morocco (the winner in 1976), to its southernmost nation, South Africa, who returned from the international wilderness to win an emotional competition in 1996. Six tournament finals have ended in exciting penalty shoot-outs, none more tense than in 1992 when an epic shoot-out saw the Ivory Coast beat Ghana 11-10. One of the most unlucky nations has to be

Zambia, who lost an entire team in a tragic 1993 airplane crash (see page 104), yet still reached the final the following year. Zambia lost the final, however, and remains a team with three third places, two second places, but no trophy win. Tunisia, with two runner-up spots and one third place, was in a similar position until the 2004 Nations Cup, when it won the title, beating Senegal, Nigeria, and Morocco. Egypt heads the winners' table with six cups after beating Cameroon in the 2008 final.

▶ *Mahamadou Diarra of Mali (left) moves past Senegal's Henri Camara at the 2004 African Nations Cup.*

THE ASIAN GAMES AND ASIAN CUP

Asia is the one continent that has two major soccer competitions for its nations—the Asian Games and the Asian Cup. Both tournaments are held every four years but in cycles that keep them two years apart.

THE ASIAN GAMES

The Asian Games is a multisport competition in which soccer is only one of a number of events. In the first tournament soccer featured alongside weight lifting, cycling, and basketball and was played in games lasting 80, not 90, minutes. India, Burma (now Myanmar), and Taiwan dominated the early competitions, with South Korea finishing runner-up three times in a row. The South Koreans have also shared the title twice, after the final was tied. Penalty shoot-outs were later introduced to decide the winner, and Iran beat North Korea 4-1 on penalties to capture the 1990 title. After a self-imposed

▲ Iran's Yahya Golmohammadi (left) and goalie Ebrahim Mirzapour run a victory lap after a shock defeat of Japan to win the 2002 Asian Games.

exile from the Asian Games in the mid-1990s, Iran powered to victories in 1998 and 2002. By the 2002 competition, the tournament had been altered to become an under-23 competition, with teams allowed to field up to three overage players. The 2006 competition, featuring soccer and more than 35 other sports, was held in and won by Qatar.

THE ASIAN CUP

First held in Hong Kong with only four competing teams, the Asian Cup has grown greatly in importance. Qualification for the 12-team tournament held in Lebanon in 2000 attracted 42 countries. The soccer-playing gap between rich and poor Asian nations was highlighted when Kuwait

◀ Zheng Zhi (left) of China and Japan's Takayuki Suzuki jump for a header during the 2004 Asian Cup final, held in Beijing, China. Japan took the trophy with a 3-1 victory.

recorded the highest-ever victory in qualifying, beating Bhutan 20-0. However, the gradual emergence of higher-quality teams from the former Soviet republics, smaller Gulf states such as Bahrain and Qatar, and countries in Southeast Asia promises to make future tournaments more competitive. In recent years the frontrunners have come from the Middle East (Iran and Saudi Arabia, for example) or the Far East (including Japan, South Korea, and China). Iran, Japan, and Saudi Arabia are the competition's most successful teams, winning the cup three times each, while Israel was a major force in the early years. It competed in the final of the first four Asian Cups, winning in 1964. In 1975, however, Israel was expelled from the Asian Football Confederation and joined UEFA in 1992.

China became the host for the first time in 2004, when the tournament was expanded to include 16 teams. There were plenty of surprise results, with popular teams Saudi Arabia and Qatar finishing at the bottom of their groups, while Uzbekistan won all of its group games. The final, between Japan and China, attracted enormous interest. The game was broadcast live to 60 nations; in China alone, the television audience was more than 250 million.

ASIAN GAMES AND ASIAN CUP WINNERS

GAMES WINNERS		CUP WINNERS	
1951	India	1956	South Korea
1954	Taiwan	1960	South Korea
1958	Taiwan	1964	Israel
1962	India	1968	Iran
1966	Burma	1972	Iran
1970	Burma and South Korea	1976	Iran
		1980	Kuwait
1974	Iran	1984	Saudi Arabia
1978	North Korea and South Korea	1988	Saudi Arabia
		1992	Japan
1982	Iraq	1996	Saudi Arabia
1986	South Korea	2000	Japan
1990	Iran	2004	Japan
1994	Uzbekistan	2007	Iraq
1998	Iran		
2002	Iran		
2006	Qatar		

THE CONCACAF CHAMPIONSHIP

Of all of the soccer-playing regions of the world, North America, Central America, and the Caribbean islands have had the most complex history of competitions. Five different tournaments have been played there, starting with the CCCF Championship in 1941.

THE GOLD CUP

For a number of years competition in the CONCACAF zone was used as a direct way of qualifying for the World Cup. In 1991 the tournament was renamed the Gold Cup, which today features 12 teams at the finals. Every Gold Cup has been hosted by the U.S., either alone or jointly with Mexico. Teams from outside CONCACAF have often been invited to play. In 1996 the Brazilian under-23 team lost to Mexico in the final.

South Korea was a guest in 2000, but it lost out on a quarterfinal place to Canada on a coin toss. Canada went on to beat another guest, Colombia, in the final. At the 2002 competition straws were drawn in a three-way tie for two quarterfinal places. Canada and Haiti progressed at the expense of Ecuador, but the tournament was eventually won by the U.S. for the first time since 1991. The 2005 competition featured guest teams Colombia and South Africa and was won by the U.S., who beat Panama in the final.

▲ Manley Junior Tabe of Vanuatu releases the ball ahead of New Zealand's Aaron Lines in the 2002 Oceanian Nations Cup.

THE OCEANIAN NATIONS CUP

Oceania's competition is the smallest and youngest of the continental championships. It has been held seven times since its conception in 1973, when the small Pacific island of Tahiti made it to the final, only to be beaten by New Zealand. In 1996 it was decided to stage the competition every two years. The 2004 tournament proved to be a major surprise when the Solomon Islands defeated New Zealand and eventually finished runner-up to Australia.

GOLD CUP WINNERS

Year	Winner
1993	Mexico
1996	Mexico
1998	Mexico
2000	Canada
2002	United States
2003	Mexico
2005	United States
2007	United States

▲ Hernan Mendford (left) of Costa Rica is fouled by Guatemala's Gustavo Cabrera. Costa Rica was the Gold Cup runner-up in 2002.

▲ Mexican captain Pavel Pardo celebrates with the CONCACAF Gold Cup in 2003 after his team's 1-0 victory over Brazil in the final.

SOCCER LEAGUES

Clubs compete in leagues that are made up of several divisions. Rules, numbers of teams, and the length of a league season vary around the world. Many top leagues—in Spain, Italy, France, and Germany, for example—have 18 or 20 teams.

NUMBERS AND BREAKS

The top divisions of Romania, Russia, and Japan each contain 16 teams. In Sweden and Poland the figure is 14, in Slovakia it is ten, and in Latvia only eight. In most leagues teams play each other twice, at home and away, during a season. In Denmark the 12 teams play each other three times. Scotland's top division has an unusual format—there are 12 teams, but the season lasts for 38 games. Teams play each other

three times before the league turns into two groups of six for a further round of games. Some leagues—in Argentina, Mexico, and Japan, for example—are split into two short seasons every year. League teams in Spain, France, Bulgaria, Hungary, and some other countries take a midwinter break, while in northern European nations, such as Russia, Norway, and Finland, the league season begins in the spring.

PROMOTION AND RELEGATION

While leagues in South Korea and the U.S. guarantee each team a place for the following season, most leagues have a system of promotion and relegation, with top and bottom teams switching places for the new season. In Uruguay relegation and promotion are determined by the performance of teams over two seasons. In Austria and Scotland one team is promoted and one relegated each season. In Hungary, the Czech Republic, and the Ukraine two

▼ Toluca (in yellow) battles with Tigres in the Mexican league. Toluca won the 2002–2003 Clausura, or winter, championship— its fourth league title since 1998.

▲ Jefferson Farfan of PSV Eindhoven runs between Feyenoord's Karim Saidi and Bruno Basto during a Dutch first division league game in 2004.

▲ South Korean Ahn Jung-Hwan, playing for Japanese team the Yokohama F Marinos, celebrates his winning goal in a J-League encounter against the Kashima Antlers.

▼ Celtic's Bobo Baldi lunges for the ball, held by Dado Prso of the Rangers, during a game between Scotland's two most successful teams.

teams go up and down, while in Germany, France, Spain, and Portugal it is three.

In Greece the third-place team in the second division contests a play-off with the team finishing 13th in the first division in order to decide who will play in the top division the following season. Other nations, such as Italy and England, hold a play-off series featuring semifinals and a final to determine which of four teams will be promoted along with others that won automatic promotion above them. In Italy play-offs are also used to determine which team joins three other relegated teams from Serie A. Play-off systems are criticized for turning an entire season into a lottery over one, two, or three games, but many people think that they maintain interest and generate high drama.

FAST RISERS

Some leagues have been dominated by a small number of teams throughout their history. For 43 seasons from 1932, the Uruguayan league title was won by either Peñarol or Nacional (Defensor was the champion in 1976). Scotland's Glasgow Rangers holds the world record for the most league championships, with a staggering 51 titles, 11 more than their arch rivals, Celtic. In some leagues small teams have

risen dramatically from humble beginnings to become champions or contenders. In Europe the now mighty Bayern Munich was not considered successful enough to join the Bundesliga in the early 1960s, but since then the team has become one of the pillars of German soccer.

FACT FILE
The Isles of Scilly, off the coast of southwestern England, are home to the Scillonian League, the world's smallest. Woolpack Wanderers and Garrison Gunners are the only two teams to play in the league, as well as two cup competitions.

▶ River Plate's Paraguayan striker Nelson Cuevas is challenged by defender German Re of Newell's Old Boys during an Argentinian first division game in Buenos Aires.

HARD FALLERS

Just as clubs can rise, they can also fall. In the 2004–2005 season 11 former champions of the English league (with 28 league titles between them) played outside the top division. A slide down the division can either be gradual or sudden. Napoli was one of Italy's soccer aristocrats and the home to Diego Maradona, winning the Italian league in 1987 and 1990 and finishing runner-up in the two intervening years. Yet, by the early 2000s, it was bankrupt and playing in Serie C, two divisions down from the top of the class.

Rarely, however, has a downturn been more dramatic than that experienced by Manchester City or Tasmania 1900 Berlin. In 1937 Manchester City was the English league champion. In the following season the team scored 80 league goals, more than any other team, but was relegated. Tasmania 1900 Berlin was joint first in the early stages of the 1965–1966 Bundesliga season. By the end, it was at the bottom and the holder of a series of unenviable records for one season, including: fewest wins (two), most losses (28), most goals against (108), and lowest points total (eight).

SERIE A

Serie A has long had a reputation as the ultimate test for the world's top players. For decades South American stars have played for its clubs; they were joined in the 1990s by great talents from Africa and Asia. Some clubs are now struggling financially as a result of their lavish spending on players. Winning Serie A is sometimes referred to as the *scudetto* ("small shield"), as the champion's shirt the following season bears a small coat of arms in Italian colors. Sometimes the quality of the league has meant that a team that is successful overseas has struggled domestically. Internazionale, for example, who won the UEFA Cup in the 1993–1994 season but could only manage 13th place in the league. Juventus is the most successful Serie A club, with 28 titles, followed by AC Milan (17), Internazionale (14), and Genoa (nine). In 2004 Serie A was expanded from 18 to 20 teams but was rocked two years later by a game-fixing scandal. Juventus was stripped of its 2005 and 2006 titles, leading to Inter being awarded the 2006 *scudetto*.

LA LIGA

The Spanish league banned foreign players between 1963 and 1973, but since then it has been the home of some of the world's greatest soccer players, from Johan Cruyff and Diego Maradona to current stars Ronaldinho, Fernando Torres, and Samuel Eto'o. The league is highly competitive. While Barcelona claimed the 2005 and 2006 titles and Real Madrid won in 2001 and 2003, Atlético Madrid, Valencia, and Deportivo La Coruña have all taken the title since 1995. La Liga has two professional divisions and a series of amateur divisions. Unlike other national leagues, the reserve teams of the major teams play in the lower divisions, not in a separate reserves' league. Real Madrid and Barcelona remain La Liga's wealthiest and most successful clubs, with a total of 47 league titles between them.

◀ *Francesco Totti of Roma (in red) clashes with Emanuele Filippini of Lazio during a Serie A derby game in 2005. Lazio won 3-0.*

▼ *Barcelona's Argentinian striker Lionel Messi (right) is one of the stars of La Liga.*

THE BUNDESLIGA

After the division of Germany into East and West following World War II, the West German Bundesliga was first contested in 1965. In 1991, after reunification, two teams from the former East Germany were admitted into the top division. Since then eastern teams have struggled—only Hansa Rostock was a regular presence in the Bundesliga until it was relegated in 2005. Bayern Munich is by far the most successful Bundesliga club, with 20 titles, followed by Borussia Mönchengladbach (five), Werder Bremen (four), and Hamburg and Borussia Dortmund (three). Hamburg is

▲ *Werder Bremen displays the German Bundesliga trophy after winning the 2003–2004 title. The team secured a league and cup double two weeks later.*

nicknamed the "Dinosaur" and is the only team to have competed in every season of the league. The Bundesliga was one of the last major leagues to adopt a system of three points for a win (in 1995), and Bayern Munich's 1997–1998 total of 78 points remains the highest. Werder Bremen came close with 74 points in 2003–2004, propelled by 27 league goals from Brazil's Ailton. His total was the highest since the early 1980s but was still short of the record 40 goals that Gerd Müller scored for Bayern in 1971–1972. Müller's total of 365 Bundesliga goals is unlikely to be beaten for many years.

HIT THE NET

www.european-football-statistics.co.uk/index1.htm
A great resource for learning more about the performances and placement of clubs in many European leagues.

www.vilacom.net/football/champions.php
Lists of league champions and cup winners from around the world.

◀ Spain's Cesc Fabregas (left) of Arsenal and the German Michael Ballack (of Chelsea) are two of the Premier League's most exciting foreign imports.

▼ Bay Area CyberRays' Brandi Chastain scores in a WUSA league game. The world's only professional women's league ran for only three seasons, although hopes for a relaunch remain.

THE ENGLISH PREMIER LEAGUE

In the early 1990s England's first division clubs broke away from league control to form the Premier League. Money has flooded into the top clubs' banks, and a wide gap has opened up between established teams and newly promoted teams, who find it very hard to stay on top. At the head of the table, Manchester United has won eight out of a possible 14 titles and never finished lower than third. The team's battle for league supremacy with Arsenal was eclipsed in 2004–2005 and 2005–2006 by a Chelsea team coached by José Mourinho and financed by Russian billionaire Roman Abramovich. Although some way short of its claim to be the best league in the world, the all-action Premiership attracts millions of viewers worldwide.

LE CHAMPIONNAT

Despite having produced some of the world's greatest players, the French league has traditionally not been as well funded as others in Europe. Its homegrown stars, such as Michel Platini, Zinedine Zidane, and Thierry Henry, usually move overseas. Despite this, French teams appear to be on the rise, reaching the final of both the Champions League and the UEFA Cup in 2004. The French league is highly competitive. Between 1983 and 2003, only three teams—Auxerre, Monaco, and Paris Saint Germain—played in the top division every season. Saint Etienne heads the list of league winners, with ten titles, but in recent years Lyon has become a major force. In 2006 it became the first team to win Le Championnat five times in a row.

ASIAN LEAGUES

The first professional league in Asia was South Korea's K-League, which began with only five teams in 1983. Featuring no relegation, it now has 14 teams and was won by the Suwon Samsung Bluewings in 2004. The K-League's most successful team is Seongnam Ilhwa Chunma, with seven titles (1993–1995 and 2001–2003 and 2006). Japan's J-League kicked off in 1993 and now has two divisions, J1 and J2. The Kashima Antlers have won four titles, while in 2004 the Yokohama F Marinos became the first club to win three J-league championships in a row. China's professional league, Jia A, has been won three times by Dalian Shide since it started in 1999.

MAJOR LEAGUE SOCCER (MLS)

Early attempts at setting up a professional league in the U.S. included the heavily financed North American Soccer League (NASL), which ran from 1968–1984 and featured global superstars such as Pelé, albeit near the end of their careers. The MLS celebrated the start of its tenth season in 2005 and focuses more on homegrown players and those from the CONCACAF region. In 2007 the number of MLS teams grew to 13, with the arrival of the Canadian team, Toronto. They play in two divisions, Eastern and Western. Unlike most leagues, there is no relegation and promotion. DC United is the most successful MLS team, with a total of four championships.

CLUB CUP COMPETITIONS

In 1872 the Wanderers beat the Royal Engineers by one goal to zero to win the first FA Cup—the oldest surviving major cup competition. Since that time hundreds of cup competitions have been introduced all over the world. Some, such as the Asian Supercup and the African Supercup, are contested between the winners of other cup competitions.

▲ Boca Juniors celebrates their penalty shoot-out victory over AC Milan in the 2003 World Club Cup. Argentinian clubs have won the competition nine times, more than any other nation.

CONTINENTAL CUP COMPETITIONS

Every continent has one or more cup competitions for its best clubs. The two most famous are the Copa Libertadores and the European Champions League (see pages 132–133). The winners of these two competitions play each other to determine the world's best team in the World Club Cup (previously called the Intercontinental Cup). Often seen as a curiosity by neutrals, the World Club Cup has suffered from withdrawals and bad-tempered games, but its staging in Japan from 1980 has kept the competition alive, despite the arrival of the World Club Championship in 2000–2001.

In Africa the African Cup Winners' Cup and the CAF Cup are only exceeded in prestige by the African Champions Cup, which was first played for in 1964. Egyptian team Zamalek has won the competition five times, while Nigeria's Enyimba recorded consecutive wins in 2003 and 2004. The Asian Cup Winners' Cup ran from 1991 to 2002 and was won by Saudi Arabian teams six times. In contrast, the Asian Champions League has seen winners from nine countries. South Korean clubs, such as 2006 winners Jeonbuk Hyundai Motors, have triumphed seven times, Saudi Arabian teams four times, while teams from Iran and Japan have won the competition three times.

COPA LIBERTADORES

South America's first international club competition was staged by Chilean club Colo Colo in 1948 and won by Brazilian team Vasco da Gama. However, it was not until 1960 that a regular competition, the Copa Libertadores, was set up. Uruguayan team Peñarol won the first two competitions but was defeated in the final of the third by Santos, thanks to two goals from Pelé. Today the Copa Libertadores begins with nine groups of four teams and culminates in a second round, quarterfinals, semifinals, and a pair of games—at home and away—between the finalists. It is open to the top teams of each South American nation, but Mexican teams were also invited to compete from 1999–2001. The Copa Libertadores has continually outshone the national team competition—the Copa America—and other South American cups in popularity and passion. This intensity has led

◄ Action from a 2005 Asian Champions League match between Al-Ain of the United Arab Emirates and Saudi Arabian team Al-Ittihad, who won the title in both 2004 and 2005.

to flare-ups on the field and in the stands. In the 1971 Copa game between Boca Juniors and Sporting Cristal, a brawl ended in the arrest of most of the players, while Colombia's Atletico Nacional was banned from the 1990 competition after a referee received death threats.

The Copa Libertadores has mainly been won by tems from Brazil, Argentina, and Uruguay. Independiente holds a stunning record of seven final appearances, all ending in wins; the only teams to have reached the final more often are Peñarol (nine times) and Boca Juniors (eight times). Uruguay's Nacional has won three Copas and been runner-up three times, as has Paraguay's Olimpia. Colombia's clubs lost seven out of eight finals before the 2004 Copa. In that year the small Colombian club Once Caldas beat Brazilian giants Santos and São Paulo and the favorite, Boca Juniors, on its way to becoming the most unexpected winner in the history of the Copa.

◄ São Paulo's Ricardo Oliveira (left) fights for the ball with Internacional's Fabiano Eller during the final of the 2006 Copa Libertadores. Internacional won the trophy and went on to stun Barcelona four months later, beating them 1-0 in the World Club Cup.

▶ Charles Coridon (left) of Lens and Samuel Johnson of Gaziantepspor battle for the ball in the 2003–2004 UEFA Cup. Lens entered the tournament via UEFA's Fair Play rule, which awards places to several clubs with the best disciplinary records in Europe the previous season.

CUPS IN EUROPE

Most leagues in Europe have one or more cup competitions for their teams to contest. Among the best-known domestic cup competitions are the English FA Cup; the Scottish Cup, which started in 1874; the Spanish Cup, which began in 1902; and the French Cup, which was first played for in 1918. From 1960 until 1999, the winners of national cup competitions in Europe played in the Cup Winners' Cup. The first and last Cup Winners' Cups were won by Italian teams (Fiorentina and Lazio), but the most successful team was Barcelona, who lifted the trophy four times. It suffered a surprising loss in the 1969 final to Slovan Bratislava (now in Slovakia), who became the first eastern European club to win a major continental cup. Since the Cup Winners' Cup was abandoned, cup winners in Europe's strongest nations have competed for the UEFA Cup.

The UEFA Cup's forerunner began in 1955 as the Inter-Cities Fairs Cup, a competition that took two years to complete. By 1960, the Fairs Cup was played over the course of one year, and for the 1971–1972 season, a new trophy and new name—the UEFA Cup—were introduced. In 1972 the European Supercup arrived and was

◄ CSKA Moscow's Venaumin Mandrikin celebrates with the 2005 UEFA Cup as his team becomes the first Russian club to win a major European trophy, beating Sporting Lisbon 3-1 in the final.

contested between the winners of the European Champions Cup and the Cup Winners' Cup. Ajax was the first winner of the Supercup. UEFA Cup winners have so far come from ten nations, with Italian clubs taking the title on nine occasions, German and English teams winning six times, and Spanish and Dutch teams four times. The competition has grown over the years, and more than 100 teams now enter the first stages of the competition. Places are granted through winning a national cup, a high league finish, being knocked out of the Champions League group stage, or doing well in the Intertoto Cup, another European competition.

EUROPEAN CHAMPIONS

European club competitions date back to 1927, when the Mitropa Cup was first contested by the leading clubs of central Europe. Sparta Prague was its first winner. The last Mitropa Cup was won by Yugoslav team Borac Banja Luka in 1992, but by then the glamour of the Mitropa had long been eclipsed by the mighty European Cup, a competition that is now known as the European Champions League.

► *Julius Aghahowa of Shakhtar Donetsk is challenged by Barcelona's Fernando Navarro in a 2004–2005 Champions League game. Aghahowa's two goals gave the Ukrainian team a surprise victory.*

◄ *Real Madrid goalie Rogelio Dominguez claims the ball during the 1959 European Cup final against French club Stade de Reims. The game ended 2-0 to Real, who lifted its fourth European Cup in a row.*

EARLY DAYS

The European Champion Clubs' Cup, usually known as the European Cup, developed out of a meeting set up by Frenchman Gabriel Hanot. Italian, Spanish, French, and Portuguese club teams were eager to take part, as were teams from many other nations. The first European Cup, held in 1955–1956, featured major names such as Real Madrid, Sporting Lisbon, Anderlecht, and AC Milan. Clubs that are less well-known today also entered—Århus GF and FC Saarbrucken, for example. English league champion Chelsea, however, was forbidden from entering, but Scottish club Hibernian reached the semifinal. The first winner of the trophy was Real Madrid.

CHANGING CHAMPIONS

Real won the first five European Cups before the tournament hit a golden age of competition in the 1960s, with Benfica, Internazionale, and AC Milan all winning the trophy. The 1970s saw both Ajax and Bayern Munich crowned champions three years in a row. English clubs won six European Cups in succession

from 1977 but were banned from European competition for five years after the 1985 Heysel Stadium disaster (see page 105). Italian, Spanish, and English clubs have won the cup ten times, while German and Dutch teams have claimed the trophy six times.

As the European Cup grew in intensity, it became more dificult to successfully defend the title. The last consecutive winner of the trophy was AC Milan in 1989 and 1990. The first year that the final went into extra time was 1958, while the first penalty shoot-out in the final was in 1984. The two finals won by eastern European teams, Steaua Bucharest (1986) and Red Star Belgrade (1991), both went to penalty shoot-outs.

EXPANSION AND DOMINATION

The format of the European Cup remained almost unchanged for its first 35 years. Teams competed in knockout rounds, playing one game at home and one away. If the scores were tied after the two games, the team with more away goals would go through. For many years the competition was open only to the league champions of each country. Today as many as four teams from each top league take part.

▲ *Nottingham Forest celebrates winning its second European Cup title in a row after winger John Robertson's single goal was enough to defeat German team Hamburg in the 1980 final.*

EUROPEAN CUP/CHAMPIONS LEAGUE WINNERS

1956	Real Madrid	1974	Bayern Munich	1992	Barcelona
1957	Real Madrid	1975	Bayern Munich	1993	Marseille (see p. 83)
1958	Real Madrid	1976	Bayern Munich	1994	AC Milan
1959	Real Madrid	1977	Liverpool	1995	Ajax
1960	Real Madrid	1978	Liverpool	1996	Juventus
1961	Benfica	1979	Nottingham Forest	1997	Borussia Dortmund
1962	Benfica	1980	Nottingham Forest	1998	Real Madrid
1963	AC Milan	1981	Liverpool	1999	Manchester United
1964	Internazionale	1982	Aston Villa	2000	Real Madrid
1965	Internazionale	1983	Hamburg	2001	Bayern Munich
1966	Real Madrid	1984	Liverpool	2002	Real Madrid
1967	Celtic	1985	Juventus	2003	AC Milan
1968	Manchester United	1986	Steaua Bucharest	2004	Porto
1969	AC Milan	1987	Porto	2005	Liverpool
1970	Feyenoord	1988	PSV Eindhoven	2006	Barcelona
1971	Ajax	1989	AC Milan	2007	Manchester United
1972	Ajax	1990	AC Milan		
1973	Ajax	1991	Red Star Belgrade		

▲ Juliano Belletti scores the winner for Barcelona against Arsenal in the 2006 Champions League final.

FACT FILE Manchester United's Ruud van Nistelrooy and José Altafini of AC Milan are the highest goal scorers in one European Cup competition, both with 14 goals.

▶ In the 2005 Champions League final Liverpool's Luis Garcia celebrates Xabi Alonso's goal that crowned a remarkable comeback. Liverpool had been 3-0 down to AC Milan but tied and then won the penalty shoot-out.

The competition was revamped as the Champions League in 1992. Group stages were introduced, guaranteeing more games and large sums of television money for the competing clubs. Champions League success is now essential for the financial health of Europe's top teams. A report in 2005 showed that taking part in the tournament can add 10–20 percent to a club's total income in one season. For a big team, failure to qualify can be a financial disaster.

The number of games in the Champions League soared from 25 in 1992–1993 to 157 in 2002–2003. From the 2003–2004 season, the number of group stages was reduced from two to one, partly owing to criticism that the competition was overblown. Yet, for every one of its critics, there are thousands of fans of the Champions League, as it pits more of the world's elite players against each other than any other club competition.

FACT FILE Up until 2004, only Dutchman Clarence Seedorf has won the European Cup with three different teams—Ajax (1995), Real Madrid (1998), and AC Milan (2003).

Celebrations get under way in Johannesburg after FIFA's announcement that South Africa will host the 2010 World Cup.

SNAPSHOT
SOUTH AFRICA 2010

South Africa came agonizingly close to hosting the 2006 World Cup but lost out to Germany by only one vote. It was a heartbreaking moment for a country that had been thrown out of FIFA in 1976 after hundreds of students were killed in an uprising in Soweto. Many other sports organizations had already barred South Africa from taking part in international competitions because of its policy of apartheid—the segregation of people of different racial backgrounds. After the dismantling of apartheid the country was allowed back into FIFA in 1992. Four years later it hosted and won the African Nations Cup. South Africa entered the race to host the 2010 World Cup alongside Egypt, Libya, Morocco, and Tunisia. On May 15, 2004 Sepp Blatter, the president of FIFA, revealed the results of the final ballot. Morocco received ten votes, but South Africa triumphed with 14—and made history by becoming the first African nation to win the right to host soccer's greatest competition.

▶ *Nelson Mandela, the former president of South Africa, celebrates with the World Cup.*

U.S. SOCCER

Soccer in the United States has a longer history than many of the European and South American soccer superpowers. Its first club team, Oneida in Boston, Massachusetts, is believed to have had an official roster of players as early as 1862. The country's first major cup competition, the American Cup, began in 1885, the same year that an unofficial national team played its first game, against Canada. The United States joined FIFA in 1914 and played its first official international game in 1916. Its governing body, the United States Soccer Federation, formed in 1913. Besides sanctioning the majority of the U.S.'s domestic leagues and competitions, it also awards the Soccer Athlete of the Year, the country's most illustrious soccer award.

LEAGUE AND CUP

Numerous attempts at establishing national leagues have come and gone, but Major League Soccer (MLS) is set to stay. Having moved into its second decade, MLS has not been without its problems and the league has been reorganized on several occasions. The 2008 season saw 14 MLS teams, with the Canadian team Toronto FC joining in 2007 and teams from Seattle and Philadelphia expected to join in future seasons. Below the MLS lie the two United Soccer Leagues (USL) divisions and the USL Premier Development League.

The U.S. Open Cup, now played for the Lamar Hunt trophy, has a 90-year history. At the current time eight teams from each of five leagues qualify for the cup: the MLS, USL division one, USL division two, the USL Premier Development League, and the United States Adult Soccer Association. Historically, teams in the dominant national leagues of their time have done well in the cup, but shocks and upsets still occur—such as the 1999 competition, which was won by USL team Rochester Ragin' Rhinos, and in 2007, when two USL teams, the Seattle Sounders and the Carolina Railhawks, reached the semifinals.

INTERNATIONAL OUTLOOK

The U.S. men's team has made great strides in recent seasons, with many of its best players opting to play in the MLS or in one of the big European leagues. The 2002 World Cup saw the team beat Portugal in the group stage and knock out their great rival, Mexico, only to lose narrowly to the eventual runner-up, Germany. At the 2006 World Cup they failed to qualify out of their group but did draw 1-1 with the eventual champions, Italy. Consolation was achieved the following year when winning their fourth CONCACAF Gold Cup, beating Mexico 2-1 with goals from Landon Donovan and Benny Feilhaber.

Based on a core of stars who have graced the game for more than a decade, including Kristine Lilly, Mia Hamm, and Brandi Chastain, the U.S. women's team has been the most successful national team on the planet, with World Cup, Olympic, and Algarve Cup wins. A successful last-gasp staging of the 2003 World Cup, when the SARS virus epidemic prevented China from hosting the event, was only spoiled by the team exiting at the semifinal stage to the eventual winner, Germany. The U.S. team would finish third for the second World Cup in a row in 2007, but they did win the 2004 Olympics and the prestigious Algarve Cup in 2005, 2007, and 2008. These and other victories helped them regain the world number-one spot in the FIFA rankings, ahead of Germany.

BOOKS AND MAGAZINES

100 Years of Football: The FIFA Centennial Book (Weidenfeld & Nicolson, 2004)
A guide to FIFA and the rise of soccer around the world, packed with rare photos.

The Encyclopedia of American Soccer History (Scarecrow Press, 2001)
The definitive guide to U.S. soccer, full of statistics, tables, and insights into the game's long and complex history.

Football in Sun and Shadow (Eduardo Galeano, 2004)
Short, poetic pieces about the passions and emotions involved in watching and playing soccer.

Go for the Gold (Perennial Currents, 2000)
A biography of U.S. soccer's most outstanding player—Mia Hamm.

Soccer America magazine (Soccer America Publishing)
Long-running U.S. magazine packed with news, features, and photographs.

The Soccer Coaching Bible (Human Kinetics Publishers, 2004)
An excellent book featuring coaching tips and drills compiled by some of the U.S.'s leading coaches.

Soccer Rules Explained, Revised and Updated (Lyons Press, 2005)
A comprehensive book on the laws of the game.

World Soccer magazine (IPC Media)
The best magazine available for fans of world soccer, with coverage of all of the major and minor leagues, as well as news and features on international competitions.

FACTS AND FIGURES

U.S. SOCCER ATHLETE OF THE YEAR

Men

1984 Rick Davis
1985 Perry van der Beck
1986 Paul Caligiuri
1987 Brent Goulet
1988 Peter Vermes
1989 Mike Windischmann
1990 Tab Ramos
1991 Hugo Perez
1992 Marcelo Balboa
1993 Thomas Dooley
1994 Marcelo Balboa
1995 Alexi Lalas
1996 Eric Wynalda
1997 Kasey Keller
1998 Cobi Jones
1999 Kasey Keller
2000 Chris Armas
2001 Earnie Stewart
2002 Brad Friedel
2003 Landon Donovan
2004 Landon Donovan
2005 Kasey Keller
2006 Oguchi Onyewu
2007 Clint Dempsey

Women

1985 Sharon Remer
1986 April Heinrichs
1987 Carin Jennings-Gabarra
1988 Joy Biefield
1989 April Heinrichs
1990 Michelle Akers
1991 Michelle Akers
1992 Carin Jennings-Gabarra
1993 Kristine Lilly
1994 Mia Hamm
1995 Mia Hamm
1996 Mia Hamm
1997 Mia Hamm
1998 Mia Hamm
1999 Michelle Akers
2000 Tiffeny Milbrett
2001 Tiffeny Milbrett
2002 Shannon MacMillan
2003 Abby Wambach
2004 Abby Wambach
2005 Kristine Lilly
2006 Kristine Lilly
2007 Abby Wambach

NATIONAL ASSOCIATION FOOTBALL LEAGUE (NAFL)

Following a failed attempt by baseball team owners to fill their stadiums in the off-season with a professional league in 1894, the NAFL kicked off the following year. It struggled at first but received a boost when the U.S. won gold in soccer at the 1904 St. Louis Olympics.

1895 Bayonne Centerville
1898 Paterson True Blues
1907 West Hudson
1908 Paterson Rangers
1909 Clark A. A.
1910 West Hudson
1911 Jersey A. C.
1912 West Hudson
1913 West Hudson
1914 Brooklyn F. C.
1915 West Hudson
1916 Alley Boys
1917 Jersey A. C.
1918 Paterson F. C.
1919 Bethlehem Steel
1920 Bethlehem Steel
1921 Bethlehem Steel

AMERICAN SOCCER LEAGUE (ASL) I AND II

Featuring teams mostly based in and around New York, New Jersey, and Philadelphia, Pennsylvania, the ASL was the first U.S. league that boasted a large financial backing, enough to attract European players. In the mid-1920s the league featured attendances that rivaled the National Football League (NFL), but infighting, disputes, and financial difficulties saw it fold in 1933. The second American Soccer League (ASL II) rose from the ashes of the former league and, like its predecessor, started with teams based in the northeastern United States before gradually expanding.

ASL I

1922 Philadelphia F. C.
1923 J. & P. Coats
1924 Fall River Marksmen
1925 Fall River Marksmen
1926 Fall River Marksmen
1927 Bethlehem Steel
1928 Boston Wonder Workers
1929 Fall River Marksmen
1929 Fall River Marksmen
1930 Fall River Marksmen
1930 Fall River Marksmen
1931 New York Giants
1932 New Bedford Whalers
1933 Fall River F. C.

ASL II

1934 Kearney Irish-Americans
1935 German-Americans
1936 New York Americans
1937 Scots-Americans
1938 Scots-Americans
1939 Newark Scots
1940 Newark Scots
1941 Newark Scots
1942 Philadelphia Americans
1943 Brooklyn Hispano
1944 Philadelphia Americans
1945 Brookhattan
1946 Baltimore Americans
1947 Philadelphia Americans
1948 Philadelphia Americans
1949 Philadelphia Nationals
1950 Philadelphia Nationals
1951 Philadelphia Nationals
1952 Philadelphia Americans
1953 Philadelphia Nationals
1954 New York Americans
1955 Uhrik Truckers (Philadelphia)
1956 Uhrik Truckers (Philadelphia)
1957 New York Hakoah
1958 New York Hakoah
1959 New York Hakoah
1960 Colombo
1961 Ukrainian Nationals (Philadelphia)
1962 Ukrainian Nationals (Philadelphia)
1963 Ukrainian Nationals (Philadelphia)
1964 Ukrainian Nationals (Philadelphia)
1965 Hartford Football Club
1966 Roma Soccer Club
1967 Baltimore St. Gerards
1968 Ukrainian Nationals (Philadelphia)
1968 Washington Darts
1969 Washington Darts
1970 Ukrainian Nationals (Philadelphia)
1971 New York Greeks
1972 Cincinnati Comets
1973 New York Apollo
1974 Rhode Island Oceaneers
1975 New York Apollo
1976 Los Angeles Skyhawks
1977 New Jersey Americans
1978 New York Apollo
1979 Sacramento Gold
1980 Pennsylvania Stoners
1981 Carolina Lightnin'
1982 Detroit Express
1983 Jacksonville Tea Men

NORTH AMERICAN SOCCER LEAGUE (NASL)

Two competing organizations were formed in the 1960s, both with the aim of establishing soccer on a level equal to baseball, basketball, and football. The National American Soccer League (NASL) changed its name to the United Soccer Association (USA) in order to avoid a name clash with its rival, the National Professional Soccer League (NPSL). Both merged in 1968 to form the North American Soccer League (NASL). After a shaky start the NASL peaked in the mid- to late 1970s with the importing of some of the biggest names in world soccer, including Pelé, Johan Cruyff, and George Best. Overexpansion, rising costs, and the lack of a national TV deal saw the league fold in 1984, although four NASL teams (Chicago, New York, Minnesota, and San Diego) joined the Major Indoor Soccer League.

1967 Los Angeles Wolves (USA Champions)
1967 Oakland Clippers (NPSL Champions)
1968 Atlanta Chiefs
1969 Kansas City Spurs
1970 Rochester Lancers
1971 Dallas Tornado
1972 New York Cosmos
1973 Philadelphia Atoms
1974 Los Angeles Aztecs
1975 Tampa Bay Rowdies
1976 Toronto Metros-Croatia
1977 New York Cosmos
1978 New York Cosmos
1979 Vancouver Whitecaps
1980 New York Cosmos
1981 Chicago Sting
1982 New York Cosmos
1983 Tulsa Roughnecks
1984 Chicago Sting

NATIONAL PROFESSIONAL SOCCER LEAGUE

Beginning its life as the American

Indoor Soccer Association in 1984, this professional indoor league changed its name in 1990. The season before it introduced an innovative scoring system where goals are worth between one and three points depending on the distance and the game situation.

1992 Detroit Rockers
1993 Kansas City Attack
1994 Cleveland Crunch
1995 St. Louis Ambush
1996 Cleveland Crunch
1997 Kansas City Attack
1998 Milwaukee Wave
1999 Cleveland Crunch
2000 Milwaukee Wave
2001 Milwaukee Wave

MAJOR LEAGUE SOCCER (MLS)

After the great interest spawned by the U.S. hosting the 1994 World Cup, the MLS kicked off in 1996 with ten teams, which later expanded to 12, then 14. Several teams and a three-division system have come and gone, but the MLS is thriving, buoyed by the attention surrounding David Beckham joining Los Angeles Galaxy at the start of the 2008 season.

1996 D. C. United (OT)
1997 D. C. United
1998 Chicago Fire
1999 D. C. United
2000 Kansas City Wizards
2001 San Jose Earthquakes (OT)
2002 Los Angeles Galaxy (OT)
2003 San Jose Earthquakes
2004 D. C. United
2005 Los Angeles Galaxy
2006 Houston Dynamo
2007 Houston Dynamo

WOMEN'S SOCCER LEAGUES

The W-League was the first of three semiprofessional or professional leagues that arose in the U.S. in the 1990s. For a while it was divided into a top and lower division (W-1 and W-2). It was joined by the WPSL and then WUSA at the turn of the century. Since WUSA has suspended operations, many players have joined or rejoined the W-League or the WPSL.

W-League

1995 Long Island Lady Riders
1996 Maryland Pride
1997 L. I. Lady Riders (OT)
1998 Raleigh Wings
1999 Raleigh Wings (OT)
2000 Chicago Cobras
 (pens. 4-2)
2001 Boston Renegades
2002 Boston Renegades
2003 Hampton Roads Piranhas
2004 Vancouver Whitecaps
 (pens. 4-2)
2005 New Jersey Wildcats
2006 Vancouver Whitecaps
2007 Vancouver Whitecaps

Women's Premier Soccer League (WPSL)

1998 Silicon Valley Red Devils
1999 California Storm
2000 San Diego WFC
2001 Ajax Southern California
2002 California Storm
2003 Utah Spiders
2004 California Storm
2005 F.C. Indiana
2006 Long Island Fury
2007 F.C. Indiana

Women's United Soccer Association (WUSA)

2001 Bay Area CyberRays
 (pens. 4-2)
2002 Carolina Courage
2003 Washington Freedom (OT)

U.S. OPEN CUP CHAMPIONSHIP

One of the oldest soccer cup competitions in the Americas, the U.S. Open Cup dates back to 1914. Only one team, Greek-American of New York, has won the cup three times in a row (1967–1969). Since 1996, a Women's Open Cup competition has also been played.

1914 Brooklyn Field Club
1915 Bethlehem Steel
1916 Bethlehem Steel
1917 Fall River Rovers
1918 Bethlehem Steel
1919 Bethlehem Steel
1920 St. Louis Ben Millers
1921 Brooklyn Robins Dry Dock
1922 St. Louis Scullins Steel
1923 Paterson F. C./St. Louis
 Scullin Steel (cochampions)
1924 Fall River Marksmen
1925 Shawsheen (MA) Indians
1926 Bethlehem Steel

1927 Fall River Marksmen
1928 New York Nationals
1929 New York Hakoah
1930 Fall River Marksmen
1931 Fall River F. C.
1932 New Bedford Whalers
1933 St. Louis Stix, Baer & Fuller
1934 St. Louis Stix, Baer & Fuller
1935 St. Louis Central Breweries
1936 Philadelphia German-
 American
1937 New York Americans
1938 Chicago Sparta
1939 Brooklyn St. Mary's Celtic
1940 Baltimore S. C./Chicago
 Sparta A & BA (cochampions)
1941 Pawtucket F. C.
1942 Pittsburgh Gallatin
1943 Brooklyn Hispano
1944 Brooklyn Hispano
1945 New York Brookhattan
1946 Chicago Vikings
1947 Fall River Ponta Delgada
1948 St. Louis Simpkins-Ford
1949 Pittsburgh Morgan S. C.
1950 St. Louis Simpkins-Ford
1951 New York German-
 Hungarians
1952 Pittsburgh Hamarville
1953 Chicago Falcons
1954 New York Americans
1955 S. C. Eintracht
1956 Pittsburgh Hamarville
1957 St. Louis Kutis
1958 Los Angeles Kickers
1959 San Pedro McIlvane
 Canvasbacks
1960 Philadelphia Ukrainian
 Nationals
1961 Philadelphia Ukrainian
 Nationals
1962 New York Hungarians
1963 Philadelphia Ukrainian
 Nationals
1964 Los Angeles Kickers
1965 New York Ukrainians
1966 Philadelphia Ukrainian
 Nationals
1967 New York Greek-American
1968 New York Greek-American
1969 New York Greek-American
1970 S. C. Elizabeth
1971 New York Hota
1972 S. C. Elizabeth
1973 Los Angeles Maccabee
1974 New York Greek-American
1975 Los Angeles Maccabee
1976 San Francisco A. C.
1977 Los Angeles Maccabee
1978 Los Angeles Maccabee

1979 Brooklyn Dodgers
1980 New York Pancyprian
 Freedoms
1981 Los Angeles Maccabee
1982 New York Pancyprian
 Freedoms
1983 New York Pancyprian
 Freedoms
1984 New York A. O. Krete
1985 San Francisco Greek-
 Americans
1986 St. Louis Kutis
1987 Washington Club España
1988 St. Louis Busch Seniors
1989 St. Petersburg Kickers
1990 Chicago A. A. C. Eagles
1991 Brooklyn Italians
1992 San Jose Oaks
1993 San Francisco C. D. Mexico
1994 San Francisco Greek-
 Americans
1995 Richmond Kickers
 (pens. 4-2)
1996 D. C. United
1997 Dallas Burn (pens. 5-3)
1998 Chicago Fire
1999 Rochester Ragin' Rhinos
2000 Chicago Fire
2001 Los Angeles Galaxy
2002 Columbus Crew
2003 Chicago Fire
2004 Kansas City Wizards (OT)
2005 Los Angeles Galaxy
2006 Chicago Fire
2007 New England Revolution

U.S. Women's Open Cup

1996 Dallas Lightning
1997 Sacramento Storm
1998 Los Angeles Ajax
1999 San Diego Auto Trader
2000 Los Angeles Ajax
2001 Detroit Rocker Hawks
2002 Southern California Blues
2003 Southern California Ajax
2004 Southern California Ajax
2005 FC Indiana
2006 Dallas Roma
2007 Ajax America Women

INDIVIDUAL AND TEAM RECORDS

Top league goal scorers (1950-2007)

1950	Joe Gaetjens	18
1951	Nick Kropfelder	17
1952	Dick Roberts	19
1953	Pito Villanon	12
1954	John Calder	19
1955	Jack Ferris	20

1956 Gene Grabowski	19
1957 George Brown	13
1958 Lloyd Monsen	22
1959 Pasquale Pepe	17
1960 Miguel Noha	22
1961 Herman Niss	17
1962 Pete Millar	18
1963 Ismael Fereyra	14
1964 Walter Czychowich	15
1965 Herculiano Riguerdo	7
1966 Walter Czychowich	27
1967 Yanko Daucik	20
1968 John Kowalik, Cirilo Fernandez	30
1969 Kaiser Motaug	16
1970 Kirk Apostolidis	16
1971 Carlos Metidieri	19
1972 Randy Horton	9
1973 Warren Archibald, Ilja Mitic	12
1974 Paul Child	15
1975 Steve David	23
1976 Derek Smethurst	20
1977 Steve David	26
1978 Giorgio Chinaglia	34
1979 Giorgio Chinaglia	26
1980 Giorgio Chinaglia	32
1981 Giorgio Chinaglia	29
1982 Ricardo Alonso	21
1983 Roberto Cabanas	25
1984 Steven Zyngul	20
1985 Josue Partillo	8
1986 Brent Goulet	9
1987 Joe Mihaljevic	7
1988 Jorge Acosta	14
1989 Ricardo Alonso, Mirko Castilo	10
1990 Chance Fry	17
1991 Jean Harbour	17
1992 Jean Harbour	13
1993 Paulinho	15
1994 Paul Wright	12
1995 Peter Hattrup	11
1996 Roy Lassiter	27
1997 Jaime Moreno	16
1998 Stern John	26
1999 Stern John, Roy Lassiter, Jason Kreis	18
2000 Mamadou Diallo	26
2001 Alex Pineda	19
2002 Carlos Ruiz	23
2003 Carlos Ruiz, Taylor Twellman	15
2004 Amado Guevara	10
2005 Taylor Zwellman	17
2006 Jeff Cunningham	16
2007 Luciano Emilio	20

MLS Most Valuable Player

1996 Carlos Valderrama, Tampa Bay Mutiny
1997 Preki, Kansas City Wizards
1998 Marco Etcheverry, D. C. United
1999 Jason Kreis, F. C. Dallas
2000 Tony Meola, Kansas City Wizards
2001 Alex Pineda Chacón, Miami Fusion
2002 Carlos Ruiz, Los Angeles Galaxy
2003 Preki, Kansas City Wizards
2004 Amado Guevara, MetroStars (New Jersey)
2005 Taylor Twellman, New England Revolution
2006 Christian Gomez, D.C. United
2007 Luciano Emilio, D.C. United

All-time MLS goal scorers (1996-2007)

Jaime Moreno, D. C. United	112
Ante Razov, Chicago Fire, LA Galaxy, etc.	109
Jason Kreis, Dallas Burn, Real Salt Lake	108
Jeff Cunningham, Columbus Crew, Toronto FC	96
Taylor Zwellman, New England Revolution	91
Roy Lassiter, D. C. United	88
Raul Diaz Arce, D. C. United	82
Carlos Ruiz, FC Dallas	81
Preki, Kansas City Wizards	79
Cobi Jones, LA Galaxy	70

Leading international appearances (men)

Cobi Jones	165
Jeff Agoos	134
Marcelo Balboa	128
Claudio Reyna	112
Paul Caligiuri	110
Eric Wynalda	106

Leading international goal scorers (men)

Landon Donovan	35
Eric Wynalda	34
Brian McBride	30
Joe-Max Moore	24
Bruce Murray	21

Leading international appearances (women)

Kristine Lilly	340
Mia Hamm	275
Julie Foudy	271
Joy Fawcett	239
Tiffeny Milbrett	205

HIT THE NET

http://www.futsal.com/index.htm
Home page of the U.S. Futsal Federation, complete with rules, tips, and news.

http://uslsoccer.com/
The official website of the United Soccer Leagues, complete with standings, tables, and news on the USL first and second divisions, the W-League, the Super-20 League, and the Super Y-League.

http://usyouthsoccer.org/
The site of the U.S. Youth Soccer Association, featuring news about young players and their coaches, as well as a list of upcoming competitions and a calendar of events.

http://www.wpsl.info/
The official website of the Women's Premier Soccer League.

www.mlsnet.com
The official website of MLS is a huge collection of history, team data, statistics, news, and opinions. Also included are the rules of the game and coaching advice.

www.soccerhall.org
The website of the National Soccer Hall of Fame is crammed full of information about great soccer players from around the world.

www.ussoccer.com
The official home of U.S. soccer in its many forms. It includes news and results from the U.S. leagues and also of U.S. players overseas.

www.ussoccerreview.com
Another strong news site split into sections devoted to MLS, U.S. national teams, U.S. players overseas, and FIFA-based news.

www.womensoccer.com
One of the most comprehensive sites on the Internet for women's soccer, with news about domestic and international competitions.

GLOSSARY

Advantage rule A rule that allows the referee to let play continue after a foul if it is to the advantage of the team that has been fouled against.

AFC The Asian Football Confederation, responsible for running soccer in Asia.

Agent A person who represents players and negotiates contracts and transfer moves.

Anchor A midfielder positioned just in front of—and who protects—the defense. An anchor player may allow other midfielders to push farther forward.

Assist A pass that releases a player to score a goal. An assist can be a pass on the ground, a flick, or a cross from which a headed goal is scored.

Away goals rule A rule used in some cup competitions. If the scores are tied over two legs, the team that has scored more goals away from home wins.

Back-pass rule A law stating that a deliberate pass backward by a player to his or her goalkeeper cannot be handled by the goalie.

CAF The Confédération Africaine de Football, which runs soccer in Africa.

Cap Recognition given to a player for each appearance in an international game for his or her country.

Catenaccio A defensive tactical system in which a sweeper plays behind a solid defense.

Caution Another word for a yellow card (a warning from the referee to a player for a foul or infringement). A player who receives two yellow cards in one game is automatically shown a red card and sent off of the field.

Central defender The defender who plays in the middle of the last line of defense.

Chip A pass propelled into the air from a player to a teammate or as a shot on goal.

CONCACAF The Confederation of North, Central American, and Caribbean Association Football, which runs soccer in North and Central America.

CONMEBOL The Confederación Sudamericana de Fútbol, which runs soccer in South America.

Counterattack A quick attack by a team after it regains possession of the ball.

Cross To send the ball from a wide position toward the center of the field, often into the opposition penalty area.

Cushioning Using a part of the body to slow down a ball in order to bring it under control.

Derby A game between two rival teams, often located in the same town or city.

Direct free kick A kick awarded to a team because of a serious foul committed by an opponent. A goal may be scored directly from the kick.

Dissent When a player uses words or actions to disagree with the referee's decision.

Distribution The way that the ball is released by a goalkeeper or is moved around the field by a team.

Dribbling Moving the ball under close control with a series of short kicks or taps.

Drop ball A way of restarting play in which the referee releases the ball for a player from each team to compete over once the ball has touched the ground.

Extra time A way of deciding a tied game. It involves two periods of additional play, usually lasting 15 minutes each.

FA (Football Association) The national soccer federation of England.

Feinting Using fake moves of the head, shoulders, and legs in order to deceive an opponent and put him or her off balance.

FIFA The Fédération Internationale de Football Association, the international governing body of soccer.

Formation The way in which a team lines up on the field in terms of the numbers of defenders, midfielders, and forwards.

Fourth official An additional game official who is responsible for displaying added-on time, checking substitutions, and aiding the referee and his or her two assistants.

Futsal A type of five-on-five soccer, supported and promoted by FIFA.

Golden Boot An award given to the player who scores the most goals in a World Cup. It is also an annual award given to the top goal scorer in European club soccer.

Golden goal A system used to decide a tied knockout game in extra time. The first goal scored wins the game.

Handball The illegal use of a hand or arm by a player.

Hat trick Three goals scored by a player in a single game.

Indirect free kick A kick awarded to a team because of a minor foul committed by an opponent. A goal cannot be scored from the kick unless the ball is first touched by a player other than the kicker.

Instep The part of a player's foot where his or her shoelaces lie.

Interception When a player gains possession of the ball by latching onto a pass made by the opposition.

Jockeying A defensive technique of delaying an attacker who has the ball.

Laws of the game The 17 main rules of soccer, established and updated by FIFA.

Libero "Free man." See also sweeper.

Man-to-man marking A system of marking in which a defender stays close to and near the goal of a single opposition player.

Marking Guarding a player to prevent him or her from advancing the ball toward the goal, making an easy pass, or receiving the ball from a teammate.

MLS Major League Soccer, the U.S. professional male league.

Narrowing the angle A technique in which a goalkeeper moves toward an attacker who has the ball in order to cut down the amount of goal that the attacker can aim a shot at.

Obstruction When a player, instead of trying to win the ball, uses his or her body to prevent an opponent from playing it.

OFC The Oceania Football Confederation, which runs soccer in Oceania.

Offside A player is offside if he or she is closer to the other team's goal than both the ball and the second-to-last opponent at the moment that the ball is played forward.

Offside trap A defensive tactic used to trick enemy attackers by leaving them offside. Defenders who play the offside trap usually move upfield together in a straight line when the ball is played toward their goal.

Overlap To run outside and beyond a teammate down the side of the field in order to create space and a possible passing opportunity.

Overload When an attacking team has more players in the opposition's half or penalty area than the defending team. An overload often leads to a goal-scoring chance.

Penalty shoot-out A method of deciding a tied game by a series of penalties, all taken at one end of the field.

Playmaker A skilled midfielder or deep-lying attacker who coordinates the attacking movements of a team.

Play-off A game, pair, or series of games used to decide a final placement. In the World Cup the two losing semifinalists contest a single play-off game for third place. In many leagues play-off games are used to decide relegation and promotion issues.

Professional foul A foul committed intentionally by a defender in order to stop an opponent who has a clear run on goal.

Referee's assistant An official who assists the referee during the game by signaling for fouls, infringements, and offsides.

Reserve team A team made up of players who are not on the first team at the club or national level.

Scout A person employed by a soccer team who attends games and training sessions to look for up-and-coming players.

Set piece A planned play or move that a team uses when a game is restarted with a free kick, penalty kick, corner kick, goal kick, throw-in, or kickoff.

Shielding A technique used by the player with the ball to protect it from a defender who is closely marking him or her. The player in possession keeps his or her body between the ball and the defender.

Silver goal A system, used at Euro 2004, to decide a tied knockout game. If a goal is scored in the first 15 minutes of extra time, it wins the game. If no goal is scored, a second period of extra time is played.

Simulation Pretending to be fouled or feigning injury in order to fool the referee. A player found guilty of simulation by the referee receives a yellow card.

Stoppage time Time added to the end of any period of a game to make up for time lost during a major halt in play—to treat an injured player, for example. Also known as added time or injury time.

Substitution Changing the team lineup on the field by replacing one player with another from the substitutes' bench.

Sweeper A defender who can play closest to his or her goal, behind the rest of the defenders, or in a more attacking role with responsibility for bringing the ball forward.

Tactics Methods of play used in an attempt to outwit and beat an opposition team.

Target man A tall striker, usually the player farthest upfield, at whom teammates aim their forward passes.

Through ball or pass A pass to a teammate that puts him or her beyond the opposition's defense and through to goal.

Total soccer A style of soccer in which players switch positions all over the field. It was made famous by the Dutch national team and Dutch teams such as Ajax.

UEFA The Union of European Football Associations, which controls soccer in Europe.

Volley Any ball kicked by a player when it is off the ground.

Wall pass A quick, short pair of passes between two players that sends the ball past a defender. Also known as a one-two pass.

Wingback A defender on the side of the field who, when the opportunity arises, makes wide runs forward in attack.

WUSA The world's first professional soccer league for women, based in the U.S.

Zonal marking A defensive system in which defenders mark opponents who enter their area of the field.

INDEX

Note: References to main entries are in **bold**.

A

Abbondanzieri, Roberto 12
Abramovich, Roman 102–103, 129
AC Milan 30, 40, 60, **82**, 100, 101, 102, 104, 128, 133
Adu, Freddy 94
advantage rule 20, **140**
AFC (Asian Football Confederation) **13**, 140
Africa 12, 13, 116, 130
African Champions League 78, 87, 88, **130**
African Cup Winners' Cup 78, **130**
African Nations Cup 77, **123**
Aghahowa, Julius 29, 132
Ahn Jung-Hwan 72, 126
Ajax 75, **89**, 94, 99
Al-Ahly 74, **78**
Al-Ain 130
al Deayea, Mohammed **36**
Alberto, Carlos 76, 77
Albrecht, Jorge 110
Aldridge, John 37
Alfonso 118
Algeria 113, 123
Al-Ittihad 130
Amokachi, Daniel 73
Anderlecht 44, **87**
Argentina 11, 12, 48, 58, 77, 108, 112, 113, 114, 121, 122, 131
Arsenal 77, **84**, 95, 96, 129, 133, 137, 138
Asante Kotoko **87**
Asia 12, 13, 109, 117, **129**, 130
Asian Cup **124**
Asian Games 34, **124**
Aston, Ken 8
Aston Villa 34, 88, 105, 137, 138
Atlético Madrid 26, 55, 67, 86, 91, 128
attacking **26–27**
Australia 12, 13, 59, 116, 125
Austria 65, 108, 110, 113, 126
Ayala, Roberto 48

B

Babayaro, Celestine 29, 73, 117, 120
back-pass rule 6, 24, 114, **140**
Baggio, Roberto 32, 33, **48**, 85
Baier, Paulo 84
Baldi, Bobo 127
ball control **16**, 24, **25**
Ballack, Michael 18, 129
Banks, Gordon **35**, 74
Barbosa, Moacir 109
Barcelona 44, 62, **78**, 99, 100, 101, 102, 133
Baresi, Franco 32, **40**, 61, 82
Baros, Milan 119
Barreto, Edgar 121
Barry, Gareth 105
Barthez, Fabien 34, 72, 97, 98
Batistuta, Gabriel 28, **55**
Basto, Bruno 126
Bayern Munich 66, 71, **86**, 100, 127, 128
beach soccer 95
Bebeto 29, 40

Beckenbauer, Franz **39**, 42, 61, 71, 108, 112
Beckham, David 16, 23, 30, **42**, 96, 97, 98, 103, 115
Belgium 11, 105, 113, 118, 121
Belletti, Juliano 133
Belodedici, Miodrag 83, 85
Benfica 23, 46, 52, 66, 79, **86**, 104
Bergkamp, Dennis **48**, 84, 89, 94
Best, George 38, **47**, 55, 79, 105
Blatter, Sepp 108, 135
Boca Juniors 23, **81**, 90, 101, 130, 131
Bojinov, Valeri 64
Bolivia 104, 122
Bonhof, Rainer 71
Boniek, Zbigniew **45**
Borussia Dortmund 38, 100, 103, 128
Borussia Mönchengladbach 46, 71, 128
Bosman ruling 103
Botafogo 43, 45, 46, 79, 84
Botasso, Juan 108
Bowyer, Lee 105
Bratseth, Rune **37**
Brazil 2, 12, 13, 19, 27, 32, 35, 54, 60, **76**, 77, 109, 110, 111, 112, 114, 115, 116, 122, 125, 130, 131
women's team 117, 121
British soccer 121, 136–139
Brocchi, Christian 30
Buffon, Gianluigi 24, 30, 34, 44
Bugaev, Alexei 22
Bundesliga 66, 86, 103, 127, **128**
Busby, Matt 79

C

Cabrera, Gustavo 125
CAF (Confédération Africaine de Football) **13**, 130, 140
Camara, Henri 62, 63, 123
Cameroon 9, **77**, 114, 120, 123
Canada 39, 113, 125
Caniggia, Claudio 114
Cannavaro, Fabio 116
Cantona, Eric 67, 95, 105
Caribbean 12
Carling Cup 138
Carragher, Jamie 88
Casillas, Iker 25, 31, 94
Castro, Hector 108
catenaccio **60–61**, 67, 80, 140
cautions **21**, 140
Cech, Petr 23, 24, 29
Celtic 20, 23, 53, 66, 83, **90**, 100, 101, 127, 137, 138
Ceni, Rogério 25
Champions League see European Cup
Chapman, Herbert 60, **66**, 84
Charisteas, Angelos 106
Charles, John **40**
Charlton, Bobby **50**, 55, 69, 74, 79, 111, 139
Chastain, Brandi 117, 129
cheating 8, **104**, 105
Chelsea 23, 62, 64, 103, 129, 132, 137, 138
Chile 12, 77, 104, 111, 120
China 10, 13, 65, 94, 115, 124, 129
women's team 12, 40, **74**, 176, 121
chip 17, **140**
Choi Jin-Chuel 72
Chrysostomos, Michael 80
Cissé, Djibril 13, 19, 94
Clarke, Steve 64

Clodaldo 76, 77
clubs 11, **78–91**, 130–131
coaches 20, 21, 58, 60, 61, 62, 63, **64–65**, **66–67**, 87, 89, 90, 106, 109, 117, 136
Cohen, George 68
Colo Colo 37, **90**, 103, 130
Colombia 12, 50, 77, 104, 122, 125, 130, 131
Coluna, Mario **46**, 86
CONCACAF (Confederation of North, Central American, and Caribbean Association Football) **12**, 75, 116, **125**, 129, 140
confederations **12–13**, 116
CONMEBOL (Confederación Sudamericana de Fútbol) **12**, 140
Copa America **122**, 131
Copa Libertadores **130–131**
Cordoba, Ivan 133
Coridon, Charles 131
Corinthians 11, 45, 79, 102
Costa Rica 12, 27, 114, 116, 122, 125
counterattacking 62, **63**
Croatia 21, 115, 119
crosses 17, 42, **140**
Cruyff, Johan 42, **47**, 67, 75, 78, 89, 94, 112
Cruyff turn 27, 47
CSKA Moscow 131
Cubillas, Teofilo 37, 112
Cuevas, Nelson 82, 127
cushioning 16, 140
Czech Republic/Czechoslovakia 76, 80, 108, 111, 118, 119, 121, 126
Czibor, Zoltan 70, 110

D

Dalglish, Kenny **51**, 89, 139
da Silva, Ze Carlos 79
Danso, Mavis, 46
de Boer, Frank and Ronald 48, 89
deaths 79, 104–5
decoy runs 18, 26
defenders 28, **37–40**, 61, 140
defending **22–23**
del Piero, Alessandro 85
derby games **101**, 105, 140
Denmark 11, 62, 63, 118, 119, 120, 126
Desailly, Marcel **37**, 72
Dhorasso, Vikash 83
di Stefano, Alfredo 14, 15, **51**, 82, 91
Diallo, Mohammed 95
Diarra, Mahamadou 123
Dick, Kerr Ladies 11, **81**
Dida 101
Diouf, El Hadji 62
distribution 25, **140**
Dominguez, Rogelio 132
dribbling 17, 27, 43, **140**
drug use 51, **105**
dummy movements 18, 27
Dyer, Kieron 105
Dynamo Kiev 50, 67, **91**, 105
Dzajic, Dragan **43**

E

Effenberg, Stefan 79
Egypt 55, 78, 108, 123
Eintracht Frankfurt 14–15, 41
Ekpo, Effioanwan 11
Elizondo, Horacio 21
Emmerich, Lothar 68

England 2, 10, 35, 60, **74**, 77, 96, 111, 114
league 127, **129**, **136**, **137**, 138
Eriksson, Sven-Goran 58, 136
Escobar, Andres 104
Esparrago, Victor 87
Esperance Sportive Tunis 23, **88**
Essien, Michael 62
Eto'o, Samuel 9, 77, 96, 97, 128
Europe 12, 13, 117, 131
European Championships 11, 12, 62, 72, 106–107, **118–119**
European Cup/Champions League 12, 14–15, 91, 131, **132–133**
European Cup Winners' Cup 78, **131**
European Supercup **131**
Eusebio **52**, 86, 109, 111
Everton 8, 96, 137, 138

F

FA (Football Association) 9, **10**, 11, 81, 140
Fabregas, Cesc 129
FA Cup 10, 51, 59, 98, 130, 131
fans 6, 21, 28, 85, **100–101**, 105, 117
Farfan, Jefferson 126
Favalli, Giuseppe 119
Ferguson, Alex 34, 59, 65, **67**, 79
Fernandez, Gaston 82
Ferreira, Edmilson 27, 28
Ferrini, Georgio 8
field 8, 66, 99
FIFA (Fédération Internationale de Football Association) 7, 9, 11, 12, 19, 135, 140
Figo, Luis **44**, 94, 103
Figueroa, Elias 37
Filippini, Emanuele 128
Fiorentina 44, 48, 64, 103, 104, 131
five-on-five soccer **19**
Flamengo 49, **79**, 84
Fluminense 54, **84**
Fontaine, Just **49**, 72, 109, 110
formations **60–61**, 62, 140
fouls 21, **22**, 24, 28, 141
fourth official 20, 140
France 11, **72**, 99, 110, 113, 115, 116, 118, 121
league 31, 41, 105, 127, 131
women's team 16
free kicks 17, 19, 24, **30**, 42, 140
Frisk, Anders 105
futsal **19**, 140

G

Galatasaray 31, 45, **85**, 101, 105
Gallagher, Dermot 20
Gallego, Americo 75
game fixing 83, 85, **104**, 128
Gao Hong **34**, 74
Garrincha 27, **43**, 105, 109, 111
Gascoigne, Paul 119
Gentile, Claudio 113
George, Finidi 89
Germany 28, 31, 37, 38, 52, 99, 108, 115, 116, 118, 119, 131
women's team 117, 121
see also West Germany
Ghana 25, 27, 46, 87, 116, 123
Giggs, Ryan 27, 67, 79, 95
Giresse, Alain **41**, 43
Giuly, Ludovic 26
Given, Shay 24
Glazer, Malcolm 102
goal area 8

ACKNOWLEDGMENTS

The publisher would like to thank the following for permission to reproduce their material. Every care has been taken to trace copyright holders. However, if there have been unintentional omissions or failure to trace copyright holders, we apologize and will, if informed, endeavor to make corrections in any future edition.

Top = *t*, bottom = *b*, center = *c*, left = *l*, right = *r*

All images supplied by Empics, with the exception of: pages 4–5 Getty/ Manchester United 2005/Matthew Peters; 8*tr* with the kind permission of Acme Whistles Limited, UK; 8*l* Getty/AFP; 9*t* Getty/Hulton/J.A. Hampton; 11*br* Getty/ Hulton/Reinhold Thiele; 12*c* Getty/Clive Mason; 16*tr* Corbis/Sygma; 19*br* Getty/ AFP/Patrick Lin; 21*cl* Getty/AFP/Patrick Hertzog; 23*cr* Getty/Stuart Franklin; 24*c* Getty/AFP/Stan Honda; 24*br* Getty/Mike Hewitt; 27*bl* Getty/AFP/Khaled Desouki; 27*br* Getty/Clive Brunskill; 28*c* Getty/Manchester United 2005/John Peters; 28*br* Getty/Bongarts/Andreas Rentz; 29*br* Getty/AFP/Patrick Herzog; 30–31*t* Corbis/ Reuters/Eric Galliard; 30*br* Corbis/Reuters; 31*br* Getty/Bongarts/Alexander Hassenstein; 42*bl* Corbis/Reuters/Eddie Keogh; 44*t* Getty/AFP/Nicolas Asfouri; 48*t* Getty/AFP/Paolo Cocco; 49*tr* Getty/Ben Radford; 60*bl* Getty/Bongarts/Christof

Koepsel; 62*tr* Getty/AFP/François-Xavier Marit; 63*cl* Corbis/Reuters/Jose Manuel Ribeiro; 67*bl* Corbis/Reuters/Ian Hodgson; 71*b* Corbis/Reuters/Grigoris Siamidis; 72*tl* Getty/Ben Radford; 77*tr* Getty/AFP; 78*t* Corbis/Liewig Media Sports/Christian Liewig; 79*tl* Corbis/Reuters; 80*r* Corbis/Reuters/Petr Josek; 82*bl* Corbis/Reuters/ Andres Stapff; 83*tr* Getty/AFP/Chi Jae-Ku; 84*tl* Corbis/Reuters/Bruno Domingos; 88*tl* Corbis/Reuters/Mohamed Hammi; 90*bl* Corbis/Reuters; 92–93 Corbis/ Sygma/Jacques Langevin; 94*bl* Getty/AFP/Oliver Lang; 95*tr* Getty/Tom Shaw; 96*cr* Getty/Shaun Botterill; 96*br* Getty/Ross Kinnaird; 98*b* Getty/Ross Kinnaird; 99*br* Corbis/Reuters/Stringer; 100*c* Getty/AFP/Mladen Antonov; 102 Getty/AFP/ Goh Chai Hin; 103*tr* Getty/AFP/Xavier Soriano; 104*br* Corbis/Sygma/Sunday Times/Joe Sefale; 105*tl* Getty/Laurence Griffiths; 105*c* Getty/Pascal Rondeau; 109*bl* Getty/AFP; 113*bl* Corbis/Bettmann; 114*t* Getty/AFP; 114*b* Getty/Simon Bruty; 116*t* Corbis/Andres Kudacki; 116*bl* Corbis/Icon SMI/Matthew Ashton; 122*bl* Corbis/ Reuters/Pilar Olivares; 123*cl* Corbis/Reuters/Radhu Sigheti; 124*tc* Corbis/Reuters; 124*bl* Corbis/Reuters/Andrew Wong; 125*tr* Getty Images; 125*bl* Corbis/Reuters; 126*br* Getty/AFP/Jiji Press; 127*br* Corbis/Reuters/Marcos Brindicci; 128*bc* Getty/ Bongarts/Stuart Franklin; 129*tl* Getty/Shaun Botterill; 129*bc* Corbis/Reuters; 130*bl* Getty/AFP/Hassan Ammar; 132*tr* Getty/Bongarts; 133*tr* Getty/Bongarts/ Martin Rose.